University of Bristol
Socio-Legal Centre
for Family Studies

Pathways to Adoption

Research Project

Mervyn Murch

Nigel Lowe

Margaret Borkowski

Rosalie Copner

Kathleen Griew

London : HMSO

ISBN 0 11 321588 6

Contents

		Page
Acknowledgements		ix
Preface		xi

Part I — The Court Record Survey

Chapter One	**Outline Method of Approach**	1
1.1	The Objective	2
1.2	Choice of Fieldwork Area	2
1.3	Collection of Data	2
1.4	Quality of Data	3
1.5	Selecting the Sample	4
1.6	Weighting the Sample	6
1.7	Representativeness of the Sample	6

Chapter Two	**A Description of the Cases Sampled**	9
2.1	Summary	10
2.2	Key Findings	10
2.3	Type of Application	11
2.4	Ratio of Freeing Applications to Adoption Applications	14
2.5	Court Usage	15
2.6	Proportion of Single Applicants for an Adoption Order	19
2.7	Inter Country Adoptions	19
2.8	Transracial Adoptions	19
2.9	The Outcome of the Case	21
2.10	Type of Order Made	22
2.11	Natural Mother's Agreement to the Application	23
2.12	Proportion of Contested Final Hearings	24
2.13	Application to Dispense with Parental Agreement	25
2.14	Definition of a Contested Case	27
2.15	Contested vs Uncontested Cases	27

Chapter Three	**A Profile of the Child in Adoption and Freeing for Adoption Proceedings**	31
3.1	Summary	32
3.2	Key Findings	32
3.3	Sex of Child	33
3.4	Legitimacy of Child	33
3.5	Religion of Child	34
3.6	Ethnic Origin of Child	34
3.7	Siblings in Birth Family	35

3.8	Sibling Groups	37
3.9	Children with Disabilities	39
3.10	Age of Child	41
3.11	The Stages in the Adoption Process	42
3.12	Routes to Adoption	44
3.13	Age Profile of Children at the Date of Current Placement	44
3.14	Age Profile of Children at the Date of Placement for Adoption	45
3.15	Age Profile of Children at Date of Panel Recommendation	46
3.16	Age Profile of Children at Date of Application to Court	48
3.17	Age Profile of Children at Date of Order	49
3.18	Age Profile of Children in Contested Cases	51

Chapter Four **Care History of Children Involved in Adoption and Freeing for Adoption Proceedings** — 53

4.1	Summary	54
4.2	Key Findings	54
4.3	Care Status of Child at Time of Application	55
4.4	The Current Care Period	55
4.5	Number of Previous Periods of Care	57
4.6	The Child's Current Placement	59
4.7	History of Previous Placements	60

Chapter Five **The Child's Court Career** — 63

5.1	Summary	64
5.2	Key Findings	64
5.3	Previous Child-Related Proceedings	64
5.4	The Frequency of Previous Court Orders	66

Chapter Six **Profile of the Birth Parents and the Adoptive Parents** — 69

6.1	Summary	70
6.2	Key Findings	70
6.3	Marital Status of the Birth Parents at Date of Application	70
6.4	Religion of the Birth Parents	72
6.5	Ethnic Origin of the Birth Parents	72
6.6	Age of the Birth Mother at the Time of the Child's Birth	73
6.7	Religion of the Adoptive Parents	74
6.8	Ethnic Origin of the Adoptive Parents	74
6.9	Age of the Adoptive Mother at the Date of Application	75
6.10	A Comparison of the Age of the Birth Mother and the Adoptive Mother	77
6.11	The Siblings in the Adoptive Family	77

		Page
Chapter Seven	**A Profile of the Adoption Agency**	79
7.1	Summary	80
7.2	Key Findings	80
7.3	Type of Agency Involved in the Current Placement	81
7.4	Inter-Agency Placements	83
7.5	Payment of Adoption Allowances	83
7.6	The Stages in the Adoption Process	84
7.7	The Length of Time from Date of Placement for Adoption to the Date of Placement Recommendation	84
7.8	The Length of Time from Date of Panel Placement Recommendation/ Agency Decision to the Date of Application to Court	86
7.9	The Length of Time from Date of Application to Court to the Date the Schedule II Report is lodged with the Court	88
7.10	The Contested Case	88
Chapter Eight	**The Court Proceedings**	91
8.1	Summary	92
8.2	Key Findings	92
8.3	The Number of Court Hearings required to reach a Final Order	93
8.4	The Number of Hearings in Relation to Court Usage	94
8.5	The Number of Hearings in Relation to Contested Cases	95
8.6	Length of Court Proceedings	96
8.7	Length of Court Proceedings in Relation to Type of Application	99
8.8	Length of Court Proceedings in Relation to Court Usage	100
8.9	Length of Court Proceedings in Contested and Uncontested Cases	101
8.10	Length of Court Proceedings in Relation to the Age of the Child at Date of Current Placement	101
8.11	Length of Time from Date of Application to Date of First Hearing in Relation to Area	102
8.12	Length of Time from Date of Application to Date of First Hearing in Relation to Court Usage	103
8.13	Length of Time from Date of Application to Date of First Hearing for Contested and Uncontested Cases	104
Chapter Nine	**An Overview of the Adoption Process**	105
9.1	Summary	106
9.2	Length of Time from Date of Placement for Adoption to Date of Order	107
9.3	Length of Time from Date of Current Placement to Date of Order	108

Page

Part II   The Practitioner Study

Introduction   113

Chapter One   Organisation Of Adoption Work in the Agencies   117

1.1   Introduction   118
1.2   Establishing Priorities   118
1.3   Inconsistent and Uncoordinated Policies and Practices Within and
        Between Agencies   119
1.4   The Issue of Specialization   123
1.5   Specialist Supervision and Support   126
1.6   Comment   127

Chapter Two   Schedule II Reports   129

2.1   Introduction   130
2.2   Social Workers' Level of Experience   131
2.3   Sources of Information   132
2.4   The Relevance of the Schedule II Report   134
2.5   Format   136
2.6   Time Allowed for Completion of Schedule II Reports   139
2.7   Should Schedule II Reports be Lodged at The Court when the Appli-
        cation is Submitted?   141
2.8   Comment   142

Chapter Three   Parental Agreement   145

3.1   Introduction   146
3.2   The Practitioner View   147
3.3   Comment   153

Chapter Four   Legal Advice and Practice   155

4.1   Introduction   156
4.2   Solicitors' Experience and Expertise in Adoption   156
4.3   Background Information   159
4.4   Legal Aid   161
4.5   Comment   163

Chapter Five   Courts Administration   165

5.1   Introduction   166
5.2   Staffing   166
5.3   Listing   169
5.4   Appointment of Reporting Officers and Guardians ad Litem   172
5.5   Comment   173

		Page
Chapter Six	**The Court Hearing**	175
6.1	Introduction	176
6.2	Practitioners' Views on the Final Hearing	177
6.3	Are Court Hearings Necessary?	180
6.4	Some Alternatives to a Court Hearing	182
6.5	Comment	184
Chapter Seven	**The Adjudication Process**	185
7.1	Introduction	186
7.2	Procedural Approach	186
7.3	The Judicial Role	188
7.4	The Judicial Manner	189
7.5	Comment	191
Chapter Eight	**The Legal Process**	193
8.1	Introduction	194
8.2	Practitioners' Knowledge of the Law	194
8.3	The Freeing for Adoption Provisions	195
8.4	Adoption Law	201
8.5	Whether Adoption Law Meets the Needs of the Parties	205
8.6	Changes to the Freeing Provisions and Adoption Law	211
8.7	Comment	214
Chapter Nine	**Open Adoption**	215
9.1	Introduction	216
9.2	The Practitioners' View About Open Adoption	218
9.3	Practitioners' Experience of Openness in Practice	223
9.4	Implications for Practice and Legislation	226
9.5	Comment	228
Chapter Ten	**Remaining Issues**	229
10.1	Introduction	230
10.2	Separate Representation for Children	230
10.3	Guardians ad Litem in Uncontested Cases	232
10.4	Legal Representation for Guardians ad Litem	233
10.5	Distinctive Roles or Reporting Officer and Guardian ad Litem	233
10.6	Ascertaining the Child's Wishes and Feelings	233
10.7	Comment	236

Page

Part III Conclusions

CONCLUSIONS
Reflections, Speculations and Proposals   239

1.   Introduction   240

2.   Reflections   240

3.   Speculations   243

4.   Proposals for Reform   246

Bibliography

Appendix A   List of Courts Covered in the Fieldwork Areas in the Mini Record
        Sample

Appendix B   The Mini Record

Appendix C   The Court Proforma

Appendix D   The Social Worker Questionnaire

Appendix E   The Private Solicitor Questionnaire

Acknowledgements

The research upon which this report is based was undertaken principally for the benefit of the Department of Health and the Law Commission's Review of Adoption Law. It was funded by the Department of Health and supported by a specially constituted Advisory Committee. This was chaired by Rupert Hughes of the Department of Health. Other members were Margaret Chiverton, Donna Sidonio, Geoffrey James and Carolyn Davies of the Department of Health; Jennifer Jenkins of the Law Commission; Chris Hammond, Director, British Agencies For Adoption And Fostering; Dr. June Thoburn, University of East Anglia; Christopher Davis, Director, Somerset Social Services Department; and Professor Roy Parker, University of Bristol. Our thanks to them all for their unfailing interest.

In addition we would like to record our special appreciation of the very professional advice and support we have received from Dr. Carolyn Davies of the Office of Research Management in the Department of Health with whom we liaised at a number of critical stages in the programme.

The work could not have been undertaken had not the Home Office, the Lord Chancellor's Department, and the President of The Family Division, Sir Stephen Brown, agreed to our being allowed privileged access to court files. In this we received the invaluable assistance of a large number of officials in the magistrates' courts, county courts and in the Principal Registry of the High Court, all of whom received us into their busy working domain with great kindness whilst we were extracting data from court records. We are also deeply indebted to all the solicitors and social workers in Birmingham, Devon, Somerset and Walsall who agreed to be interviewed and who, for obvious reasons, cannot be named. We also record our thanks to the following adoption agencies who supported the research and permitted their staff to be interviewed: Birmingham Social Services Department; Walsall Social Services Department; Solihull Social Services Department; Devon Social Services Department; Somerset Social Services Department; Council for Christian Care; National Children's Home; Father Hudson's Society; Barnardos; Catholic Children's Society; The Children's Society.

The research itself, although a team effort, was largely conducted by our research associates, Margaret Borkowski and Rosalie Copner. We wish to pay special tribute to them for their remarkable perseverance and commitment to the project even through periods of serious medical indisposition. Margaret Borkowski organised and conducted the main interview programme, while Rosalie Copner did likewise with the Court Record Survey. We were particularly fortunate to have expert back-up assistance on many points in the study from Daphne Norbury, a former Assistant Director of BAAF. Dr. Rosie Collins and Alice Pringle also assisted the project at crucial times and ensured the work kept to schedule. Our colleague, Kathleen

Griew, systems analyst, designed and managed the statistical aspects of the study and was well supported by Andrew Chalmers.

The clerical and administrative load of a project of this kind is formidable: Linda Van Sant helped us launch the project, Sara Gourlay took over through the main fieldwork stages, and Tina Beattie, supported by Doreen Bailey, Rose Jacobs and Iris Murch, coped magnificently with all the pressures associated with producing the report on time. All of these colleagues have tackled the work involved with skill and good humour. We have greatly enjoyed working with them and learnt much from them.

Whatever errors and deficiencies the report may contain are our responsibility as co-Directors of the Project and should not be held against any of our colleagues and advisers.

Nigel Lowe
Professor of Law
Cardiff Law School
University of Wales
(formerly Reader in Law,
University of Bristol)

Mervyn Murch
Professor in Law
Cardiff Law School
University of Wales
(formerly Senior Research Fellow,
Socio-Legal Centre, University of Bristol)

April 1991

Preface

This research report is intended not only for members of the Adoption Law Review, which is being undertaken by the Department of Health and the Law Commission, but for anyone with an interest in the process of adopting children.

It sets out the findings of a research project conducted between July 1988 and March 1991 which sought to:

(i)   examine the legal pathways in adoption and related processes;

(ii)   expose the general areas of difficulty which may arise in the course of these processes.

These objectives emerged from negotiations between personnel from the Department of Health, some of whom are members of the Adoption Law Review, and the co-Directors of the project, Mervyn Murch and Nigel Lowe, together with the principal researchers, Margaret Borkowski and Rosalie Copner.

In pursuit of these objectives, it was agreed with the Department of Health that the following tasks would be undertaken:

(i)   the establishment of hard 'quantifiable' information drawn from court records concerning both adoption and freeing for adoption cases.[1]

(ii)   a survey of social workers who had prepared Schedule II reports and of solicitors involved in a sample of cases drawn from the Court Record Survey in order to record and describe their views concerning the adoption process and the law relating to it.[2]

In effect, two separate but related studies were undertaken. The results from each form the basis of this report—the Court Record Survey (Part I), and the Practitioner Study (Part II). The research strategy was to provide a sound quantitative base from which to move to an examination of qualitative issues involved in the study of social worker and solicitor perspectives.

---

[1]   The need for this was increased by the abandonment in 1990 of the OPCS/Department of Health scheme to collect routine statistics in Adoption via the A100 unit returns (see LAC (90)2).

[2]   The researchers also considered it essential to the overall task to record the views of consumers, since their perception of the process would be different from those of the practitioners and would act as a balance to them. After discussions with the Department of Health it did not prove possible to include this as an integral part of the Pathways project. However the ESRC has agreed to sponsor a two year Consumer Study which commenced on 1 April 1991. It is hoped that findings from this follow-on study will be available in time to be considered by the Adoption Law Review before changes to the legislation are concluded.

The Limitations of the Research

Although we have striven to be true to the material and to present it in as balanced a way as possible, it has some obvious limitations:

(i)   The main surveys were conducted in only five fieldwork areas in England: the predominantly rural south west counties of Devon and Somerset; the predominantly urban areas of the city of Birmingham and the Metropolitan Borough of Walsall in the West Midlands; and in selected courts in six London Boroughs. All three types of court with an adoption jurisdiction were sampled, namely magistrates' courts, county courts and the High Court.[3]

(ii)   The courts in these areas, their facilities, practices and procedures, are bound to be varied and, to some extent, idiosyncratic. The economic, cultural and demographic composition of each area is very different. In terms of this research we were not able to explore what, if any, influence these factors might have on court usage and the adoption process.

(iii)   The practitioner view is confined to those social workers who had prepared the Schedule II report and to the solicitors each of whom were involved in a sample of cases drawn from the Court Record Study. In our discussions with the Department of Health which preceded the research, the researchers advocated the importance of seeking the views of Reporting Officers and Guardians ad Litem involved in the cases to complement these perspectives. But in the event, because of limitations in time and funding, it was agreed with the Department of Health to exclude this dimension.

(iv)   It should also be borne in mind that in the Practitioner Study we recorded the social workers' and solicitors' perceptions about the process. We had no way of independently confirming the validity of their views since we were not able to study the adoption process in both the agencies and courts at first-hand ourselves.

(v)   We are particularly concerned that in the time available it was not possible to encompass the views of the consumer, but our new ESRC project should be able to remedy this.[4]

(vi)   We should emphasise that this report as drafted is not to be regarded as a discursive academic text. The focus is on the presentation of the findings and their policy implications for the Adoption Law Review. As such we hope it complements the review of research which has a bearing on adoption or alternatives to adoption which the Department of Health has received from June Thoburn, one of our advisers (Thoburn 1990).

---

[3]   A list of courts visited is given in Appendix 4.

[4]   A two year research project "Adoption Proceedings—The Consumer View" commenced on 1 April 1991 funded by the ESRC.

PART I
The Court Record Survey

CHAPTER 1   # Outline Method of Approach

1.1   The Objective

1.2   Choice of Fieldwork Area

1.3   Collection of Data

1.4   Quality of Data

1.5   Selecting the Sample

1.6   Weighting the Sample

1.7   Representativeness of the Sample

1.1   The Objective

We conducted a survey of court records as part of a wider investigation into the obstacles affecting the outcome to successful adoption. The aim was to elicit empirical data concerning the children placed for adoption, the practice of the adoption agencies, the various courts used and their related procedures, the size of the courts' adoption workload, and the length of proceedings. This would then provide a backcloth of quantifiable data against which to consider the more qualitative information about adoption practices to be obtained from a survey of practitioners[1]. We also hoped that this information would help to compensate, albeit in a limited way, for the failure of the OPCS/Department of Health Unit Return Scheme for Adoption Proceedings, which was abandoned in 1990 (see LAC (90)2).

1.2   Choice of Fieldwork Area

Given constraints of finance and research staff time, it was decided to conduct this part of the investigation in five fieldwork areas in England: the predominantly rural south-west counties of Devon and Somerset; two urban areas in the West Midlands, the city of Birmingham and the Metropolitan Borough of Walsall; and in selected courts in London.[2] All three types of court with an adoption jurisdiction were sampled, namely magistrates' courts, county courts and the High Court. A list of courts visited is given in Appendix A.

1.3   Collection of Data

Data on the process of adoption was extracted directly from the court records using two research tools. First, we designed a data-collection sheet known as the **mini record** which recorded information such as details of the application, outcome of the case and the court proceedings, together with a brief profile of the child including his/her court career.

The second tool, known as the **court proforma**, was designed both to collect information on subjects in the adoption process not covered by the mini record, for example details of the birth parents and prospective adopters, and to provide further details on certain aspects already mentioned in the mini record, such as the care history of the child.

A court proforma was completed for every case in the mini record sample except those which involved a non-agency placement. Thus, adoptions by

---

[1]   The Court Record Survey will also provide useful background information for the projected study, funded by the ESRC, on the consumer view of adoption proceedings.

[2]   It should be noted that the data from the London courts cannot be used as a reliable indicator of local authority practice, since the county courts examined drew applications from a number of different local authorities which might have totally different policies with regard to the use of the freeing provisions.

step parents were excluded, together with those cases where children being adopted were from overseas and where relations had made private arrangements to adopt a child. For reasons of finance and research staff time we also excluded cases from the London courts in the court proforma sample. The fieldwork areas in this sub sample were therefore Devon, Somerset, Birmingham and Walsall.

1.4   Quality of Data

Before starting on the main fieldwork, we spent some time testing both the research tools.[3] This pilot stage enabled us to eliminate questions that were proving difficult to answer, once we had established what information was generally available from the files. The data we sought were extracted mainly from the application form (and the Statement of Facts if the parents were not agreeing to the application), the Schedule II report, the court order, and the report prepared by the Reporting Officer or Guardian ad Litem, all these being documents that almost without fail could be found in the court records.

In the course of the main fieldwork, we experienced few problems with missing documents. However, the reports were sometimes difficult to locate because the papers were often filed in no chronological or systematic order. Furthermore, we noticed a lack of consistent information on issues that we considered could be important, such as whether or not any of the parties had received legal aid and details of the court hearings. Where a record of the court hearings had been kept, it was often handwritten in shorthand form, which made it impossible for anyone (except its author) to ascertain, for instance, who had attended the hearing, how long the hearing had lasted, and what evidence was heard. Perhaps the most important piece of information that was unavailable in the majority of cases in the magistrates' and county court files was whether or not the hearing had been contested and if so, by whom.

In general, we found the Schedule II report to be the most useful document for the purposes of our survey. Sometimes however, especially in complex cases, details of the child's previous care history and placements were recorded in a confusing and inconsistent way. Occasionally, information recorded in the Schedule II report appeared to be at odds with case history details noted in other documents, for example the Guardian ad Litem report.

---

3   We are grateful to the clerks of the local courts who allowed us access to their court files for this purpose.

1.5 Selecting the Sample

Bearing in mind the resources we had available in terms of funding and staff time, we were able to calculate the approximate number of cases that could be examined within the period of the study. However, due to the lack of available reliable data published on adoption and freeing for adoption, we were unable to ascertain with any degree of certainty the total number of applications made within any one year to the courts in any of the selected fieldwork areas. It was thus not possible to sample randomly. However, we judged from the available statistics that about twice as many cases occurred in each area as we were able to examine within the study period. We therefore decided to take a systematic sample.

Thus the sample size was arrived at by first taking *every other* application for either an adoption order or a freeing for adoption order made to the magistrates' court and county court. Secondly, with respect to the High Court cases sampled at the Principal Registry of the Family Division in London, *every* application arising from Devon, Somerset, Birmingham and Walsall was included. Thirdly, with regard to High Court cases arising from the selected county court areas in London,[4] *every other* case was recorded due to the unexpectedly large number of such cases and to time constraints.

Using the mini record, data were collected from a total of 650 court records relating to applications for adoption or freeing for adoption covering the period 1st July 1986 to 30th June 1988.

Figure 1a illustrates the actual size of the **mini record** sample in each of the five fieldwork areas broken down by the type of court (see Part I, section 2.5 Table 2.5(b), for equivalent data on the weighted sample). The majority of cases were taken from the London, Birmingham and Devon courts. In each area the greatest proportion of cases was sampled in the county courts. Perhaps not surprisingly in view of its geographical convenience, the highest proportion of High Court cases was found in London.

The mini record sample provided a number of agency placement adoption applications almost exactly equal to the proposed sample size. A court proforma was thus completed for every previously selected case (excepting London), where the records could be found. A total of 258 court proformas were completed, 204 in respect of applications for adoption and 54 in respect of applications for freeing for adoption. **To avoid confusion with the mini record sample, the adoption applications in the court proforma sample will be termed 'agency' adoptions for the remainder of the report.**

---

4   The researchers working on the records in the chosen London Courts used the London County Courts Directory to determine which High Court cases fell within the jurisdiction of the six London County Courts in the survey (Bloomsbury, Bow, Clerkenwell, Lambeth, Wandsworth and Woolwich).

Figure 1a:
Actual number of mini record cases sampled by area and type of court

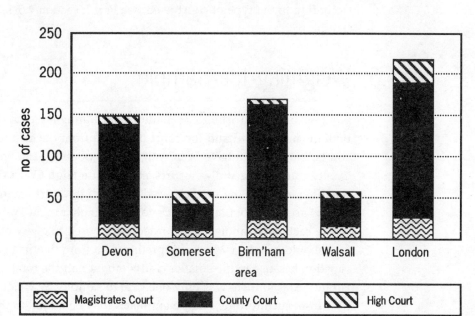

A picture of the actual number of cases sampled using the **court proforma** by area and according to the type of court used is shown in Figure 1b. Birmingham and Devon provided the largest number of cases in the court proforma sample. Few High Court cases were included from the Midland areas. Birmingham appeared to have the highest proportion of agency adoption and freeing cases taken to the magistrates' court. As in the mini

Figure 1b:
Actual number of court proforma cases sampled by area and type of court

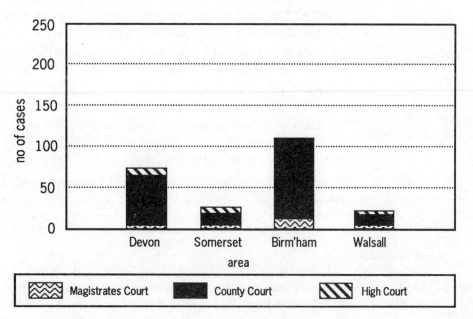

record sample, the greatest proportion of cases in each area was found in the county court. For a further regional analysis of the weighted sample according to the type of court used, see Part I, section 2.5 Tables 2.5(c) and 2.5(d).

1.6   Weighting the Sample

For a useful comparison to be made incorporating the data collected using both the mini record and the court proforma from the different types of courts, the raw data have been weighted by doubling the figures for the county courts, magistrates' courts and London High Court. This allows for the different sampling method used in the High Court regarding applications arising from Somerset, Devon, Birmingham and Walsall, that is, where each application was recorded as opposed to every other one. Some care should be taken when interpreting data from the magistrates' courts in isolation because in the smaller courts (about half the total number of magistrates' courts) there was only one case to sample. By weighting the raw data from such records, undue emphasis may be added to the figures in the order of 2–3%.

1.7   Representativeness of the Sample

Figure 2a shows how the pattern of adoption in England and Wales has changed over 16 years in relation to the age of the child.[5] The total number of children being adopted has fallen by about two thirds since 1970. Nearly twice as many babies were being adopted in 1970 as in 1986. On the other hand, the proportion of older children being adopted has increased since 1970. Figure 2b illustrates the number of children who were the subject of adoption proceedings in the Pathways to Adoption sample (taken between 1986 and 1988) according to the age of the child when adopted. Comparing that with the national data for 1986 in Figure 2a, we see that the relative proportions of children being adopted are similar. We therefore feel able to assume that our sample of children being adopted in the five fieldwork areas is in this respect representative of the national population. Figure 2b also shows the proportion of 'no relation' adoptions[6] found in our sample according to the age of the child when adopted. It is interesting to note that these are very similar to the pattern of adoptions overall established in 1970, as shown in Figure 2a. The changing face of adoption may be due in some part to the increase in the number of step parent adoptions taking place.

---

[5]   Taken from a leaflet produced by BAAF on Adoption and Fostering: Information for Schools.

[6]   A 'no relation' adoption is one where the applicant to adopt the child is not related to the child in any way, either by marriage (as in step parent adoptions), or by blood (as in adoption by an aunt/uncle/grandparent).

Figure 2a:
Number of children adopted in England and Wales 1970 and 1986

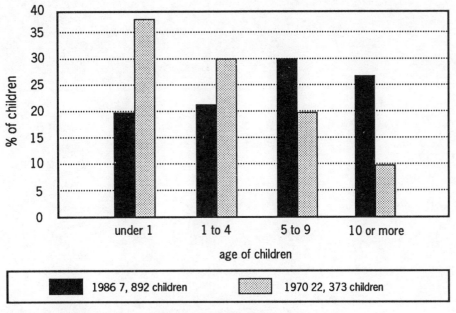

Source: Houghton Report (1972) and OPCS Monitors (1972, 1988)

Figure 2b:
Number of children adopted in Pathways to Adoption Sample 1986–1988

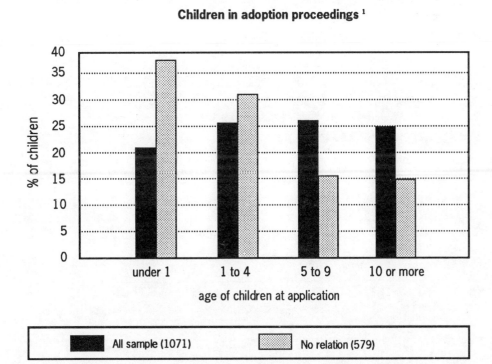

1 excluding freeing for adoption proceedings and cases where the age of the child was not known.

CHAPTER 2   A Description of the Cases Sampled

2.1   Summary

2.2   Key Findings

2.3   Type of Application

2.4   Ratio of Freeing Applications to Adoption Applications

2.5   Court Usage

2.6   Proportion of Single Applicants for an Adoption Order

2.7   Inter Country Adoptions

2.8   Transracial Adoptions

2.9   The Outcome of the Case

2.10   Type of Order Made

2.11   Natural Mother's Agreement to the Application

2.12   Proportion of Contested Final Hearings

2.13   Application to Dispense with Parental Agreement

2.14   Definition of a Contested Case

2.15   Contested vs Uncontested Cases

2.1   Summary

In this chapter we give a detailed description of the cases sampled using the mini record and the court proforma. We identify four different types of application made in adoption proceedings; namely

:   application for adoption by parent and step parent **(STEP PARENT)**. This type of application was not included in the court proforma sample.

:   application for adoption by a relative other than a parent/step parent **(OTHER RELATION)**

:   application for adoption by parties unrelated to the child **(NO RELATION)**

:   application to free child for adoption **(FREEING)**

The incidence of these four types of application is analysed both regionally and according to court usage. The ratio of freeing applications to adoption applications is investigated and areas identified that have made differing use of the freeing provisions. We look at the proportion of cases in our sample where an application to adopt was made by a single person, as well as the incidence of inter country adoptions and transracial adoptions. An analysis is made of the outcome of the cases together with the types of order made. Finally, we investigate the differences between those cases where an element of contest was found and those where the application was made with parental agreement. We identify several measurable criteria which for the purposes of this study may identify a contested case.

2.2   Key Findings

2.2.1   The incidence of the different types of application varied by region (2.3). Somerset was found to have the highest proportion of step parent adoptions (2.3). A high use of the freeing provisions was found in Birmingham and none at all in Somerset (2.4).

2.2.2   A wide variation in court usage was found for the different types of application. The majority of no relation adoption and freeing applications was heard in the county court. The magistrates' courts tended to deal with more step parent adoptions than the higher courts. Some regional variation was found in the use of the different courts (2.5).

2.2.3   Our sample contained very few applications for adoption made by a single applicant (2.6).

2.2.4   The large majority of adoption and freeing applications resulted in an order (2.9). Very little evidence was found of adoption orders made with access conditions attached (2.10).

2.2.5   The majority of freeing applications was made without the natural mother's consent (2.11)[1]. As far as adoption is concerned, most baby adoptions proceeded with the mother's agreement (2.11); the older the child the less likely the adoption application was to have been made with the mother's agreement (2.11).

2.2.6   Freeing cases were more likely to be actively contested (at the final hearing) than no relation adoptions (2.12). Some regional variation was found in the proportion of contested and uncontested adoption and freeing cases (2.13).

2.2.7   Contesting an application appeared to have little effect on the outcome of the case (2.13).

2.3   Type of Application

The data from the mini record presented in Table 2.3 below show that just under half the applications made in Somerset were step parent adoptions (45%), a higher proportion than for any of the other areas. Furthermore, no freeing applications were recorded in the Somerset courts during the period covered by our study. Birmingham recorded the lowest proportion of step parent adoptions (26%) among our areas but had the highest proportion of freeing applications made (23%).

Table 2.3
Type of Application Made in Each Area (Mini Record)

| | AREA | | | | | | | | | | |
| | DEVON | | SOMERSET | | BIRMINGHAM | | WALSALL | | LONDON | | ALL | |
TYPE OF APPLICATION	NO.	(%)	NO.	(%)	NO.	(%)	NO.	(%)	NO.	(%)	NO.	(%)
Step parent	104	(36)	46	(45)	90	(26)	42	(40)	144	(34)	426	(34)
Other relation	13	(5)	0	–	15	(4)	14	(13)	40	(9)	82	(7)
No relation	151	(52)	56	(55)	162	(47)	43	(41)	198	(47)	610	(48)
Freeing	21	(7)	0	–	80	(23)	7	(7)	42	(10)	150	(12)
All	**289**	**(100)**	**102**	**(100)**	**347**	**(100)**	**106**	**(100)**	**424**	**(100)**	**1268**	**(100)**

Figures 3a and 3c represent the data in Table 2.3 graphically. It is evident that there is a wide variation in the use of the freeing provisions in the five fieldwork areas.[2] This confirms impressions gathered from our earlier free-

---

[1]   It is legally correct to refer to the parental **consent** to a freeing application being made and to parental **agreement** to adoption or freeing orders being made.

[2]   Practitioners' views on the freeing provisions are described in Part II of this Report. In Chapter 8 (The Legal Process), sections 8.3 and 8.6.1 we suggest some possible explanations for these variations.

Figure 3a:
Type of application by area (mini record)

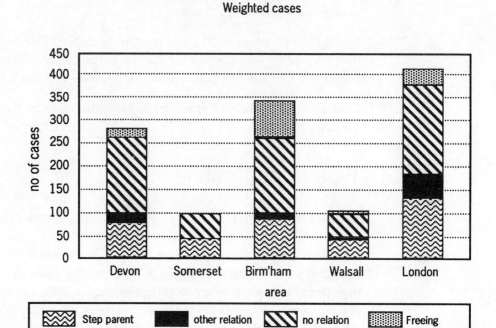

Figure 3b:
Type of application by area (court proforma)

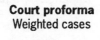
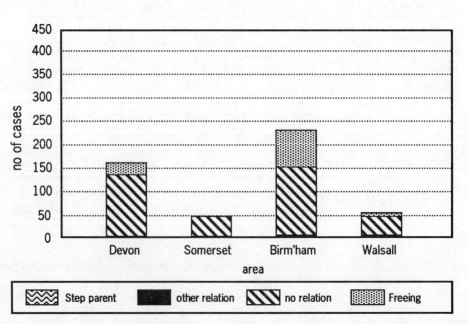

Figure 3c:
Type of application by area (mini record)

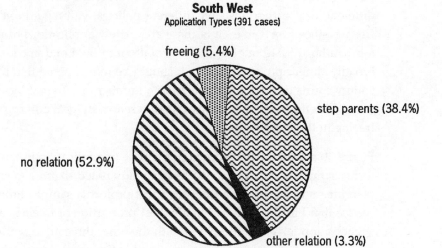

South West
Application Types (391 cases)

freeing (5.4%)

step parents (38.4%)

no relation (52.9%)

other relation (3.3%)

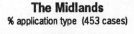

The Midlands
% application type (453 cases)

freeing (19.2%)

step parent (29.1%)

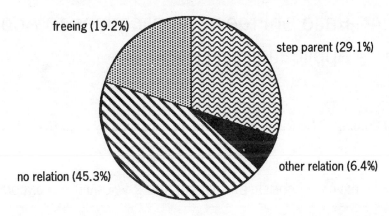

no relation (45.3%)

other relation (6.4%)

London
% application type (424 cases)

freeing (9.9%)

step parent (34.0%)

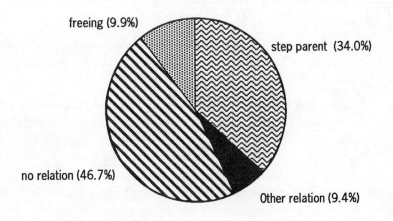

no relation (46.7%)

Other relation (9.4%)

ing for adoption study.[3] In this study we found that Birmingham had the highest proportion of freeing to all other adoption applications (1:3), compared with 1:13 in Devon and 1:14 in Walsall. These data suggest that different local authorities have different policies with regard to the use of freeing, since courts in each of these areas drew applications from a single local authority. Although overall our data from the London courts show a broadly similar proportion (1:9), it should be remembered that the London county courts drew applications from a number of different local authorities. This effectively masks possible differences in local authority use of freeing in the London area.

Figure 3b shows the breakdown of the type of application in the court proforma sample for each area. We have already noted that non-agency placements were excluded from the court proforma sample. From Figure 3b we see that Birmingham had the highest proportion of freeing cases to agency adoption cases compared with the other three areas, with few freeing cases found in Walsall and none at all in Somerset. Nearly three times as many agency adoption cases were sampled in Devon and Birmingham as in Somerset and Walsall.

2.4 Ratio of Freeing Applications to Adoption Applications

Table 2.4(a)
Proportion of Freeing to No Relation Adoption Applications by Area (Mini Record)

	AREA										
	DEVON		**SOMERSET**		**BIRMINGHAM**		**WALSALL**		**LONDON**		**ALL**	
TYPE OF APPLICATION	NO.	(%)	NO.	(%)	NO.	(%)	NO.	(%)	NO.	(%)	NO.	(%)
Freeing	21	(12)	0	–	80	(33)	7	(14)	42	(17)	150	(20)
No relation adoption	151	(88)	56	(100)	162	(67)	43	(86)	198	(83)	610	(80)
All	**172**	**(100)**	**56**	**(100)**	**242**	**(100)**	**50**	**(100)**	**240**	**(100)**	**760**	**(100)**

Table 2.4(a) above correlates the number and proportion of freeing applications to no relation applications in the mini record sample by area, thus excluding adoptions by step parents and by other relations. It confirms that

---

3   See Report of the Research into the Use and Practice of the Freeing for Adoption Provisions (Chapter 2) (Lowe, 1991).

in this study Birmingham was the area with the highest actual and proportionate incidence of freeing. Further analysis of the data revealed that 15% of the sample of children involved in no relation adoptions had been previously freed for adoption, (see Table 2.4(b)).

Table 2.4(b)
No Relation Type Adoptions:
Proportion of Previously Freed Cases by Area (Mini Record)

	AREA											
	DEVON		SOMERSET		BIRMINGHAM		WALSALL		LONDON		ALL	
PREVIOUSLY FREED	NO.	(%)	NO.	(%)	NO.	(%)	NO.	(%)	NO.	(%)	NO.	(%)
Yes	21	(14)	4	(7)	32	(20)	10	(23)	24	(12)	91	(15)
No	130	(86)	52	(93)	130	(80)	33	(77)	164	(83)	509	(83)
Not Recorded	0	–	0	–	0	–	0	–	8	(4)	8	(1)
Not known	0	–	0	–	0	–	0	–	2	(1)	2	*
All	**151**	**(100)**	**56**	**(100)**	**162**	**(100)**	**43**	**(100)**	**198**	**(100)**	**610**	**(100)**

*=Less than 1%

Bearing in mind that not all the children in our sample had been placed by the same local authority that had freed them, it seems from Tables 2.4(a) and 2.4(b) that both Birmingham and Walsall made relatively high use of the freeing provision in comparison with Somerset and Devon. As we have already mentioned, the data from the London courts cannot be used as a reliable indicator of local authority practice (see part I (*ante*) footnote at section 1.2).

2.5   Court Usage

Table 2.5(a)
Type of Application by Court Usage (Mini Record)

	TYPE OF COURT							
	MAGISTRATES'		COUNTY		HIGH		ALL	
TYPE OF APPLICATION	NO.	(%)	NO.	(%)	NO.	(%)	NO.	(%)
Step parent	118	(63)	298	(30)	10	(11)	426	(34)
Other relation	16	(8)	48	(5)	18	(20)	82	(7)
No relation	46	(25)	512	(52)	52	(58)	610	(48)
Freeing	8	(4)	132	(13)	10	(11)	150	(12)
All	**188**	**(100)**	**990**	**(100)**	**90**	**(100)**	**1268**	**(100)**

Figure 4:
Type of application by court usage (mini record)

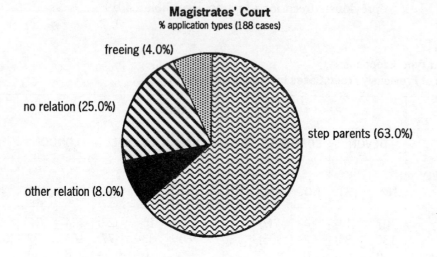

Magistrates' Court
% application types (188 cases)

freeing (4.0%)

no relation (25.0%)

step parents (63.0%)

other relation (8.0%)

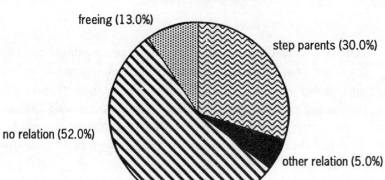
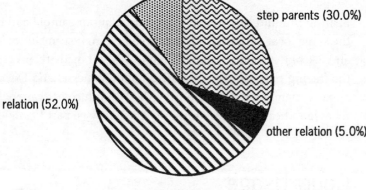

County Court
% application types (990 cases)

freeing (13.0%)

step parents (30.0%)

no relation (52.0%)

other relation (5.0%)

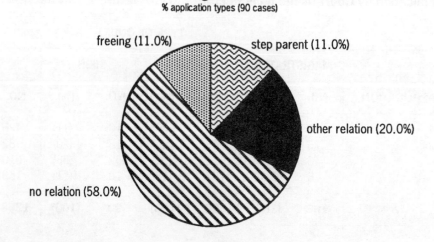

High Court
% application types (90 cases)

freeing (11.0%)

step parent (11.0%)

other relation (20.0%)

no relation (58.0%)

We see from Table 2.5(a) and Figure 4 that a relatively small percentage (4%) of adoption work in the magistrates' court is concerned with freeing applications, with most of the business (63%) involving adoption applications by step parents. On the other hand, adoption proceedings heard in either the county court or the High Court were less likely to be applications made by step parents and more likely to be no relation adoptions. The High Court also heard a comparatively high proportion of applications for adoption made by relatives (other than step parents) of the child. For both the county court and the High Court about one tenth of their business in the adoption field involved freeing applications.

Table 2.5(b)
Court Usage by Area (Mini Record)

	AREA										
	DEVON		**SOMERSET**		**BIRMINGHAM**		**WALSALL**		**LONDON**		**ALL**	
TYPE OF COURT	**NO.**	**(%)**	**NO.**	**(%)**	**NO.**	**(%)**	**NO.**	**(%)**	**NO.**	**(%)**	**NO.**	**(%)**
Magistrates' Court	40	(14)	20	(20)	48	(14)	28	(26)	52	(12)	188	(15)
County Court	236	(82)	74	(72)	292	(84)	74	(70)	314	(74)	990	(78)
High Court	13	(4)	8	(8)	7	(2)	4	(4)	58	(14)	90	(7)
All	**289**	**(100)**	**102**	**(100)**	**347**	**(100)**	**106**	**(100)**	**424**	**(100)**	**1268**	**(100)**

The breakdown between the types of court given in Table 2.5(b) above shows a remarkably consistent pattern in all areas, (see Figure 1a (Part I, section 1.5) for a graphical picture of this breakdown for the unweighted sample). The great preponderance of cases in the county court for all areas will be noted. A larger proportion of High Court applications was made in London—14% compared with an overall average of 7%. Walsall was revealed as an area with an overall greater propensity to use the magistrates' court (26%) for adoption than other areas.[4] This confirms other family jurisdiction studies (Davidoff [1984], and Murch, Borkowski, Copner and Griew [1987]), which show local variations in the resort to the magistrates' court where there is a choice of jurisdictions. Such studies also indicate a general preference for county court adjudication.

Further analysis using the court proforma data (see Table 2.5(c) and 2.5(d)) revealed a noticeable difference between the areas in the use of the courts according to the type of application made, that is an agency adoption or a freeing application.

---

[4]   However, see Tables 2.5(c) and 2.5(d) which show that the greatest proportional use of the magistrates' court by agencies was found in Birmingham, (see also Figure 1b (Part I, section 1.5)).

In the Practitioner Study we formed the impression that the majority of social workers and lawyers, despite their misgivings about the county court, clearly preferred that adoptions be heard in that forum rather than in the magistrates' court. They had major reservations about the High Court. Their views are reported variously in Part II of this Report in Chapters 5, 6 and 7.

Table 2.5(c)
Court Usage for Agency Adoption Applications by Area (Court Proforma)

	AREA									
	DEVON		SOMERSET		BIRMINGHAM		WALSALL		ALL	
TYPE OF COURT	NO.	(%)	NO.	(%)	NO.	(%)	NO.	(%)	NO.	(%)
Magistrates'	4	(3)	4	(8)	20	(13)	4	(8)	32	(8)
County	130	(94)	40	(77)	134	(86)	42	(88)	346	(88)
High	4	(3)	8	(15)	1	(1)	2	(4)	15	(4)
All	**138**	**(100)**	**52**	**(100)**	**155**	**(100)**	**48**	**(100)**	**393**	**(100)**

From Table 2.5(c) one can see that the highest use of the magistrates' court for agency adoption applications was made in Birmingham (13%), and the lowest in Devon (3%). It is perhaps interesting to note that a higher propro-tion (15%) of agency adoption applications made in Somerset were lodged in the High Court compared with the other areas.

Table 2.5(d)
Court Usage for Freeing Applications by Area (Court Proforma)

	AREA							
	DEVON		BIRMINGHAM		WALSALL		ALL	
TYPE OF COURT	NO.	(%)	NO.	(%)	NO.	(%)	NO.	(%)
Magistrates'	0	–	8	(11)	0	–	8	(8)
County	16	(76)	66	(89)	6	(86)	88	(86)
High	5	(24)	0	–	1	(14)	6	(6)
All	**21**	**(100)**	**74**	**(100)**	**7**	**(100)**	**102**	**(100)**

Table 2.5(d) shows the variance in the use of the different types of courts for freeing applications made in Devon, Birmingham and Walsall. As we noted earlier, no freeing applications were made to the Somerset courts during the period covered by the project. It appears that Birmingham is the

only area in our study that used the magistrates' court for freeing applications (11%). On the other hand, although the numbers are small, nearly a
quarter of freeing applications (24%) in Devon were made to the High
Court (and 14% in Walsall). No such cases from Birmingham were recorded
in the High Court for the period of our study.[5]

2.6 Proportion of Single Applicants for Adoption Order

From the more detailed information collected in the court proforma, we
were able to ascertain that the overwhelming majority of applications (98%)
for an adoption order were made jointly by a married couple. Only 2% of
cases in the court proforma sample involved a single applicant and none of
these concerned a baby for adoption. There was some evidence to show
that applications by single people were more likely to involve older
children. Further analysis revealed that all such applications were in
Birmingham and that applicants were living as single females, that is, they
were not living with a partner, either married or unmarried, or as part of a
homosexual couple. Some practitioners interviewed in the Practitioner
Study voiced some concern at what they regarded as inflexibility in certain
aspects of adoption, the marital status of applicants being one. However,
there was a suggestion that attitudes were changing in this respect, (see
Part II Chapter 8—The Legal Process section 8.4.2).

2.7 Inter Country Adoptions

Table 2.7 below shows the proportion of cases from the mini record that
were inter country adoptions, a total of 3%. The incidence of inter county
adoptions was higher in London where 6% of such cases were recorded.
Overall however, the evidence suggests that these cases are uncommon,
although no doubt when they occur they can present complex practice
problems.

2.8 Transracial Adoptions

We hoped to discover the incidence of transracial adoptions that occurred
in our sample, and to that end the mini record included a question to cover
this point.[6] However, our researchers found that in the majority of cases
(73%), information on the race of the child and/or his/her adoptive parents

---

[5]   For further discussion on the differential use of the freeing provisions in the different levels of courts, refer to Lowe
(1991) Report of the Research into the Use and Practice of the Freeing for Adoption Provisions (Chapter 3).

[6]   See q. 14 of the mini record (Appendix B).

Table 2.7
Proportion of Inter Country Adoptions by Area (Mini Record)

	AREA											
	DEVON		SOMERSET		BIRMINGHAM		WALSALL		LONDON		ALL	
INTER COUNTRY ADOPTION	**NO.**	**(%)**	**NO.**	**(%)**	**NO.**	**(%)**	**NO.**	**(%)**	**NO.**	**(%)**	**NO.**	**(%)**
Yes	10	(2)	2	(2)	1	*	0	–	26	(6)	39	(3)
No	258	(89)	100	(98)	302	(87)	100	(94)	370	(87)	1130	(89)
Other[1]	0	–	0	–	2	(1)	2	(2)	2	*	6	*
Not known	0	–	0	–	0	–	0	–	6	(1)	6	*
Not recorded	21	(7)	0	–	42	(12)	4	(4)	20	(5)	87	(7)
All	**289**	**(100)**	**102**	**(100)**	**347**	**(100)**	**106**	**(100)**	**424**	**(100)**	**1268**	**(100)**

1   Cases recorded in this category related to children who, although born overseas, had not been brought into this country specifically for the purpose of adoption.

*=Less than 1%

was not recorded in the court files. We are therefore unable to present any reliable data for analysis on the frequency of transracial adoptions, or indeed on cases where same-race placements had occurred.

2.9   The Outcome of the Case

Table 2.9
Outcome of the Case by Type of Application (Mini Record)

	TYPE OF APPLICATION										
OUTCOME	STEP PARENT		OTHER RELATION		NO RELATION		FREEING		ALL	
	NO.	**(%)**	**NO.**	**(%)**	**NO.**	**(%)**	**NO.**	**(%)**	**NO.**	**(%)**
Order made	347	(81)	66	(80)	588	(96)	126	(84)	1127	(89)
Withdrawn	42	(10)	2	(2)	4	(1)	8	(5)	56	(4)
Refused-no order made	0	–	0	–	0	–	2	(1)	2	*
Pending/adjourned s.d.	24	(6)	9	(11)	14	(2)	12	(8)	59	(5)
Other	13	(3)	2	(2)	4	(1)	2	(1)	21	(2)
Not known	0	–	2	(2)	0	–	0	–	2	*
Not recorded	0	–	1	(1)	0	–	0	–	1	*
All	**426**	**(100)**	**82**	**(100)**	**610**	**(100)**	**150**	**(100)**	**1268**	**(100)**

*=Less than 1%

Figure 5:
The outcome of the application for cases in the mini record sample

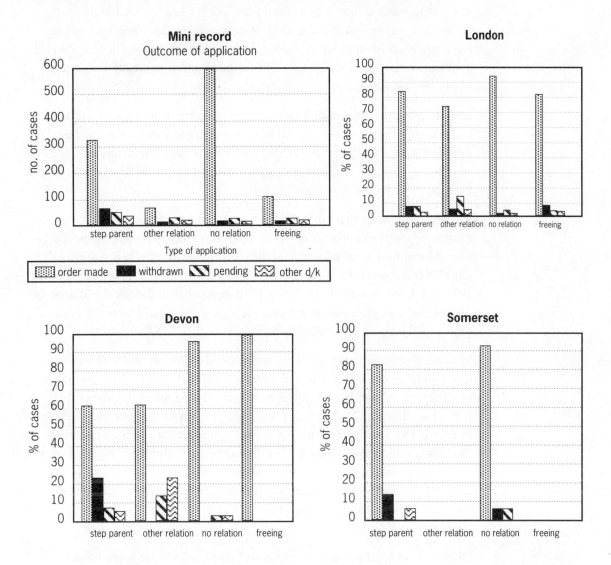

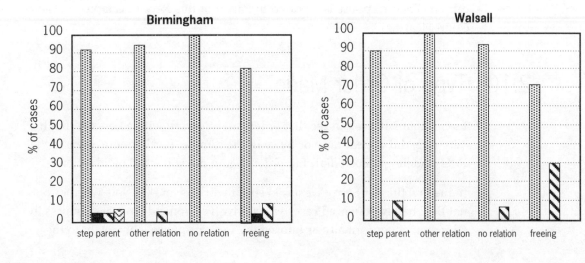

The most important point to emerge from Table 2.9 above is that for the majority (89%) of all adoption applications an order was made. Virtually none were refused and only a small proportion were withdrawn (4%) or pending or adjourned sine die (5%). With regard to no relation adoptions, the proportion of 'successful' cases was even higher (96%). These would of course have included some cases where the children had been previously subject to successful freeing applications.

Although the proportion of 'successful' freeing applications was a little lower (84%), the number was still high. 5% of freeing cases were withdrawn, 1% refused, and 8% were left pending or adjourned sine die. This reflects the suggestion that freeing cases are perhaps more likely to have been contested at some stage.

It is also noticeable that 10% of the applications by step parents were withdrawn or not proceeded with. One reason for this may be that some courts seen reluctant to grant an adoption order in those cases where a joint custody order might be more suitable. Indeed, under the Adoption Act 1976 s.14(3) (to be repealed by the Children Act 1989), the court is bound to dismiss such an application if it considers that this would be *better* dealt with as a joint custody application.

Figure 5 illustrates graphically the outcome of the application for each area in the mini record sample. It confirms our finding that the vast majority of applications in each area resulted in an order being made, whatever the type of application. However, a greater proportion of step parent adoptions appeared to be withdrawn in Devon and Somerset than in the other areas. No cases at all in Walsall were recorded as being withdrawn. Figure 5 also shows a regional variation in the outcome of freeing cases. Withdrawn applications were found only in London and Birmingham, while Walsall recorded the highest proportion of such cases that were pending or adjourned sine die.

Given the high proportion of 'successful' applications, we were prompted to ask practitioners how they viewed the court hearing and whether or not they considered a court hearing to be necessary in uncontested applications. Their response is reported in Part II of this Report, Chapter 6 (The Court Hearing).

2.10 Type of Order Made

From Table 2.10 we can see that orders for adoption with access, although very rare, did appear once or twice in the sample. Furthermore, there is little evidence of custodianship orders being made instead of adoption.

In the Practitioner Study we asked social workers and lawyers whether or not they had experienced cases which involved some degree of openness in adoption, either formally or informally. Their response lent weight to the

Table 2.10
Type of Order Made by Area (Mini Record)

	AREA											
	DEVON		**SOMERSET**		**BIRMINGHAM**		**WALSALL**		**LONDON**		**ALL**	
TYPE OF ORDER	NO.	(%)	NO.	(%)	NO.	(%)	NO.	(%)	NO.	(%)	NO.	(%)
Freeing	21	(9)	0	–	68	(21)	5	(5)	34	(9)	128	(11)
Adoption—no access	223	(91)	88	(96)	255	(78)	92	(95)	334	(90)	992	(88)
Adoption with access conditions	0	–	2	(2)	0	–	0	–	2	*	4	*
Custodianship	0	–	0	–	0	–	0	–	2	*	2	*
Other	0	–	2	(2)	2	(1)	0	–	0	–	4	*
All	**244**	**(100)**	**92**	**(100)**	**325**	**(100)**	**97**	**(100)**	**372**	**(100)**	**1130[1]**	**(100)**

*=Less than 1%

1   The total number of orders made in this Table is higher than the figure quoted in Table 2.9 (no.=1127), because cases coded as 'other' in Table 2.9 included some where an order had been made.

fact that formal arrangements are rare. However, informal arrangements appear to be more common, (see Part II of the Report, Chapter 9—Open Adoption).

2.11   Natural Mother's Agreement to the Application

It was not always easy to determine from court records whether or not an application was contested. Moreover, people disagree about the definition of a contested application—is it sufficient for agreement to the making of an order to be withheld, or does this issue have to be fought in court? We approached the matter first by recording on the mini record whether or not the application was made with the positive agreement of the natural mother. These data are given in Table 2.11 below.

It will be noted that lack of mother's agreement occurred most frequently in the freeing cases (67%) compared with only 21% in the no relation adoptions.

Analysis of the age of the child by whether or not the natural mother gave her agreement to the adoption suggested that the mother's agreement was much more likely to be given when the child was under one year old. Only 6% of cases in this group showed clear evidence of agreement being withheld, while in the remainder it was clearly given. By contrast, in the 1 up to

Table 2.11
Application with Natural Mother's Agreement by Type of Application (Mini Record)

WITH MOTHER'S AGREEMENT	TYPE OF APPLICATION									
	STEP PARENT		OTHER RELATION		NO RELATION		FREEING		ALL	
	NO.	(%)	NO.	(%)	NO.	(%)	NO.	(%)	NO.	(%)
Yes	5	(1)	51	(62)	333	(54)	48	(32)	437	(35)
No	0	–	10	(12)	128	(21)	100	(67)	238	(19)
N/A—whereabouts unknown	2	*	0	–	2	*	0	–	4	*
N/A—dead	4	(1)	17	(21)	26	(4)	0	–	47	(4)
N/A—step parent	415	(97)	0	–	0	–	0	–	415	(33)
N/A—other	0	–	2	(2)	117	(19)[1]	0	–	119	(9)
Not known	0	–	2	(2)	4	(1)	2	(1)	8	(1)
All	**426**	**(100)**	**82**	**(100)**	**610**	**(100)**	**150**	**(100)**	**1268**	**(100)**

*=Less than 1%

[1]   The comparatively high figure of 19% of no relation applications being coded as 'N/A—Other' included those cases where the mother's agreement was not required as the child was already freed for adoption.

5 year old group, the comparable figure was 49% withheld and 51% given; and for the cases in the 5 up to 10 year old group the figures are respectively 60% withheld and 40% given.

In Part II, Chapter 3 (Parental Agreement) section 3.2, we report practitioners' views on the issue of parental agreement and how it can affect the progress of a case. We shall also be seeking further information on this issue in our projected study on the Consumer View in Adoption Proceedings.[7]

2.12 Proportion of Contested Final Hearings

We also examined the court records for indications as to whether or not the final hearing had been contested. Unfortunately we found that many contained little, if any, information about the hearing itself. Thus in nearly half the records (41%), it was not possible to establish the matter with any certainty. Also, such was the lack of clarity in some of the records that it was difficult to maintain consistency. Despite these reservations, the definite information we were able to record on the mini record shown in Table 2.12 below suggests that freeing applications were more likely to be contested than no relation adoptions.

[7]   This project funded by the ESRC commenced on 1 April 1991.

Table 2.12
Proportion of Contested to Uncontested Final Hearings (Mini Record)

	TYPE OF APPLICATION									
	STEP PARENT		OTHER RELATION		NO RELATION		FREEING		ALL	
	NO.	(%)	NO.	(%)	NO.	(%)	NO.	(%)	NO.	(%)
Contested	6	(2)	2	(3)	27	(4)	28	(22)	63	(6)
Uncontested	204	(59)	41	(61)	281	(48)	47	(37)	573	(51)
Other	0	–	0	–	22	(4)	2	(2)	24	(2)
Not recorded	0	–	0	–	8	(1)	0	–	8	(1)
Not known	139	(40)	24	(36)	250	(43)	49	(39)	462	(41)
All	**349**	**(100)**	**67**	**(100)**	**588**	**(100)**	**126**	**(100)**	**1130[1]**	**(100)**

1   These figures do not total 1268, since not all cases in the sample had reached a final hearing.

2.13 Application to Dispense with Parental Agreement

On the court proforma we recorded whether the application to adopt or to free for adoption was accompanied by an application to dispense with parental agreement and if so, on what grounds. These data help to give an indication of the proportion of cases in the court proforma sample that could be said to contain an element of contest.

Table 2.13(a) shows that overall nearly a quarter (23%) of adoption applications were accompanied by an application to dispense with the birth mother's agreement. It appeared that relatively few baby adoption applications (10%) were contested by the birth mother. Excluding the 10–18 year old age group (where the number in the sample was very small) it seems that the older the child the more likely the mother was to withhold agreement to the adoption. This might be explained in part by the probability that the older the child the more likely it would be that the birth mother would find it difficult to relinquish the established bond with her child.[8]

Analyis of the data with regard to applications to dispense with the agreement of the birth father shows that only 11% were ready to contest the adoption of their child. However, this finding must be tempered with the fact that paternal agreement is less often legally required. Unmarried fathers, unless they have a custody or parental rights and duties order in their favour, or are otherwise a guardian, do not have a right to agree or withhold agreement to adoption, (see *Re M (An Infant)* [1955] 2 QB 479).

---

8   Our study on the Consumer View of Adoption Proceedings, funded by the ESRC, may shed some light on this matter.

Table 2.13(a)
Application Made to Dispense with Natural Mother's Agreement by Age of Child at Date of Current Placement—Agency Adoption Applications (Court Proforma)

| | AGE OF CHILD AT DATE OF CURRENT PLACEMENT[1] | | | | | | | | | | | |
| | UP TO 1 YR | | 1–5 YRS | | 5–10 YRS | | 10–18 YRS | | NOT KNOWN | | TOTAL | |
APPLICATION MADE TO DISPENSE	NO.	(%)	NO.	(%)	NO.	(%)	NO.	(%)	NO.	(%)	NO.	(%)
Yes	20	(10)	46	(34)	19	(51)	4	(50)	0	–	89	(23)
No	167	(81)	59	(43)	16	(43)	4	(50)	6	(100)	252	(64)
Other[2]	18	(9)	32	(23)	2	(5)	0	–	0	–	52	(13)
All	**205**	**(100)**	**137**	**(100)**	**37**	**(100)**	**8**	**(100)**	**6**	**(100)**	**393**	**(100)**

1   The definition 'age of child at date of current placement' refers to the age of the child at the time s/he entered the placement that was current when the application was made, regardless of the original purpose of that placement.

2   Where 'other' was recorded, a high proportion of these cases involved children already freed for adoption and thus parental agreement was not required. In the remainder of the 'other' cases the birth mother had died prior to the application being made.

Table 2.13(b)
Application Made to Dispense with Natural Mother's Agreement by Age of Child at Date of Current Placement—Freeing Applications (Court Proforma)

| | AGE OF CHILD AT DATE OF CURRENT PLACEMENT | | | | | | | | | | | |
| | UP TO 1 YR | | 1–5 YRS | | 5–10 YRS | | 10–18 YRS | | NOT KNOWN | | TOTAL | |
APPLICATION MADE TO DISPENSE	NO.	(%)	NO.	(%)	NO.	(%)	NO.	(%)	NO.	(%)	NO.	(%)
Yes	14	(56)	30	(70)	14	(70)	0	–	10	(100)	68	(67)
No	11	(44)	13	(30)	6	(30)	4	(100)	0	–	34	(33)
All	**25**	**(100)**	**43**	**(100)**	**20**	**(100)**	**4**	**(100)**	**10**	**(100)**	**102**	**(100)**

In Table 2.13(b) we can see that in two thirds of freeing cases, applications were made to dispense with the birth mother's agreement. This was nearly three times as many compared with agency adoption cases. The proportion of freeing applications involving babies where the mother withheld her agreement (56%) was somewhat lower than it was for children over 1 year old. This suggests that fewer freeing applications involving babies are contested by the birth mother than those involving older children. This finding may be a reflection of the way that freeing is being used by the adoption agencies. However, the fact that in 56% of cases where babies were being freed for adoption the mother's agreement was being dispensed with shows how out of line the current use of the freeing provisions is with the original predictions made by the Houghton Committee (1972).

Interrogation of the data concerning dispensation of the birth father's agreement revealed that 29% of freeing applications were accompanied by such an application. Once again, (excluding the 10–18 year age group where the number is small), the older the child the more likely it was that the birth father would withhold his consent to the application to free the child for adoption.

2.14 Definition of a Contested Case

By combining the information collected on the mini record with that recorded on the more detailed court proforma, we established for the purposes of our analysis a definition of a contested case as having one or more of the following conditions:—

— application made without birth mother's and/or birth father's agreement;[9]

— application made to dispense with birth mother's and/or birth father's agreement;

— contested final hearing.

2.15 Contested VS Uncontested Cases

The following analysis of contested cases relates only to those included in our court proforma sample. Thus cases involving non-agency placements are excluded.

Using our criteria for a contested case set out above, we found that about a quarter (26%) of all agency adoption applications and three quarters (75%) of freeing applications were contested.

Table 2.15(a) shows that Devon and Birmingham had the same proportion of contested (25%) adoption applications. However, fewer contested cases than average were found in Somerset (17%), whilst more were found in Walsall (37%).

Again, (see Table 2.15(b)), little difference was found between Devon (76%) and Birmingham (73%) in the proportion of contested freeing cases. However, although numerically small (n = 7), all the freeing cases in our sample

---

9   It has already been noted (at Part I section 2.2.5), that it is correct to refer to the parental **consent** to a freeing application being made and to parental **agreement** to an adoption application or freeing or adoption orders being made. For clarity, when referring to both freeing and adoption cases we have stated it as parental agreement to such applications.

Table 2.15(a)
Proportion of Contested Cases by Area—Agency Adoption Applications (Court Proforma)

	AREA									
	DEVON		SOMERSET		BIRMINGHAM		WALSALL		ALL	
	NO.	(%)	NO.	(%)	NO.	(%)	NO.	(%)	NO.	(%)
Contested	35	(25)	9	(17)	39	(25)	18	(37)	101	(26)
Not contested or not known	103	(75)	43	(83)	116	(75)	30	(63)	292	(74)
All	138	(100)	52	(100)	155	(100)	48	(100)	393	(100)

Table 2.15(b)
Proportion of Contested Cases by Area—Freeing Applications (Court Proforma)

	AREA							
	DEVON		BIRMINGHAM		WALSALL		TOTAL	
	NO.	(%)	NO.	(%)	NO.	(%)	NO.	(%)
Contested	16	(76)	54	(73)	7	(100)	77	(75)
Not contested or not known	5	(24)	20	(27)	0	–	25	(25)
All	21	(100)	74	(100)	7	(100)	102	(100)

from Walsall had been recorded as contested by one or both birth parents at some stage of the proceedings.

Although overall almost all agency adoption applications result in a final order (98%), Table 2.15(c) below shows that this occurs in slightly fewer contested cases (95%).

Surprisingly, no difference was found between the proportion of freeing cases that were contested and those that were not which resulted in a final order (84%)—see Table 2.15(d). A few (3%) contested freeing applications were refused and a further 13% were pending or adjourned. No uncontested application for a freeing order had been refused but we found that 16% had been withdrawn.[10]

Evidence from the following two tables suggests that contesting an application appears to have little effect on the outcome of the case and the vast majority of applications result in an order being made.

---

[10]   For further discussion of this point refer to Lowe (1991), Report of the Research into the Use and Practice of the Freeing for Adoption Provisions (Chapter 3).

Table 2.15(c)
Proportion of Contested Cases by Outcome of Application—Agency Adoption Applications (Court Proforma)

OUTCOME	CONTESTED		NOT CONTESTED/ NOT KNOWN		ALL	
	NO.	(%)	NO.	(%)	NO.	(%)
Order made	96	(95)	290	(99)	386	(98)
Pending/adjourned, s.d.	3	(3)	2	(1)	5	(1)
Other	2	(2)	0	–	2	(1)
All	**101**	**(100)**	**292**	**(100)**	**393**	**(100)**

Table 2.15(d)
Proportion of Contested Cases by Outcome of Application—Freeing Applications (Court Proforma)

OUTCOME	CONTESTED		NOT CONTESTED/ NOT KNOWN		ALL	
	NO.	(%)	NO.	(%)	NO.	(%)
Order made	65	(84)	21	(84)	86	(84)
Withdrawn	0	–	4	(16)	4	(4)
Refused	2	(3)	0	–	2	(2)
Pending/adjourned, s.d.	10	(13)	0	–	10	(10)
All	**77**	**(100)**	**25**	**(100)**	**102**	**(100)**

CHAPTER 3   A Profile of the Child in Adoption and Freeing for Adoption Proceedings

3.1   Summary

3.2   Key Findings

3.3   Sex of Child

3.4   Legitimacy of Child

3.5   Religion of Child

3.6   Ethnic Origin of Child

3.7   Siblings in Birth Family

3.8   Sibling Groups

3.9   Children with Disabilities

3.10   Age of the Child

3.11   The Stages in the Adoption Process

3.12   Routes to Adoption

3.13   Age Profile of Children at Date of Current Placement

3.14   Age Profile of Children at the Date of Placement for Adoption

3.15   Age Profile of Children at Date of Panel Recommendation

3.16   Age Profile of Children at Date of Application to Court

3.17   Age Profile of Children at Date of Order

3.18   Age Profile of Children in Contested Cases

3.1 Summary

In this chapter we study the child who is the subject of freeing or adoption applications. Using information from the mini record and where necessary the court proforma, we try to construct a picture of these children in terms of their sex and their legitimacy at the time of birth, as well as looking at their religion and ethnic origin. We look at the child's natural siblings, their involvement in child-related proceedings, including whether or not they are the subjects of a parallel application. The incidence of children with disabilities in our sample is analysed. Finally, the age profile of the child is investigated, looking for any regional variation as well as how the age profile may vary at different stages of the adoption process, and according to whether or not the case was contested.

3.2 Key Findings

3.2.1   The majority of children involved in no relation adoptions were illegitimate at the time of birth. Children being freed were a little less likely to be illegitimate. About half the children in step parent adoptions were legitimate at birth (3.4).

3.2.2   Children, especially babies, being adopted tended to come from smaller families with either one or no other sibling. The older the child being adopted, the more likely it was that the child came from larger families (3.7).

3.2.3   Children in freeing cases tended to come from larger families in general. Furthermore, the siblings of children being freed were more likely than siblings of children being adopted to have been or to be involved in child-related proceedings (3.7).

3.2.4   Over a third of children being freed were part of a sibling group with parallel applications, a higher proportion than those being adopted. The older the child, the more likelihood there was that s/he would be part of such a sibling group (3.8).

3.2.5   The majority of children in both adoption and freeing cases were classified as having no disability. The older the child being freed or adopted, the greater the likelihood was that the child had some form of disability (3.9).

3.2.6   A difference in the age profiles of the children at the time of application was noted according to the type of application. Children involved in no relation adoptions were, on the whole, much younger than children being adopted by step parents or by other relatives. Children being freed tended to be in the pre-school age range (1–5 years old) (3.10).

3.2.7   Regional variations were found in the age profiles of children being freed when analysed at different stages of the adoption process, which may reflect differing agency practices in the use of the freeing provisions (3.13–3.17).

3.2.8   We also found regional variations in the ages of children being adopted at the different stages of the adoption process, a finding which suggests that some agencies may have an adoption policy for placement of older children centred on long-term fostering with a view to adoption (3.13–3.17).

3.2.9   Children in contested freeing cases tended to be about two years younger than children in contested adoptions (3.18).

3.3 Sex of Child

We see from Table 3.3 that there was little difference in the proportion of boys to girls being adopted overall. Slightly more boys than girls were subject to freeing applications, whereas the reverse was true for adoptions by step-parents and other relations.

Analysis of the court proforma data confirmed these findings from the mini record in relation to the ratio of boys to girls being freed. It also showed that more girls (57%) than boys (43%) were being adopted as babies, whereas the opposite was true for children over 1 year old.

Table 3.3
Sex of Child by Type of Application (Mini Record)

	TYPE OF APPLICATION									
	STEP PARENT		OTHER		NO REL.		FREEING		ALL	
	NO.	(%)	NO.	(%)	NO.	(%)	NO.	(%)	NO.	(%)
Male	200	(47)	33	(40)	302	(49)	82	(55)	617	(49)
Female	226	(53)	49	(60)	308	(51)	68	(45)	651	(51)
All	**426**	**(100)**	**82**	**(100)**	**610**	**(100)**	**150**	**(100)**	**1268**	**(100)**

3.4 Legitimacy of Child

Table 3.4 records the legitimacy of the child at birth for each type of application. When interpreting the data we need to remember that over a quarter of all children are currently being born illegitimate, (OPCS 1989). The table shows nevertheless that in no relation adoptions illegitimate children made up over three quarters (78%) of the total. More children involved in freeing proceedings were legitimate, 37% compared with 18%

Table 3.4
Legitimacy of Child by Type of Application (Mini Record)

	TYPE OF APPLICATION									
	STEP PARENT		OTHER REL		NO REL		FREEING		ALL	
	NO.	(%)	NO.	(%)	NO.	(%)	NO.	(%)	NO.	(%)
Legitimate	210	(49)	27	(33)	108	(18)	55	(37)	400	(32)
Illegitimate	192	(45)	45	(55)	476	(78)	88	(59)	801	(63)
Illegitimate and subsequently legitimized	8	(2)	6	(7)	12	(2)	5	(3)	31	(2)
Other	0	–	0	–	2	*	0	–	2	*
Not known	14	(3)	4	(5)	12	(2)	2	(1)	32	(3)
Not recorded	2	*	0	–	0	–	0	–	2	*
All	426	(100)	82	(100)	610	(100)	150	(100)	1268	(100)

* = Less than 1%

in the no relation adoptions.[1] It is interesting but not surprising to note that half the children in step parent adoptions (49%) were legitimate at birth.

3.5 Religion of Child

We recorded details of the child's religion on the court proforma. We found that around half the children did not have any particular religious affiliation (49% of agency adoption cases and 57% of freeing cases).

26% of children in adoption applications were affiliated to the Church of England,[2] 9% were Roman Catholic and 3% were affiliated to other Christian denominations. A small percentage of children were either Muslim or Sikh.

In freeing cases 22% of the children were affiliated to the Church of England and 11% Roman Catholic. A few children were either Muslim or affiliated to other Christian denominations.

3.6 Ethnic Origin of Child

Little useful information was obtained from the court record survey on the child's ethnic origin because this factor was seldom recorded on any document found in the court files.

[1] For a possible explanation of this finding refer to Lowe (1991), Report of the Research into the Use and Practice of the Freeing for Adoption Provisions (Chapter 3).

[2] The term 'Church of England' is used in this report to define the Churches of England, Wales, Ireland, and the Episcopal Church of Scotland.

Thus, for instance, the race of the child cannot be identified in 72% of agency adoption applications in our court proforma sample. However, given this limitation we found that 13% of the children were of mixed ethnic origin and 10% white. A small percentage of children were of either Indian, West Indian or African origin.

Similarly for freeing applications in the court proforma sample, no information was found on the child's ethnic origin in 74% of cases. Of the total sample of freeing cases, 12% of the children were recorded as white and 10% as being of mixed origin.

3.7   Siblings in Birth Family

We recorded on the court proforma details of the child's siblings in the birth family, including their number, sex, relationship to the child and whether or not they were subject to a parallel application.

Table 3.7a
Number of Siblings by Age of Child at Date of Current Placement—Agency Adoption Applications (Court Proforma)

	AGE OF CHILD AT DATE OF CURRENT PLACEMENT[1]										
	UP TO 1 YR		1–5 YRS		5–10 YRS		10–18 YRS		NOT KNOWN		TOTAL	
NO. OF SIBLINGS	NO.	(%)	NO.	(%)	NO.	(%)	NO.	(%)	NO.	(%)	NO.	(%)
None	111	(54)	25	(18)	6	(16)	4	(50)	0	–	146	(37)
One	40	(20)	26	(19)	8	(22)	0	–	4	(67)	78	(20)
Two	18	(9)	32	(23)	4	(11)	0	–	0	–	54	(14)
Three	14	(7)	14	(10)	2	(5)	0	–	0	–	30	(8)
Four	8	(4)	20	(15)	13	(35)	0	–	0	–	41	(11)
Five or more	14	(7)	18	(13)	4	(11)	4	(50)	2	(33)	42	(11)
Not known	0	–	2	(1)	0	–	0	–	0	–	2	(1)
All	**205**	**(100)**	**137**	**(100)**	**37**	**(100)**	**8**	**(100)**	**6**	**(100)**	**393**	**(100)**

[1]   See Part I Table 2.13(a) for the definition of 'Age at Date of Current Placement'

From Table 3.7(a) one can see that over a third (37%) of children involved in agency adoption applications had no siblings, the majority of those being babies when placed in their current home. Whereas in general over half of the children in adoption proceedings (57%) had either only one or no siblings, 46% of the older children aged between 5 and 10 years when currently placed came from larger families with four or more siblings. Perhaps not surprisingly, the trend appears to be that the older the child the more likely it is s/he is part of a larger birth family. Further analysis of

Table 3.7b
Number of Siblings by Age of Child at Date of Current Placement—Freeing Applications (Court Proforma)

NO. OF SIBLINGS	AGE OF CHILD AT DATE OF CURRENT PLACEMENT											
	UP TO 1 YR		1–5 YRS		5–10 YRS		10–18 YRS		NOT KNOWN		TOTAL	
	NO.	(%)	NO.	(%)	NO.	(%)	NO.	(%)	NO.	(%)	NO.	(%)
None	8	(32)	4	(9)	0	–	0	–	0	–	12	(12)
One	3	(12)	9	(21)	0	–	0	–	2	(20)	14	(14)
Two	4	(16)	10	(23)	2	(10)	0	–	0	–	16	(16)
Three	10	(40)	6	(14)	4	(20)	2	(50)	2	(20)	24	(24)
Four	0	–	6	(14)	10	(50)	0	–	2	(20)	18	(18)
Five or more	0	–	8	(19)	4	(20)	2	(50)	4	(40)	18	(18)
All	**25**	**(100)**	**43**	**(100)**	**20**	**(100)**	**4**	**(100)**	**10**	**(100)**	**102**	**(100)**

these data revealed that the greater the number of birth siblings, the more likely it was that these siblings were half brothers or sisters to the child being adopted.

A comparison of the children in agency adoption applications with the children in freeing applications in respect of number of birth siblings shows that children being freed came from larger families in general. From Table 3.7(b) it can be seen that only 12% of children in freeing cases had no siblings and the greater proportion of children (60%) have 3 or more siblings. Indeed, in contrast to baby adoptions, 40% of babies being freed came from families having four children.[3] Further analysis of the data in terms of the relationship between the siblings and the child being freed showed that the proportion of half-siblings to full siblings was approximately equal with little difference noted according to the size of the family.

In the mini record survey we noted whether or not the child had other birth siblings who were or had been involved in child-related proceedings[4] (for example, civil care proceedings (s.1(2) Children and Young Persons Act 1969), proceedings under the Guardianship Acts 1971 and 1973, wardship proceedings, etc.). The result, as seen in Table 3.7(c) below, shows that the majority of children (62%) in freeing cases had siblings who were or had been involved in child-related proceedings, compared with 42% in 'ordinary' adoption cases and 39% in step parent adoptions. Although these figures cannot be compared directly with those from the court proforma

---

3   This point is developed further in Lowe (1991), Report of the Research into the Use and Practice of the Freeing for Adoption Provisions (Chapter 3).

4   Cases where the sibling was the subject of a parallel application are included in this description (see following section 3.8).

since the latter sample excludes all non-agency placements, they seem to confirm the impression that children in freeing cases are more likely to come from larger families with a history of experience with the social services and the family justice system.

Table 3.7(c)
Number of Siblings Involved in Child-Related Proceedings by Type of Application (mini record)

	TYPE OF APPLICATION									
	STEP PARENT		OTHER REL		NO REL		FREEING		ALL	
SIBLINGS INVOLVED IN CHILD-RELATED PROCEEDINGS	NO.	(%)	NO.	(%)	NO.	(%)	NO.	(%)	NO.	(%)
Yes	164	(39)	17	(21)	254	(42)	93	(62)	528	(42)
No	178	(42)	43	(52)	167	(27)	39	(26)	427	(34)
Not recorded	2	*	4	(5)	2	*	0	–	8	(1)
No other sibs.	30	(7)	2	(2)	108	(18)	8	(5)	148	(12)
Not known	52	(12)	16	(20)	79	(13)	10	(7)	157	(12)
All	**426**	**(100)**	**82**	**(100)**	**610**	**(100)**	**150**	**(100)**	**1268**	**(100)**

* = Less than 1%

3.8   Sibling Groups

A record was made on the court proforma with siblings who were the subject of a parallel application, that is, an application for the same type of order made by the same applicants at the same time.

18% of children in agency adoption cases had one or more siblings who were the subject of a parallel application (see table 3.8(a)). There were relatively few babies (7%) who were part of such a sibling group compared with just under half (46%) of children aged between 5 and 10 years when placed for adoption who have siblings subject to a parallel application. These figures for older children are perhaps not so remarkable when one considers that around 80% of children in care have at least one sibling (who may or may not be in care).

In the Practitioner Study, social workers in particular considered it desirable that wherever possible and appropriate, sibling groups should be placed in the same adoptive home. They also felt that consideration should be given to the possibility of some kind of sibling contact being maintained when siblings are separated by adoption (see Part II Chapter 9 (Open Adoption)).

Table 3.8(a)
Children as Part of a Sibling Group by Age of Child at Date of Current Placement—Agency Adoption Applications (Court Proforma)

| | AGE OF CHILD AT DATE OF CURRENT PLACEMENT | | | | | | | | | | |
| | UP TO 1 YR | | 1–5 YRS | | 5–10 YRS | | 10–18 YRS | | NOT KNOWN | | TOTAL | |
NO. OF SIBLINGS IN PARALLEL APPLICATION	NO.	(%)	NO.	(%)	NO.	(%)	NO.	(%)	NO.	(%)	NO.	(%)
None	191	(93)	99	(72)	20	(54)	8	(100)	2	(33)	320	(81)
One	14	(7)	32	(23)	14	(38)	0	–	4	(67)	64	(16)
Two	0	–	6	(4)	3	(8)	0	–	0	–	9	(2)
All	**205**	**(100)**	**137**	**(100)**	**37**	**(100)**	**8**	**(100)**	**6**	**(100)**	**393**	**(100)**

Table 3.8(b)
Children as Part of a Sibling Group by Age of Child at Date of Current Placement—Freeing Applications (Court Proforma)

| | AGE OF CHILD AT DATE OF CURRENT PLACEMENT | | | | | | | | | | |
| | UP TO 1 YR | | 1–5 YRS | | 5–10 YRS | | 10–18 YRS | | NOT KNOWN | | TOTAL | |
NO. OF SIBLINGS IN PARALLEL APPLICATION	NO.	(%)	NO.	(%)	NO.	(%)	NO.	(%)	NO.	(%)	NO.	(%)
None	21	(84)	29	(67)	10	(50)	2	(50)	2	(20)	64	(63)
One	0	–	10	(23)	2	(10)	0	–	6	(60)	18	(18)
Two	4	(16)	0	–	4	(20)	0	–	0	–	8	(8)
Three	0	–	2	(5)	2	(10)	2	(50)	2	(20)	8	(8)
Four	0	–	2	(5)	2	(10)	0	–	0	–	4	(4)
All	**25**	**(100)**	**43**	**(100)**	**20**	**(100)**	**4**	**(100)**	**10**	**(100)**	**102**	**(100)**

38% of children in freeing cases had one or more siblings who were the subject of a parallel application. Only 16% of babies were members of such a group compared with 33% of children aged 1–5 years old and 50% of children aged between 5 and 10 years old when they entered their current placement.[5]

---

[5]   The significance of this finding is discussed in Lowe (1991), Report of the Research into the Use and Practice of the Freeing for Adoption Provisions (Chapter 3).

3.9   Children with Disabilities

Disability is only one potential hurdle to successful placement, and in other sections we have looked at race, and sibling groups (Part I *ante* at sections 3.6 and 3.8 respectively), all factors that may be termed special needs in relation to placement for adoption.

Using the information contained in the Schedule II report, four different categories of disabilities were recorded.[6]

(a)   Long term physical illness or disability

(b)   Mental handicap

(c)   Emotional or behavioural difficulties requiring specialist services[7]

(d)   Learning difficulties requiring specialist school.

While the large majority (89%) of children in agency adoption cases from our sample were recorded as having no disability, the remaining 12% of children may be classified as disabled in some respect (see Table 3.9(a)). A

Table 3.9(a)

Children with One or More Disabilities by Age of Child at Date of Current Placement—Agency Adoption Applications (Court Proforma)

| | AGE OF CHILD AT DATE OF CURRENT PLACEMENT | | | | | | | | | | |
| | UP TO 1 YR | | 1–5 YRS | | 5–10 YRS | | 10–18 YRS | | NOT KNOWN | | TOTAL | |
NO. OF DISABILITIES	NO.	(%)	NO.	(%)	NO.	(%)	NO.	(%)	NO.	(%)	NO.	(%)
None	189	(92)	123	(90)	29	(78)	4	(50)	6	(100)	351	(89)
One	8	(4)	10	(7)	4	(11)	0	–	0	–	22	(6)
Two	5	(2)	0	–	2	(5)	0	–	0	–	7	(2)
Three	3	(1)	2	(1)	2	(5)	0	–	0	–	7	(2)
Four	0	–	2	(1)	0	–	4	(50)	0	–	6	(2)
All	**205**	**(100)**	**137**	**(100)**	**37**	**(100)**	**8**	**(100)**	**6**	**(100)**	**393**	**(100)**

small proportion of babies and younger children (1–5 years old) being adopted had one or more disabilities (8% and 9% respectively). Older children appear to be more likely to have some form of disability, with 21% of

---

6   These categories (with the exception of (d)), were taken from the Adoption Proceedings Unit Return (Form A100) issued by the OPCS in 1984.

7   This category may include children who have been subject to various types of abuse and thus require some form of specialist service. Since we were relying on the Schedule II report for such information, our data in this category are to some extent dependent on the judgement of the social worker writing the report, as to whether or not such children would be included.

Table 3.9(b)
**Children with One or More Disabilities by Age of Child at Date of Current Placement—
Freeing Applications (Court Proforma)**

| NO. OF DISABILITIES | AGE OF CHILD AT DATE OF CURRENT PLACEMENT | | | | | | | | | | |
| | UP TO 1 YR | | 1–5 YRS | | 5–10 YRS | | 10–18 YRS | | NOT KNOWN | | TOTAL | |
	NO.	(%)	NO.	(%)	NO.	(%)	NO.	(%)	NO.	(%)	NO.	(%)
None	23	(92)	28	(65)	14	(70)	2	(50)	6	(60)	73	(72)
One	2	(8)	11	(26)	0	–	2	(50)	0	–	15	(15)
Two	0	–	2	(5)	4	(20)	0	–	4	(40)	10	(10)
Three	0	–	2	(5)	0	–	0	–	0	–	2	(2)
Four	0	–	0	–	2	(10)	0	–	0	–	2	(2)
All	**25**	**(100)**	**43**	**(100)**	**20**	**(100)**	**4**	**(100)**	**10**	**(100)**	**102**	**(100)**

children aged between 5 and 10 years old when they entered their current placement having one or more disabilities and (although the number is small), 50% of children aged between 10 and 18 years old having all four types of disability.

Analysis of these data by area showed that there was little difference between the areas in the proportion of children with disabilities who were being adopted.

We find from Table 3.9(b) that just under three quarters (72%) of children in freeing cases were recorded as having no disabilities (as defined in this survey). Analysis of the data by age of the child at the date of current placement revealed that relatively few babies being freed were disabled (8%), whereas about one third of children between 1 and 10 years old had one or more disabilities. When the incidence of children being freed with disabilities was analysed by area we found that just under a half (44%) of children being freed in Devon had some form of disability, compared with a third (33%) in Walsall and a quarter (24%) in Birmingham.

Further interrogation of the court proforma data to determine the frequency of the different types of disability revealed that only 5% of children overall had either a long-term physical illness or disability or some form of mental handicap or indeed both. There was little difference in this respect between children being freed or being adopted. However, roughly four times as many children being freed as those being adopted suffered some emotional or behavioural difficulty requiring specialist services. Furthermore, around three times as many children being freed as those being adopted had some learning difficulty requiring a specialist school.

3.10   Age of Child

The mini record data presented in Table 3.10 below shows that two-thirds of the no relation adoption cases involved younger children under the age of five. Of these, 37% involved babies under a year old and a further 30% involved pre-school children between the ages of 1 and 5 years old. All told, under fives made up 67% of this mainstream category of adoption—a figure nearly matched by the children in the freeing category, although here it will be noted that proportionately more babies were subject to adoption than freeing proceedings. It will also be noted that in the 5–10 year old age range the freeing group (32%) was more than double the proportion involved in the no relation group.[8] Of interest to point out is the finding that adoption by relatives and step parents mostly concerned children over five, comprising almost 80% of the step parent group and 56% in the 'other relation' group.

Table 3.10
Age of Child at Date of Application by Type of Application (Mini Record)

| | TYPE OF APPLICATION | | | | | | | | | |
| | STEP PARENT | | OTHER RELATION | | NO RELATION | | FREEING | | ALL | |
AGE	NO.	(%)	NO.	(%)	NO.	(%)	NO.	(%)	NO.	(%)
Up to 1 yr	3	(1)	8	(10)	226	(37)	18	(12)	255	(20)
1–5 yrs	74	(17)	22	(27)	182	(30)	74	(49)	352	(28)
5–10 yrs	175	(41)	26	(32)	90	(15)	48	(32)	339	(27)
10–18 yrs	164	(38)	20	(24)	81	(13)	6	(4)	271	(21)
Not known	10	(2)	6	(7)	31	(5)	4	(3)	51	(4)
All	**426**	**(100)**	**82**	**(100)**	**610**	**(100)**	**150**	**(100)**	**1268**	**(100)**

Figure 6 illustrates graphically these differences in the age profiles of the child according to the type of application.

We decided to investigate further the age profiles of these children at various stages of the adoption process, using data available from the court proforma. In particular, we were interested in how the age profile of the children may vary according to the area, the type of court used and whether or not the proceedings were contested.

---

8   The significance of these findings in relation to freeing is taken up in Lowe (1991), Report of the Research into the Use and Practice of the Freeing for Adoption Provisions (Chapter 3).

Figure 6:

Age of child (at date of application) for each type of application

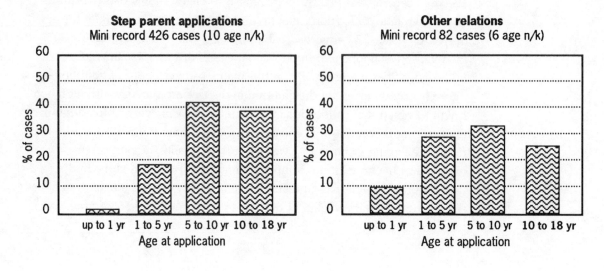

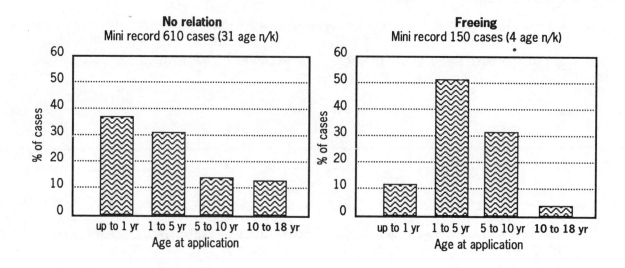

3.11   Stages in the Adoption Process

There are of course many stages reached and decisions taken on the future of the child in care, prior to being placed for adoption. The first definitive stage on the route to adoption is the point at which the Adoption Panel identifies the child as suitable for adoption and recommends that s/he should be placed for adoption (or in the case of freeing that the child should be freed for adoption). The adoption agency then carries out a home-finding and 'matching' exercise to find suitable adopters for the child following which the actual placement is recommended by the Adoption Panel. Long term foster children may well have been with the family for some time before the foster parents make the decision to adopt in which case these two stages coincide. The application for an adoption order is made to the court by the prospective adoptive parents and following at least one court hearing a decision is made by the court. In the case of freeing the application to the court for a freeing order is made by the adoption agency.

The date of placement for adoption is defined for the purposes of this study as the date when the child was actually placed for adoption with the prospective adopters. Where the child had been placed on a long term fostering basis either with a view to adoption, or where the foster parents had subsequently decided to adopt, the date of placement for adoption has been taken for these purposes as the date when the Adoption Panel recommended that those caring for the child could proceed with their application to adopt. In these cases therefore, and in most others, the date of placement for adoption is the same as or within a few days of the date of panel recommendation. In a few cases the child had been placed in the adoptive home prior to the date of panel recommendation, whereas in other cases the panel made their recommendation prior to the actual placement for adoption. We should not forget that the date of placement for adoption probably represents little change to the child's actual situation. As far as the child is concerned, the date s/he entered his/her current placement has much more significance.

In our court proforma sample we found that, where the information was available from the court records, for the majority of cases the date of placement for adoption coincided with the date of the panel recommendation. In a handful of cases (2%), the child had been placed for adoption some months before the Adoption Panel had formally recommended the placement. In a few more instances, (3%), the placement of the child for adoption followed the date of the panel placement recommendation by weeks or even months.

In this study we decided to take five reference points in the adoption process. For children being adopted these points are:—

—   date when current placement began, that is the date the child entered the placement that was current at the date of application, regardless of the original purpose of that placement;

—   date of placement for adoption;

—   date of Adoption Panel recommendation of this placement;

—   date of application to court;

—   date of court order.

Where freeing is concerned the reference points in the process have been defined as:—

— date when the current placement began;

— date of Adoption Panel recommendation to make freeing application;[9]

— date of application to court;

— date of court order.

3.12   Routes to Adoption

For the purpose of this secondary analysis we have categorised the children in our court proforma sample according to which route to adoption had been selected for them and at which point on that route they had reached; that is,

— Children for whom an application has been made to free for adoption (FREEING).

— Children who previously have been freed and for whom an application has now been made to adopt (ADOPT/PREV. FREED).

— Children who are going straight to adoption and for whom an application has been made to adopt (ADOPTION).

3.13   Age Profile of Children at Date of Current Placement

In general, we see from Table 3.13 that children being freed entered their current placement aged on average three and a half years. Children who are to be adopted appeared to be a year or so younger than children being freed at this stage. It is perhaps interesting to note that in Walsall, where the child being adopted had already been freed, the average age of such children was around six months, which is in marked contrast to children in the same category of application from the other areas, who were on average at least two years old.

Table 3.13
Mean Age of Child at Date of Entering into Current Placement By Area (Court Proforma)

AREA	TYPE OF APPLICATION					
	FREEING		ADOPT/PREV FREED		ADOPTION	
	(YEARS)		(YEARS)		(YEARS)	
Devon	2.97	(n = 17)	2.11	(n = 21)	1.26	(n = 115)
Somerset	–	–	5.45	(n = 4)	1.52	(n = 46)
Birmingham	3.68	(n = 68)	2.04	(n = 28)	2.31	(n = 125)
Walsall	2.09	(n = 7)	0.52	(n = 10)	2.65	(n = 38)
All	**3.43**	**(n = 92)**	**2.04**	**(n = 63)**	**1.86**	**(n = 324)**
[Missing cases]	[10 (9%)]		[0]		[6 (2%)]	

3.14   Age Profile of Children at the Date of Placement for Adoption

We next examined the age profile of the children at the time they were placed for adoption. We have excluded from this analysis those children who were being freed for adoption because at the time of application they were not necessarily placed for adoption.

The data in Table 3.14(a) show that just under half (46%) the agency adoption applications in our sample involved children who were under one year old when placed for adoption. Nearly a quarter (23%) of the children were of school age, of which a small proportion (9%) was over ten years old.

Table 3.14(a)
Age of Child when Placed for Adoption by Area—All Agency Adoptions (Excluding Freeing) (Court Proforma)

	AREA									
	DEVON		SOMERSET		BIRMINGHAM		WALSALL		TOTAL	
	NO.	(%)	NO.	(%)	NO.	(%)	NO.	(%)	NO.	(%)
Up to 1 yr	68	(49)	26	(50)	68	(44)	18	(38)	180	(46)
1–5 yrs	43	(31)	8	(15)	53	(34)	14	(29)	118	(30)
5–10 yrs	17	(12)	14	(27)	16	(10)	8	(17)	55	(14)
10–18 yrs	10	7	2	(4)	16	(10)	8	(17)	36	(9)
Not known	0	–	2	(4)	2	(1)	0	–	4	(1)
Total	**138**	**(100)**	**52**	**(100)**	**155**	**(100)**	**48**	**(100)**	**393**	**(100)**

Further analysis revealed little regional variation—Devon and Somerset had slightly higher proportions of baby adoptions than Birmingham and Walsall.

The data in Table 3.14(b) shows that on average children placed for adoption without previously being freed were slightly older than children placed for adoption who had already been freed. It is worth noting that in Walsall, unlike the other areas in our study, the average age of previously freed children being placed for adoption was around nine months, these children being considerably younger at placement than children from the same area going straight to adoption, who were on average around five and a half years old. This finding, together with that in Part I, section 3.13 *ante*, suggests that Walsall may have adopted a different practice from the other areas in relation to the "straightforward" agency adoption.

Table 3.14(b)
Mean Age of Child when Placed for Adoption by Area (Court Proforma)

AREA	TYPE OF APPLICATION			
	ADOPT/PREV. FREED		ADOPTION	
	(YEARS)		(YEARS)	
Devon	2.49	(n = 21)	2.71	(n = 117)
Somerset	5.37	(n = 4)	2.70	(n = 46)
Birmingham	2.13	(n = 28)	3.05	(n = 125)
Walsall	0.73	(n = 10)	5.45	(n = 38)
All	**2.24**	**(n = 63)**	**3.16**	**(n = 326)**

[missing cases]   [0]   [4 (1%)]

3.15 Age Profile of Children at Date of Panel Placement Recommendation/Agency Decision

From Table 3.15 we see that at the time of recommendation children being freed were in general somewhat older than children being adopted. However, once again in Walsall the converse was true, where the average age of children being adopted (without being freed first) was four years older than the average age (just over two years old) of children being freed at the date of the placement recommendation.

Table 3.15
Mean Age of Child at Date of Panel Placement Recommendation/Agency Decision by Area (Court Proforma)

	TYPE OF APPLICATION					
AREA	**FREEING**		**ADOPT/PREV. FREED**		**ADOPTION**	
	(YEARS)		**(YEARS)**		**(YEARS)**	
Devon	3.08	(n = 15)	2.62	(n = 18)	2.76	(n = 109)
Somerset	–		6.13	(n = 4)	2.80	(n = 43)
Birmingham	4.20	(n = 68)	2.11	(n = 26)	3.18	(n = 115)
Walsall	2.37	(n = 7)	0.73	(n = 10)	6.32	(n = 30)
All	**3.87**	**(n = 90)**	**2.31**	**(n = 58)**	**3.29**	**(n = 297)**
[missing cases]	(12 (12%)		[5 (8%)]		[33 (10%)]	

A more detailed analysis of the age of children at the point when an application for freeing is recommended reveals that only 10% of these children were babies. Furthermore in Devon during the study period we found that none of the children in our sample were babies at that time, (compared with 11% of children in Birmingham and 29% in Walsall). Around a third (35%) of the sample of children in Birmingham were five years old or over when recommended for freeing, compared with 10% in Devon and none at all in Walsall.

As can be seen from Table 3.15, we found that overall, children in agency adoption applications who had not been previously freed were on average a little older (just over three years old) at the time of the recommendation than the previously free group (around two and a quarter years old on average). This difference was very much more marked in Walsall where the average age of children being adopted who had previously been freed was under one year old, compared with an average age of about six and a quarter years for children going straight to adoption. Indeed, further analysis revealed that 80% of children in Walsall who were being adopted having been previously freed were under one year old at the time of the panel placement recommendation (compared with 29% in Birmingham and none at all in Devon and Somerset). On the other hand, we found that Walsall had the smallest percentage (16%) of babies being recommended for adoption without previously being freed (compared with an average for the four areas of 47%).

These data raise the question of whether Walsall, unlike the other areas in our study, has a policy of freeing babies for adoption, as well as a different policy for older children who are more likely to be placed in a long term foster home with a view to adoption.

3.16 Age Profile of Children at Date of Application to Court

We took as the fourth step in the adoption process the date when the application for adoption or freeing for adoption was lodged in the court. By this stage an unknown number of children may have "fallen by the wayside", in the sense that although a recommendation to place the child for adoption had been made or, in the case of freeing, the child had been recommended for a freeing application, an application was never made to the court for a variety of reasons. Since it was agreed to select our sample from applications made to the courts, these children are inevitably missing from our study.

As one would predict having seen the data in Table 3.15 (*ante*, section 3.15), the figures in Table 3.16(a) show that in general, children being freed were slightly older on average (about four and a quarter years old), at the time of application than those being adopted, especially those children in our sample who had previously been freed (just under three years old). This finding suggests that the children in our sample who were currently being freed were different, at least in terms of their age, from the sample of children who were being adopted following a freeing order. This may reflect changes in agency policy and practice since the implementation of the freeing provisions. Once again, the exception to this is Walsall where there was a wide difference in the average ages between children being freed (about two and a half years old) and those going straight to adoption who were just over seven years old at the time the adoption application was made.

Table 3.16(a)
Mean Age of Child at Date of Application by Area (Court Proforma)

AREA	TYPE OF APPLICATION					
	FREEING		ADOPT/PREV. FREED		ADOPTION	
	(YEARS)		(YEARS)		(YEARS)	
Devon	3.66	(n = 19)	3.27	(n = 21)	3.53	(n = 109)
Somerset	–		7.03	(n = 4)	2.90	(n = 46)
Birmingham	4.72	(n = 72)	2.89	(n = 28)	3.79	(n = 125)
Walsall	2.53	(n = 7)	1.06	(n = 10)	7.11	(n = 37)
All	**4.36**	**(n = 98)**	**2.99**	**(n = 63)**	**3.96**	**(n = 317)**

[missing cases]   (4 (4%)   [0]   [13 (4%)]

From Table 3.16(b) an interesting pattern emerges relating to court usage according to the type of application being made. It appears in the case of applications to the High Court (although the number of children is small) that the child is on average younger in freeing proceedings compared with

Table 3.16(b)
Mean Age of Child at Date of Application by Type of Court (Court Proforma)

COURT	TYPE OF APPLICATION					
	FREEING		ADOPT/PREV. FREED		ADOPTION	
	(YEARS)		(YEARS)		(YEARS)	
Magistrates'	4.54	(n = 8)	2.79	(n = 12)	2.54	(n = 20)
County	4.47	(n = 84)	3.06	(n = 50)	4.00	(n = 284)
High	2.55	(n = 6)	1.94	(n = 1)	5.27	(n = 13)
All	**4.36**	**(n = 98)**	**2.99**	**(n = 63)**	**3.96**	**(n = 317)**

[missing cases]	(4 (4%)	[0]	[13 (4%)]

adoption proceedings (without a prior freeing order). The magistrates' court tends to deal with younger children being adopted without previously being freed (average age of about two and a half years). There is little difference in the average ages of children appearing before the county court and the magistrates' court for a freeing order, (about four and a half years old).

3.17   Age Profile of Children at Date of Order

The fifth and final stage in the adoption process is the granting of the court order.

Table 3.17
Mean Age of Child at Date of Order by Area (Court Proforma)

AREA	TYPE OF APPLICATION					
	FREEING		ADOPT/PREV. FREED		ADOPTION	
	(YEARS)		(YEARS)		(YEARS)	
Devon	4.45	(n = 21)	3.56	(n = 21)	3.84	(n = 115)
Somerset	–		7.37	(n = 4)	3.52	(n = 46)
Birmingham	4.44	(n = 60)	3.13	(n = 28)	4.22	(n = 127)
Walsall	3.51	(n = 5)	1.35	(n = 10)	7.16	(n = 35)
All	**4.39**	**(n = 86)**	**3.26**	**(n = 63)**	**4.30**	**(n = 323)**

[missing cases]	[16 (16%)]	[0]	[7 (2%)]

There was little difference in the average ages of children (around 4 years 4 months) being freed and those being adopted (without previously being freed) at the time they reached the order. However, those children who had

Figure 7:

Age range of children at various stages in the adoption process for each type of application (court proforma)

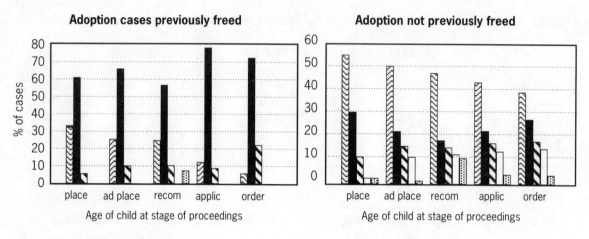

Adoption cases previously freed — Adoption not previously freed

Age of child at stage of proceedings

Key to abbrerviations

place -　　date of current placement

ad place -　date of current placement for adoption

recom -　　date of panel placement
　　　　　　recommendation/agency decision

applic -　　date of application

order -　　date of order

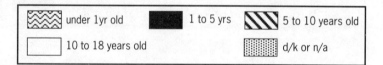

under 1yr old　　1 to 5 yrs　　5 to 10 years old

10 to 18 years old　　d/k or n/a

Freeing cases
Court proforma

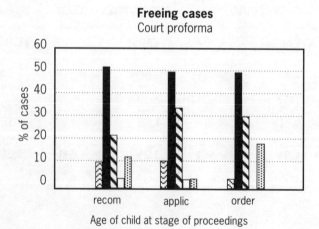

Age of child at stage of proceedings

been adopted having previously been freed were on average over a year younger than children being freed. This reinforces our earlier observation (see *ante* Part I at section 3.16) that the two groups of children in our sample who either are being freed or have been freed already have different characteristics, at least in terms of their age. The group of children who have been freed and are now involved in adoption proceedings appear to be younger than children who are now involved in the freeing process. This may be a reflection of the changing practices in the use of freeing provisions amongst the agencies.[10]

Figure 7 illustrates the age profiles of the children for each category of application at the different stages of the adoption process. The relatively high proportion of babies in mainstream agency adoption cases (where the child was not already freed), compared with adoption cases where the child had been freed is to be noted together with the fact that in freeing cases the greatest proportion of children were aged between one and five years.

3.18   Age Profile of Children in Contested Cases

We have described earlier (see *ante* Part I, section 2.14) the criteria adopted in the study to define a contested case. In this section we examine the variation in the age profiles of the children according to whether or not the case was contested. Adoption applications relating to children who have previously been freed are excluded from this analysis, because in these cases after the granting of a freeing order the birth parents are no longer involved in the proceedings.

We already have found (Table 3.15 *ante* at section 3.15) that the overall tendency seemed to be for children being recommended by the adoption panel for freeing to be somewhat older than children going straight to adoption. However, from Table 3.18 we see that children in contested freeing cases were just under three and a half years old on average, which was roughly two years younger than the average age of children in contested adoption cases (just over five and a half years old). Conversely, the older the child the less likely the freeing application was to be contested, with an average age of just over five years for children in uncontested freeing cases. Children in uncontested adoption cases were on average aged about two years four months.

Social workers and solicitors in the Practitioner Study talked about the changes that have taken place in adoption in recent years. They felt that older children and children with disabilities who would previously have

---

10   A fuller analysis of the differing lengths between these stages of the adoption process and how they vary between area, type of court and whether the case was contested or not is described later in Part I, Chapters 7, 8 and 9.

Table 3.18

Mean Age of Child at Date of Panel Placement Recommendation/Agency Decision in Contested and Uncontested Cases (Court Proforma)

	TYPE OF APPLICATION			
	FREEING		ADOPTION	
	(YEARS)		(YEARS)	
Contested	3.38	(n = 65)	5.66	(n = 85)
Not contested/not known	5.13	(n = 25)	2.34	(n = 212)
All	**3.87**	**(n = 90)**	**3.29**	**(n = 297)**

[missing cases]	[12 (12%)]	[33 (10%)]

languished in care are now more likely to have adoption as one of the options open to them. The profile of children in the Court Record Survey offers some further proof of these changes. A consequence of this, and one of particular concern to the practitioners, was the need to consider the possibility of more open adoption for some of the older children who may have established a bond with birth family members prior to adoption proceedings. Practitioners' views are described in Part II, Chapter 9 (Open Adoption).

CHAPTER 4   Care History of Children Involved in Adoption and Freeing for Adoption Proceedings

4.1   Summary

4.2   Key Findings

4.3   Care Status of Child at time of Application

4.4   The Current Care Period

4.5   Number of Previous Periods in Care

4.6   The Child's Current Placement

4.7   History of Previous Placements

4.1 Summary

In this chapter we describe the care history of the children who are the subject of adoption and freeing for adoption applications. As well as examining various aspects of the current (at the time of the application) care period, if the child was in care at that time, we also look back at any previous periods of care. We describe the type of placement the child was in at the time of application, as well as examining the frequency and nature of previous placements.

4.2 Key Findings

4.2.1   In comparison with step parent adoptions where very few of the children were in care at the time of the application, the great majority of children in no relation adoption or freeing proceedings were in care (either voluntary or compulsory) at that time (4.3).

4.2.2   Around half the sample of children in agency adoption proceedings were in compulsory care at the time of the application. A higher proportion of children being freed were in compulsory care. Furthermore, the older the child the more likely it was that s/he was in compulsory care at the time of the application (4.4).

4.2.3   The majority of children in agency adoption cases, although in care at the time of the adoption application, had not been in care before. However, these were more likely to be babies. Older children being adopted tended to have had one or more previous periods in care. Furthermore, over twice as many children being freed as those being adopted had been in care previously (4.5).

4.2.4   Few babies being adopted had experienced more than one other placement prior to their placement for adoption (4.7). The older the child, the more likely that he or she had been placed originally in the current placement on a long-term fostering basis before the foster parents made the decision to adopt (4.6).

4.2.5   Children being freed were more likely to be in a short term fostering placement at the time of the application, although around one fifth of the sample had already been placed with an adoptive family (4.6). Just over half the sample of children being freed had experienced two or more moves, more often than not involving short term foster parents, since separation from their birth family (4.7).

4.3   Care Status of Child at Time of Application

Table 4.3
Status of Child at Date of Application by Type of Application (Mini Record)

	TYPE OF APPLICATION									
	STEP-PARENT		OTHER REL.		NO REL.		FREEING		ALL	
STATUS OF CHILD	NO.	(%)	NO.	(%)	NO.	(%)	NO.	(%)	NO.	(%)
Voluntary care	2	*	4	(5)	204	(33)	40	(27)	250	(20)
Compulsory care[1]	0	–	10	(12)	290	(48)[2]	108	(72)	408	(32)
Not in care	418	(98)	68	(83)	112	(18)	2	(1)	600	(47)
Other	0	–	0	–	4	(1)	0	–	4	*
Not known	6	(1)	0	–	0	–	0	–	6	(1)
All	**426**	**(100)**	**82**	**(100)**	**610**	**(100)**	**150**	**(100)**	**1268**	**(100)**

* =less than 1%

1   Children who had been subject to s. 3 parental rights resolutions were considered as being in compulsory care.

2   Theoretically once children are free for adoption they cease to be in compulsory care, but for the purposes of this investigation they were still classified as being so.

Almost all children subject to freeing applications and the great majority of those involved in no relation adoptions were in either compulsory or voluntary care, in marked contrast to those cases where children were being adopted by step parents or other relations.

Further investigation using the court proforma data revealed that in this sub-sample (where all non-agency placements are excluded), 8% of children in agency adoption proceedings were not in care at the time of application, all of whom were babies when placed for adoption. This finding probably relates to different agency practices, where some agencies always receive babies into care before placing them for adoption and others do not.

4.4   The Current Care Period

If the child was in care, we also recorded the way s/he had come into care for the current care period.

From Table 4.4(a) we see that just under half (47%) of children involved in agency adoption proceedings and who were currently in care came into care under a court order, with a similar proportion who were received into the voluntary care of a local authority (47%). The remainder were received into the care of a voluntary organisation (6%).

Table 4.4(a)

How the Child Came into Care by Age of Child at Date of Current Placement—Agency Adoption Applications (Court Proforma)

	AGE OF CHILD AT DATE OF CURRENT PLACEMENT											
	UP TO 1 YR		1–5 YRS		5–10 YRS		10–18 YRS		NOT KNOWN		TOTAL	
	NO.	(%)	NO.	(%)	NO.	(%)	NO.	(%)	NO.	(%)	NO.	(%)
Received into care voluntarily by LA	114	(66)	37	(27)	11	(30)	6	(75)	2	(33)	170	(47)
Received into care voluntarily by voluntary organisations	18	(10)	2	(1)	0	–	0	–	0	–	20	(6)
Came into care under court order	41	(24)	98	(72)	26	(70)	2	(25)	4	(67)	171	(47)
All	**173**	**(100)**	**137**	**(100)**	**37**	**(100)**	**8**	**(100)**	**6**	**(100)**	**361[1]**	**(100)**

1   The total number of children (n=361) in this table is less than the total number of children in agency adoption applications (n=393) since some children were not in care at the time of applicaton.

Around three quarters (76%) of babies in care had been received into care voluntarily for the current care period, compared with just over a quarter (28%) of children aged between one and five years old and 30% of children aged between five and ten years old. This finding once again emphasises the existence of two different types of adoption that are currently taking place—the adoption of babies and that of older children. It should be mentioned however that a high proportion (75%) of older children (ten years and over) had been received into voluntary care. The number of children in this age cateogry is too small (n=8) to warrant further investigation.

Children who had been received into care voluntarily by the local authority and subsequently had been the subject of a parental rights resolution should not be overlooked. We found from information in the court proforma that nearly a quarter of children being freed (23%) had been the subject of a parental rights resolution, a higher proportion than children in agency adoptions (13%).

It is evident when comparing Table 4.4(a) with Table 4.4(b) that a higher proportion of children in freeing proceedings had come into care under a court order (63%) compared with those children in adoption proceedings. More than half the babies involved in freeing cases had been received into care voluntarily (52%), whereas older children being freed were more likely to have been taken into compulsory care.

Table 4.4(b)
**How the Child Came into Care by Age of Child at Date of Current Placement—Freeing
Applications (Court Proforma)**

	AGE OF CHILD AT DATE OF CURRENT PLACEMENT										
	UP TO 1 YR		1–5 YRS		5–10 YRS		10–18 YRS		NOT KNOWN		TOTAL	
	NO.	(%)	NO.	(%)	NO.	(%)	NO.	(%)	NO.	(%)	NO.	(%)
Received into care voluntarily by LA	9	(36)	12	(28)	6	(30)	0	–	2	(20)	29	(28)
Received into care voluntarily by voluntary organisation	4	(16)	1	(2)	0	–	0	–	0	–	5	(5)
Came into care under court order	12	(48)	30	(70)	14	(70)	2	(50)	6	(60)	64	(63)
Other	0	–	0	–	0	–	2	(50)	2	(20)	4	(4)
All	**25**	**(100)**	**43**	**(100)**	**20**	**(100)**	**4**	**(100)**	**10**	**(100)**	**102**	**(100)**

4.5   Number of Previous Periods in Care

From data recorded on the court proforma, we ascertained the number of
previous care periods that these children had experienced.

Table 4.5(a) reveals that only 15% of children in care and placed for adoption had been in care once before and even fewer (4%) had been in care
twice or more before. The majority of children (67%) although in care at the
time of the adoption application had not been in care before. However,
these were mostly babies and, perhaps not surprisingly, children who had
been in care previously tended to be aged between five and ten years old.
9% of children aged from one to five years old and 14% of children aged
from five to ten years old had experienced two or more previous periods of
care.

We see from Table 4.5(b) that just under half (43%) the children in freeing
proceeding had been in care previously, 25% having been in care once
before, 5% twice before and 13% three or more times previously. The older
the child (save for the ten to eighteen year old age group where our sample
is too small to be significant) the more likely it appeared that s/he had
been in care before this current period.

Comparing these figures for freeing proceedings with those for adoption, it
will be seen that twice as many children involved in freeing had been in
care before this current period (43%) as those being adopted (19%).

Table 4.5(a)
Number of Times Previously in Care by Age of Child at Date of Current Placement—Agency Adoption Applications (Court Proforma)

NO. OF TIMES IN CARE	AGE OF CHILD AT DATE OF CURRENT PLACEMENT											
	UP TO 1 YR		1–5 YRS		5–10 YRS		10–18 YRS		NOT KNOWN		TOTAL	
	NO.	(%)	NO.	(%)	NO.	(%)	NO.	(%)	NO.	(%)	NO.	(%)
None	160	(78)	83	(61)	12	(32)	6	(75)	2	(33)	263	(67)
One	9	(4)	31	(23)	16	(43)	2	(25)	0	–	58	(15)
Two	0	–	7	(5)	4	(11)	0	–	2	(33)	13	(3)
Three	0	–	3	(2)	1	(3)	0	–	0	–	4	(1)
Four	0	–	2	(1)	0	–	0	–	0	–	2	*
Five	0	–	2	(1)	0	–	0	–	0	–	2	*
Not recorded[1]	32	(16)	8	(6)	4	(11)	0	–	0	–	46	(12)
Not known	2	(1)	1	(1)	0	–	0	–	2	(33)	5	(1)
All	**205**	**(100)**	**137**	**(100)**	**37**	**(100)**	**8**	**(100)**	**6**	**(100)**	**393**	**(100)**

* =less than 1%

1   Cases in this category included those where the child was not in care at the time of the application.

Table 4.5(b)
Number of Times Previously in Care by Age of Child at Date of Current Placement—Freeing Applications (Court Proforma)

NO. OF TIMES IN CARE	AGE OF CHILD AT DATE OF CURRENT PLACEMENT											
	UP TO 1 YR		1–5 YRS		5–10 YRS		10–18 YRS		NOT KNOWN		TOTAL	
	NO.	(%)	NO.	(%)	NO.	(%)	NO.	(%)	NO.	(%)	NO.	(%)
None	16	(64)	17	(40)	4	(20)	2	(50)	2	(20)	41	(40)
One	7	(28)	13	(30)	6	(30)	0	–	0	–	26	(25)
Two	1	(4)	4	(9)	0	–	0	–	0	–	5	(5)
Three	0	–	2	(5)	2	(10)	0	–	4	(40)	8	(8)
Four	1	(4)	0	–	0	–	0	–	0	–	1	(1)
Five or more	0	–	0	–	2	(10)	0	–	2	(20)	4	(4)
Not recorded[1]	0	–	4	(9)	2	(10)	2	(50)	2	(20)	10	(10)
Not known	0	–	3	(7)	4	(20)	0	–	0	–	7	(7)
All	**25**	**(100)**	**43**	**(100)**	**20**	**(100)**	**4**	**(100)**	**10**	**(100)**	**102**	**(100)**

1   Cases in this category included those where the child was not in care at the time of the application.

4.6   The Child's Current Placement[1]

We see from Table 4.6(a) that in agency adoption cases, as one would expect, for the majority of children (68%) the original purpose of the current placement was adoption. A further 20% had originally been placed with long term foster parents who had subsequently made the decision to adopt. A breakdown of the data in Table 4.6(a) by the child's age reveals that the original purpose of the current placement was adoption for a high proportion of babies (84%). However, the older the child the more likely it was that s/he had entered his or her current placement initially on a long-term fostering basis before the foster parents made the decision to adopt. This finding may well reflect agency policy. In some cases involving older children, although an adoption placement may be sought, the child is placed on a long-term fostering basis initially in order that, given the irreversible nature of adoption, enough time is allowed for settling in and unhurried decisions to be made, as well as perhaps to enable payments to be made to the care givers.

Table 4.6(a)
Original Purpose of Current Placement by Age of Child at Date of Current Placement—Agency Adoption Applications (Court Proforma)

	AGE OF CHILD AT DATE OF CURRENT PLACEMENT										
	UP TO 1 YR		1–5 YRS		5–10 YRS		10–18 YRS		NOT KNOWN		TOTAL	
PURPOSE OF PLACEMENT	NO.	(%)	NO.	(%)	NO.	(%)	NO.	(%)	NO.	(%)	NO.	(%)
Placed for adoption	172	(84)	80	(58)	15	(40)	2	(25)	0	–	269	(68)
Long-term* fostering	17	(8)	43	(31)	14	(38)	4	(50)	2	(33)	80	(20)
Short-term fostering	10	(5)	6	(4)	2	(5)	2	(25)	0	–	20	(5)
Other	6	(3)	8	(6)	6	(16)	0	–	0	–	20	(5)
Not known	0	–	0	–	0	–	0	–	4	(67)	4	(1)
All	**205**	**(100)**	**137**	**(100)**	**37**	**(100)**	**8**	**(100)**	**6**	**(100)**	**393**	**(100)**

* We recorded the placement as long-term or short-term fostering according to how it was described in the Schedule II report. We realize that this definition has shortcomings since local authorities may have different criteria.

We found that in 80% of the cases where the original purpose of the current placement had been short term fostering, the placement evolved into a long-term fostering one before the decision to adopt was taken.

We did not find *any* change recorded in the child's placement situation during the course of the adoption proceedings (compared with freeing proceedings, see below).

---

[1]   For the purpose of this study we defined a placement as an agency arrangement made by either a local authority or a voluntary organisation, as opposed to a 'private' arrangement.

Table 4.6(b)

Original Purpose of Current Placement by Age of Child at Date of Current Placement—Freeing Applications (Court Proforma)

PURPOSE OF PLACEMENT	AGE OF CHILD AT DATE OF CURRENT PLACEMENT											
	UP TO 1 YR		1–5 YRS		5–10 YRS		10–18 YRS		NOT KNOWN		TOTAL	
	NO.	(%)	NO.	(%)	NO.	(%)	NO.	(%)	NO.	(%)	NO.	(%)
Placed for adoption	3	(12)	6	(14)	8	(40)	2	(50)	2	(20)	21	(21)
Long-term fostering	3	(12)	10	(23)	2	(10)	2	(50)	2	(20)	19	(19)
Short-term fostering	17	(68)	19	(44)	2	(10)	0	–	6	(60)	44	(43)
Other	2	(8)	6	(14)	8	(40)	0	–	0	–	16	(16)
Not known	0	–	2	(5)	0	–	0	–	0	–	2	(2)
All	**25**	**(100)**	**43**	**(100)**	**20**	**(100)**	**4**	**(100)**	**10**	**(100)**	**102**	**(100)**

The data presented in Table 4.6(b) show that just under half (43%) of children in freeing cases were currently placed with short term foster parents. A smaller proportion (19%) of children were with long term foster parents and a similar proportion (20%) of children in freeing applications had already been placed in an adoptive home.

A closer examination of the court proforma data revealed that for about a quarter of children in freeing cases their placement situation had changed during the course of the proceedings. However, no pattern emerged from an investigation of these freeing cases in terms of the child's age or the length of the proceedings. Further analysis revealed that over a third of this sub sample of children (35%) had been placed in an adoptive home during the course of the proceedings before a decision on the freeing application had been made.

4.7   History of Previous Placements

Table 4.7(a) shows the number of previous placements experienced by children who were being adopted by the age of the child at the date s/he entered his or her current placement.

Just over half the children in agency adoption cases had had **one** previous placement (53%) and a third (34%) of children had experienced **two or more** moves in their lives in between being separated from their birth family and entering their current placement. If one examines these data in terms of ages of the children, whereas only 8% of babies had had two or more previous placements, over half (57%) of the children aged between 1

Table 4.7(a)

Number of Previous Placements by Age of Child at Date of Current Placement—Agency Adoption Applications (Court Proforma)

NO. OF PREVIOUS PLACEMENTS	AGE OF CHILD AT DATE OF CURRENT PLACEMENT											
	UP TO 1 YR		1–5 YRS		5–10 YRS		10–18 YRS		NOT KNOWN		TOTAL	
	NO.	(%)	NO.	(%)	NO.	(%)	NO.	(%)	NO.	(%)	NO.	(%)
None	29	(14)	14	(10)	2	(5)	2	(25)	0	–	47	(12)
One	159	(78)	45	(33)	4	(11)	0	–	2	(33)	210	(53)
Two	13	(6)	42	(31)	12	(32)	2	(25)	0	–	69	(18)
Three	4	(2)	17	(12)	4	(11)	2	(25)	2	(33)	29	(7)
Four	0	–	16	(12)	7	(19)	0	–	0	–	23	(6)
Five or more	0	–	2	(2)	8	(22)	2	(25)	0	–	12	(3)
Not known	0	–	1	(1)	0	–	0	–	2	(33)	3	(1)
All	**205**	**(100)**	**137**	**(100)**	**37**	**(100)**	**8**	**(100)**	**6**	**(100)**	**393**	**(100)**

and 5 years, and the great majority of children aged between 5 and 10 years (84%) and of children 10 years and over (75%) had experienced two or more placements before being moved to their current home.

A few (12%) of the children had been placed directly for adoption. In the case of babies, we may suppose that they had been placed with their prospective adoptive parents direct from hospital. However, a small number of older chidren were also found to have been placed directly for adoption without any intermediary placement. Further investigation would be needed to discover their situation prior to placement for adoption.

Closer analysis of the pattern of previous placements revealed that, where the child to be adopted had had a previous placement, the large majority (84%) of first placements were with short term or interim foster parents. Only a few children (4%) had been originally placed in a children's home, although it seems that older children were more likely to experience a children's home as their first placement.

Where the child had experienced two previous placements, the second such placement was also likely to be with short term or interim foster parents (64%). 12% of the children had their second placement in a children's home, this occurrence being more likely the older the child. A few children (4%) had already been placed with prospective adopters, but that placement had subsequently broken down.

In Table 4.7(b) the number of previous placements experienced by children in freeing cases is analysed by the age of the child when s/he entered the current placement.

Table 4.7(b)
Number of Previous Placements by Age of Child at Date of Current Placement—Freeing Applications (Court Proforma)

	AGE OF CHILD AT DATE OF CURRENT PLACEMENT										
	UP TO 1 YR		1–5 YRS		5–10 YRS		10–18 YRS		NOT KNOWN		TOTAL	
NO. OF PREVIOUS PLACEMENTS	NO.	(%)	NO.	(%)	NO.	(%)	NO.	(%)	NO.	(%)	NO.	(%)
None	14	(56)	6	(14)	0	–	2	(50)	0	–	22	(22)
One	4	(16)	14	(33)	2	(10)	2	(50)	0	–	22	(22)
Two	4	(16)	16	(37)	6	(30)	0	–	0	–	26	(26)
Three	2	(8)	4	(9)	0	–	0	–	4	(40)	10	(10)
Four	1	(4)	0	–	2	(10)	0	–	4	(40)	7	(7)
Five or more	0	–	2	(5)	6	(30)	0	–	2	(20)	10	(10)
Not known	0	–	1	(2)	4	(20)	0	–	0	–	5	(5)
All	**25**	**(100)**	**43**	**(100)**	**20**	**(100)**	**4**	**(100)**	**10**	**(100)**	**102**	**(100)**

Just under a quarter of children (22%) in freeing cases had had no previous placement and a similar proportion had only one previous placement. The remainder of the children (53%) from our sample had experienced two or more moves since separation from their birth family. As with children in adoption proceedings, the older the child (excluding the ten to eighteen year old age group where the number in our sample is too small to be significant), the more likely it appeared to be that s/he would have had several previous placements. Furthermore, it should be remembered that children in freeing cases may not yet have gained a permanent placement. With adoption, a worryingly high proportion of children aged between one and five years (51%) had experienced two or more moves in their brief lives since being separated from their birth family.

Further investigation into the pattern of previous placements revealed that the large majority (80%) of children in freeing proceedings who had had one or more previous placements had perhaps predictably usually been placed with short term or interim foster parents.

Where there had been three or more previous placements for both adoption and freeing applications (involving 16% and 27% of our sample respectively), analysis revealed that these children had more often than not experienced a succession of moves involving short term foster parents.

CHAPTER 5   The Child's Court Career

5.1   Summary

5.2   Key Findings

5.3   Previous Child-related Proceedings

5.4   The Frequency of Previous Court Orders

5.1   Summary

As well as obtaining a picture of the care career and placement history of children being adopted or freed for adoption, we were also interested in discovering the different routes through the courts that those children had travelled before an application for adoption or freeing for adoption was made. In this chapter we look at the frequency of previous child-related proceedings that the child had experienced, together with the frequency and pattern of court orders of which the child may have been the subject[1].

5.2   Key Findings

5.2.1   More than half the children in our mini record sample had been involved in previous child-related proceedings. For children being freed that figure rises to over two thirds (5.3).

5.2.2   Just under half the sample of children being freed had experienced at least two or more previous child-related proceedings, a higher proportion of children than in the no relation adoption group (5.3).

5.2.3   For all types of proceedings, the older the child involved the more likely s/he was to have been the subject to one or more court orders. However, startingly a small number of babies being freed in our sample had already been the subject of five court orders (5.4).

5.3   Previous Child-Related Proceedings

We ascertained from the mini record data the proportion of children in the sample who had been involved in previous child-related proceedings.

It will be seen from Table 5.3(a) that more than half the children (55%) in the mini record sample had been involved in previous child-related proceedings, a figure that rises to 68% in the freeing group. Table 5.3(b) shows the breakdown of the number of previous child-related proceedings by type of case.

We have already seen from the mini record data displayed in Table 5.3(a) that children being freed were more likely than children in no relation adoptions to have been involved in previous child-related proceedings. It appears from Table 5.3(b) that, where previous proceedings had occurred, a higher proportion of children in freeing cases (71%) had experienced at least two or more previous child-related proceedings, compared with children in no relation adoptions (61%). This is not surprising, since a number

---

1   For a more detailed examination of these previous proceedings experienced by children being freed or adopted, see Murch and Griew (1991) Monograph on Charting the Pathways to Adoption (to be published).

Table 5.3(a)
Has the Child been Involved in Other Child-Related Proceedings Prior to This Application? (Mini Record)

	TYPE OF APPLICATION									
	STEP PARENT		OTHER REL.		NO REL.		FREEING		ALL	
	NO.	(%)	NO.	(%)	NO.	(%)	NO.	(%)	NO.	(%)
Yes	253	(59)	29	(35)	314	(52)	102	(68)	698	(55)
No	153	(36)	53	(65)	296	(48)	48	(32)	550	(43)
Other	4	(1)	0	–	0	–	0	–	4	*
Not known	16	(4)	0	–	0	–	0	–	16	(1)
All	**426**	**(100)**	**82**	**(100)**	**610**	**(100)**	**150**	**(100)**	**1268**	**(100)**

* =less than 1%

Table 5.3(b)
The Number of Previous Child-Related Proceedings by Type of Application (Mini Record)

	TYPE OF APPLICATION									
	STEP PARENT		OTHER REL.		NO REL.		FREEING		ALL	
NO. OF PROCEEDINGS	NO.	(%)	NO.	(%)	NO.	(%)	NO.	(%)	NO.	(%)
At least one	167	(66)	17	(59)	113	(36)	29	(28)	326	(47)
At least two	62	(25)	10	(35)	113	(36)	33	(32)	218	(31)
At least three	14	(6)	2	(7)	55	(17)	28	(27)	99	(14)
At least four	4	(2)	0	–	14	(5)	8	(8)	26	(4)
At least five	0	–	0	–	6	(2)	4	(4)	10	(1)
More than five	0	–	0	–	2	(1)	0	–	2	*
Not known	6	(2)	0	–	11	(3)	0	–	17	(2)
All	**253**	**(100)**	**29**	**(100)**	**314**	**(100)**	**102**	**(100)**	**698**	**(100)**

* =less than 1%

of children being freed may have been involved in care proceedings preceded by a place of safety order and followed by further care proceedings. It must also be remembered that some of the children in the latter category (15%) will have been the subject of previous freeing proceedings[2], (see Part 1, section 2.4).

---

[2]   For further discussion and analysis of these previous child-related proceedings, see Murch and Griew (1991) Monograph on Charting the Pathways to Adoption.

5.4   The Frequency of Previous Court Orders

Further investigation using the court proforma data was carried out looking at the frequency of the child's previous court orders in terms of the age of the child at the date of the current placement.

From our court proforma sample of children involved in agency adoption applications, (see Table 5.4(a)), just half (50%) of such children had not been the subject of any previous court orders. These data confirm the mini record information displayed in Table 5.3(b) (*ante* at section 5.3). On the other hand, just over a third (39%) of children had been the subject of at least two court orders, those children tending to be in the one to five years and five to ten years age groups. A noticeable 16% of children aged from five to ten years when entering their current placement had been the subject of five or more court orders.

Table 5.4(a)
Number of Previous Court Orders by Age of Child at Date of Current Placement—Agency Adoption Applications (Court Proforma)

	AGE OF CHILD AT DATE OF CURRENT PLACEMENT											
	UP TO 1 YR		1–5 YRS		5–10 YRS		10–18 YRS		NOT KNOWN		TOTAL	
NO. OF PREVIOUS COURT ORDERS	NO.	(%)	NO.	(%)	NO.	(%)	NO.	(%)	NO.	(%)	NO.	(%)
None	156	(76)	26	(19)	7	(19)	6	(75)	2	(33)	197	(50)
One	11	(5)	23	(17)	8	(22)	0	–	2	(33)	44	(11)
Two	14	(7)	36	(26)	8	(22)	2	(25)	2	(33)	62	(16)
Three	13	(6)	39	(29)	6	(16)	0	–	0	–	58	(15)
Four	9	(4)	2	(1)	2	(5)	0	–	0	–	13	(3)
Five or more	2	(1)	11	(8)	6	(16)	0	–	0	–	19	(5)
All	**205**	**(100)**	**137**	**(100)**	**100**	**(100)**	**8**	**(100)**	**6**	**(100)**	**393**	**(100)**

Confirming what we have already found (Table 5.3(b) *ante* at Part I, section 5.3), we see from Table 5.4(b) that a smaller proportion of children in freeing cases than in agency adoptions had not been the subject of a previous court order (28%). At the same time, a higher percentage of these children had been the subject of two or more court orders (58%). Again, the older the child (save for the ten to eighteen year old age group where the number in our sample is too small to be significant), the more likely it is that s/he will have been the subject of a greater number of court orders, although it is noticeable that a sizeable proportion (16%) of babies being free, although numerically very small, had already been the subject of at least five court orders.

Table 5.4(b)
Number of Previous Court Orders by Age of Child at Date of Current Placement—Freeing Applications (Court Proforma)

	AGE OF CHILD AT DATE OF CURRENT PLACEMENT										
	UP TO 1 YR		1–5 YRS		5–10 YRS		10–18 YRS		NOT KNOWN		TOTAL	
NO. OF PREVIOUS COURT ORDERS	NO.	(%)	NO.	(%)	NO.	(%)	NO.	(%)	NO.	(%)	NO.	(%)
None	12	(48)	8	(19)	2	(10)	2	(50)	4	(40)	28	(28)
One	3	(12)	8	(19)	4	(20)	0	–	0	–	15	(15)
Two	4	(16)	11	(26)	6	(30)	2	(50)	0	–	23	(22)
Three	2	(8)	8	(19)	6	(30)	0	–	2	(20)	18	(18)
Four	0	–	3	(7)	2	(10)	0	–	4	(40)	9	(9)
Five or more	4	(16)	5	(12)	0	–	0	–	0	–	9	(9)
All	**25**	**(100)**	**43**	**(100)**	**20**	**(100)**	**4**	**(100)**	**10**	**(100)**	**102**	**(100)**

CHAPTER 6 # Profile of the Birth Parents and the Adoptive Family

6.1   Summary

6.2   Key Findings

6.3   Marital Status of the Birth Parents at Date of Application

6.4   Religion of the Birth Parents

6.5   Ethnic Origin of the Birth Parents

6.6   Age of the Birth Mother at the Time of the Child's Birth

6.7   Religion of the Adoptive Parents

6.8   Ethnic Origin of the Adoptive Parents

6.9   Age of the Adoptive Mother at the Date of Application

6.10 A Comparison of the Age of the Birth Mother and the Adoptive Mother

6.11 The Siblings in the Adoptive Family

6.1   Summary

In this chapter we first describe the birth parents of children being adopted or freed for adoption, collated from information recorded in the court proforma. The parents' marital status, their religion and ethnic origin are discussed. The age of the birth mother at the time the child was born is analysed. Secondly we look at the prospective adoptive family. We have omitted a profile of the parents of such children who, although placed with a view to adoption, were the subject of freeing applications, as it was sometimes difficult to ascertain from the court files the exact status of the child at the time of application and the timing of the adoption placement. The religion and ethnic origin of the adoptive parents are described. We analyse the age profile of the adoptive mother at the date of application and a comparison in age is made between the birth mother and the adoptive mother. Finally, we look at the siblings in the prospective adoptive family in relation to their number and status, (that is, whether natural, fostered or adopted).

6.2   Key Findings

6.2.1   The majority of birth parents of children in agency adoptions were single and not cohabiting at the time of the application. Children being freed tended more to come from families where the parents either were or had been married at the time of the application (6.3).

6.2.2   Around three quarters of the children from the court proforma sample, whether the subject of adoption or freeing applications, were born to mothers aged 25 years or under (6.6).

6.2.3   A comparison of the ages of the birth mother and adoptive mother revealed that in the large majority of agency adoption cases the birth mother was yonger than the adoptive mother, perhaps by 15 years or more (6.10).

6.2.4   Pre school children (aged from one to five years), were more likely to be placed for adoption with a family that already had children, unlike babies and older children (6.11).

6.3   Marital Status of the Birth Parents at Date of Application

The majority (68%) of the birth parents of children in agency adoption proceedings were single and were not cohabiting at the time the adoption application was made, this being especially so in the case of babies being adopted. From Table 6.3(a) one can see that the older the child being

Table 6.3(a)
Marital Status of Birth Parents by Age of Child at Date of Current Placement—Agency Adoption Applications (Court Proforma)

	AGE OF CHILD AT DATE OF CURRENT PLACEMENT											
	UP TO 1 YR		1–5 YRS		5–10 YRS		10–18 YRS		NOT KNOWN		TOTAL	
MARITAL STATUS	No.	(%)	No.	(%)	No.	(%)	No.	(%)	No.	(%)	No.	(%)
Married	9	(4)	13	(9)	4	(11)	0	–	0	–	26	(7)
Divorced	0	–	18	(13)	6	(16)	4	(50)	2	(33)	30	(8)
Married and separated	4	(2)	8	(6)	8	(22)	0	–	0	–	20	(5)
Never married	172	(84)	78	(57)	15	(41)	2	(25)	2	(33)	269	(68)
Cohabiting	14	(7)	4	(3)	2	(5)	0	–	0	–	20	(5)
Widowed	0	–	2	(2)	0	–	0	–	0	–	2	(1)
N/A	2	(1)	0	–	0	–	0	–	0	–	2	(1)
Other[1]	2	(1)	8	(6)	2	(5)	2	(25)	0	–	14	(4)
Not known	2	(1)	6	(4)	0	–	0	–	2	(33)	10	(2)
All	**205**	**(100)**	**137**	**(100)**	**37**	**(100)**	**8**	**(100)**	**6**	**(100)**	**393**	**(100)**

[1] In all but one of the cases in this category, one or both of the parents (who were not married to each other) had died before the application was made. In the remaining case the parents had divorced but were still cohabiting.

Table 6.3(b)
Marital Status of Birth Parents by Age of Child at Date of Current Placement—Freeing Applications (Court Proforma)

	AGE OF CHILD AT DATE OF CURRENT PLACEMENT											
	UP TO 1 YR		1–5 YRS		5–10 YRS		10–18 YRS		NOT KNOWN		TOTAL	
MARITAL STATUS	No.	(%)	No.	(%)	No.	(%)	No.	(%)	No.	(%)	No.	(%)
Married	4	(16)	11	(26)	4	(20)	2	(50)	4	(40)	25	(24)
Divorced	0	–	3	(7)	2	(10)	0	–	2	(20)	7	(7)
Married and separated	2	(8)	2	(5)	4	(20)	2	(50)	2	(20)	12	(12)
Never married	13	(52)	19	(44)	8	(40)	0	–	2	(20)	42	(41)
Cohabiting	4	(16)	6	(14)	2	(10)	0	–	0	–	12	(12)
Other	0	–	2	(5)	0	–	0	–	0	–	2	(2)
Not known	2	(8)	0	–	0	–	0	–	0	–	2	(2)
All	**25**	**(100)**	**43**	**(100)**	**20**	**(100)**	**4**	**(100)**	**10**	**(100)**	**102**	**(100)**

adopted, the more likely it was that the child's birth parents had either separated or divorced.

About a quarter of the sample of children in freeing proceedings (24%) came from families where the parents were still married at the time the freeing application was made. Just under half the sample (41%) came from a background where the birth parents were single and not cohabiting (a smaller proportion than in adoption). In the case of babies being freed for adoption, about a half of them originated from such relationships but approximately a third of the babies (33%) came from families where the parents were still together whether or not they were married. This pattern is repeated in the age group 1–5 years old, but is less pronounced in the age group 5–10 years old where 30% of the children came from homes where the parents had either separated or divorced.

6.4 Religion of the Birth Parents

In agency adoption cases nearly half of the birth mothers (46%) declared themselves to be affiliated to the Church of England. 15% said they had no religious affiliation and 13% were Roman Catholic. A small proportion of them were either affiliated to other Christian denominations, or were of Sikh or Muslim faith. As far as the birth fathers were concerned, the religious affiliation of about half of them was unknown. Of the remainder, 25% were affiliated to the Church of England, 8% were Roman Catholic, and 11% had no religious affiliation.

Nearly half (46%) of the mothers of children being freed declared their religious affiliation to be Church of England, 18% were Roman Catholic, 21% had no religious affiliation, and a small percentage (2%) were Muslim. The religious affiliation of the birth father was unknown for quite a high proportion of cases (38%), but a further 18% of fathers were Roman Catholic, 16% Church of England and 8% Muslim. 17% had no religious affiliation.

6.5 Ethnic Origin of the Birth Parents

It is disappointing to have to report that, as with the data on the child's ethnic origin, generally speaking there was little information available from the court records on the ethnic origin of the birth parents.

In about four fifths of agency adoption cases information on the ethnic origin of the parents was unavailable. Where it was known, we found that half the birth mothers were white with the remainder being of mixed race, West Indian or Indian origin with a few of African origin. An equal proportion of birth fathers were of white or mixed race origin, while the remainder had Indian, West Indian and African origins.

Very little information could be gathered on the racial origin of birth parents of children being freed. In 85% of the cases their race was not stated. Where it was known, the birth mother was either of white or mixed race background, whereas there was a wider spread of ethnicity connected with the birth father (mixed race, white, West Indian, Indian and Arab).

6.6   Age of the Birth Mother at the Time of the Child's Birth

From Table 6.6(a) we see that around three quarters of the children in our court proforma sample (74%) involved in agency adoption applications were born to mothers aged 25 years old or under, and more than half of those were aged under 20. In only 9% of cases were the birth mothers 30 years old or over at the time of the child's birth.

Table 6.6(a)
Age of the Birth Mother at Date of Child's Birth by Age of Child at Date of Current Placement—Agency Adoption Applications (Court Proforma)

	AGE OF CHILD AT DATE OF CURRENT PLACEMENT											
	UP TO 1 YR		1–5 YRS		5–10 YRS		10–18 YRS		NOT KNOWN		TOTAL	
AGE OF BIRTH MOTHER	NO.	(%)	NO.	(%)	NO.	(%)	NO.	(%)	NO.	(%)	NO.	(%)
20 yrs and under	94	(46)	53	(30)	17	(46)	4	(50)	4	(67)	172	(44)
21–25 yrs	52	(26)	50	(36)	14	(38)	2	(25)	0	–	118	(30)
26–30 yrs	32	(16)	16	(12)	4	(11)	0	–	0	–	52	(13)
31–35 yrs	16	(8)	8	(6)	0	–	2	(25)	0	–	26	(7)
36–40 yrs	7	(3)	2	(2)	0	–	0	–	0	–	9	(2)
41–65 yrs	2	(1)	0	–	0	–	0	–	0	–	2	–
Not known	2	(1)	8	(6)	2	(5)	0	–	2	(33)	14	(4)
All	**205**	**(100)**	**137**	**(100)**	**37**	**(100)**	**8**	**(100)**	**6**	**(100)**	**393**	**(100)**

There was little difference to be found in the age profile of birth mothers whose children were being freed for adoption (see Table 6.6(b)). In just under three quarters (73%) of these cases the mother was 25 years old or under when her child was born. 13% of children in freeing proceedings were born when their mothers were 30 years old or more.

A comparison of the ages of the birth mother and adoptive mother is made later in this chapter, (section 6.10).

Table 6.6(b)
Age of the Birth Mother at Date of Child's Birth by Age of Child at Date of Current Placement—Freeing Applications (Court Proforma)

| | AGE OF CHILD AT DATE OF CURRENT PLACEMENT | | | | | | | | | | | |
| | UP TO 1 YR | | 1–5 YRS | | 5–10 YRS | | 10–18 YRS | | NOT KNOWN | | TOTAL | |
AGE OF BIRTH MOTHER	**NO.**	**(%)**	**NO.**	**(%)**	**NO.**	**(%)**	**NO.**	**(%)**	**NO.**	**(%)**	**NO.**	**(%)**
20 yrs and under	11	(44)	14	(33)	8	(40)	4	(100)	4	(40)	41	(40)
21–25 yrs	6	(24)	20	(47)	4	(20)	0	–	4	(40)	34	(33)
26–30 yrs	4	(16)	4	(9)	4	(20)	0	–	0	–	12	(12)
31–35 yrs	2	(8)	3	(7)	2	(10)	0	–	0	–	7	(7)
36–40 yrs	0	–	2	(5)	0	–	0	–	2	(20)	4	(4)
41–65 yrs	2	(8)	0	–	0	–	0	–	0	–	2	(2)
Not known	0	–	0	–	2	(10)	0	–	0	–	2	(2)
All	**25**	**(100)**	**43**	**(100)**	**20**	**(100)**	**4**	**(100)**	**10**	**(100)**	**102**	**(100)**

6.7 Religion of the Adoptive Parents

Just over half of adoptive mothers (53%) and adoptive fathers (55%) declared that their religious affiliation was Church of England. Around one tenth of the sample were Roman Catholic (10% mothers, 8% fathers) and a few more were affiliated to other Christian denominations (12% mothers, 13% fathers). A further one tenth of the sample declared no religious affiliation. A small percentage (1–2%) declared themselves to be of Jewish,[1] Muslim of Sikh faith.

6.8 Ethnic Origin of the Adoptive Parents

Once again, unfortunately there was little information available in the court files on ethnic origin of the adoptive parents. In about 90% of the cases the ethnic origin was not stated in any of the documents on record. Where reported, the adoptive mother was of white, Indian or mixed race origin, with a small proportion being West Indian or African. The adoptive father was generally of either white or Indian origin, with a few being West Indian, African or mixed race origin.

---

[1]   It is perhaps worth noting that affiliation to the Jewish faith was positively identified from the files only in these cases concerning the adoptive parents.

6.9   Age of the Adoptive Mother at the Date of Application

Table 6.9
Age of the Adoptive Mother at Date of Application by Age of Child when Placed for Adoption (Court Proforma)

AGE OF ADOPTIVE MOTHER	AGE OF CHILD AT DATE OF CURRENT PLACEMENT FOR ADOPTION											
	UP TO 1 YR		1–5 YRS		5–10 YRS		10–18 YRS		NOT KNOWN		TOTAL	
	NO.	(%)	NO.	(%)	NO.	(%)	NO.	(%)	NO.	(%)	NO.	(%)
26–30 yrs	34	(19)	18	(15)	4	(7)	2	(6)	0	–	58	(15)
31–35 yrs	80	(44)	30	(25)	10	(18)	2	(6)	2	(50)	124	(32)
36–40 yrs	50	(28)	49	(42)	13	(24)	6	(17)	0	–	118	(30)
41–65 yrs	10	(16)	18	(15)	24	(44)	26	(72)	2	(50)	80	(20)
Other	6	(3)	3	(2)	4	(7)	0	–	0	–	13	(3)
All	**180**	**(100)**	**118**	**(100)**	**55**	**(100)**	**36**	**(100)**	**4**	**(100)**	**393**	**(100)**

The large majority (82%) of adoptive mothers were over thirty years old at the time the adoption application was made, with roughly a third of the total number of mothers aged betwen 31 and 35 years old and a third aged between 36 and 40 years old. A fifth of all adoptive mothers (20%) were over forty years old when the adoption application was made. In the case of babies being adopted, just under half (44%) of the adoptive mothers were aged between 31 and 35 years old at the time of application. Just over a third of mothers adopting babies (34%) were over 35 years old, compared with 57% of mothers in the same age range adopting children between one and five years old and 68% adopting children aged between five and ten years old. Furthermore, the large majority (89%) of mothers in the sample adopting older children (over ten years old) were over 35 years old at the time of application.

One must bear in mind when interpreting these data the effect of agency policy in relation to the age of the prospective parent. Many agencies tend to use age as a rationing device to restrict application for healthy baby adoptions, whereas for older children the age of the mother is less relevant. Age restrictions imposed by adoption agencies were an issue of concern to some practitioners, as we report in Part II at Chapter 8 (The Legal Process) section 8.4.2.

Figure 8:

A comparison in age of the birth mother and adoptive mother

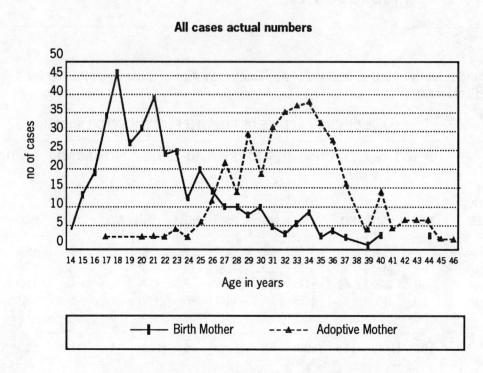

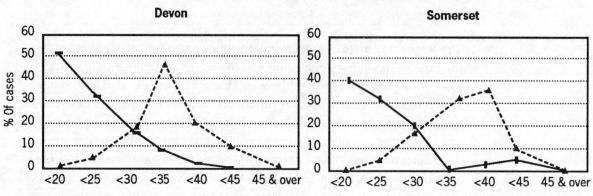

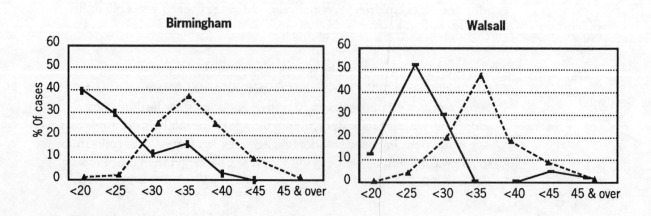

6.10   A Comparison of the Age of the Birth Mother and the Adoptive Mother

Further interrogation of the data to compare the ages of the birth mother with the adoptive mother revealed that in 85% of the cases the birth mother was younger than the adoptive mother. In 7% of the cases the adoptive mother was younger than the birth mother and in 4% of the cases there was little or no difference between their ages.

Where the natural mother was younger than the adoptive mother the difference was of 5 years or less in 5% of the cases. In 26% of the cases the difference was more than 5 years but less than 10 years, and in 31% of the cases the difference was more than 10 years but less than 15 years. In approximately a fifth of the cases (19%) the adoptive mother was over 15 years older than the child's birth mother.

Figure 8 illustrates graphically a comparison of the age of the birth and adoptive mother at the date of the child's birth both overall and for each area in the study. There appear to be regional variations but caution is needed when making any deductions from these findings as complex issues concerning family recruitment and placement practice are involved.

6.11   The Siblings in the Adoptive Family

Details of the siblings in the prospective family were recorded on the court proforma, including their age, sex and status, (that is, whether natural, fostered, adopted, etc.)

From Table 6.11 we can see that just under half (45%) of children in agency adoption proceedings were in an adoptive home where there were no other adoptive siblings. Only 18% of children had been placed for adoption in a family where there were two or more siblings.

A little over half the babies placed for adoption (52%) were placed with adoptive couples with no other children and 13% of babies were in an adoptive family with two or more other siblings. On the other hand, of the children aged between 1 and 5 years at the time they had been placed, roughly a third (33%) were with adoptive couples with no other children and 26% had been placed in a family with at least two other children. One may deduce from these data that these pre-school children, unlike babies and older children, were more likely to be placed for adoption with a family that already has children.[2]

---

[2]   However, see *ante* Part I section 3.8 where we discuss the incidence of sibling groups in our sample.

Table 6.11
Number of Adoptive Siblings by Age of Child at Date of Current Placement (Court Proforma)

NO. OF SIBLINGS[1]	AGE OF CHILD AT DATE OF CURRENT PLACEMENT											
	UP TO 1 YR		1–5 YRS		5–10 YRS		10–18 YRS		NOT KNOWN		TOTAL	
	NO.	(%)	NO.	(%)	NO.	(%)	NO.	(%)	NO.	(%)	NO.	(%)
None	107	(52)	45	(33)	18	(49)	4	(50)	1	(17)	175	(45)
One	70	(34)	56	(41)	12	(32)	4	(50)	2	(33)	144	(37)
Two	9	(4)	17	(12)	5	(13)	0	–	2	(33)	33	(8)
Three	10	(5)	14	(10)	2	(5)	0	–	0	–	26	(7)
Four	5	(2)	4	(3)	0	–	0	–	0	–	9	(2)
Five or more	4	(2)	1	(1)	0	–	0	–	0	–	4	(1)
Not recorded	0	–	0	–	0	–	0	–	0	–	1	*
Not known	0	–	0	–	0	–	0	–	1	(17)	1	*
All	**205**	**(100)**	**137**	**(100)**	**37**	**(100)**	**8**	**(100)**	**6**	**(100)**	**393**	**(100)**

*=less than 1%

[1]   Including siblings placed together for adoption.

Further interrogation revealed that in cases where the child was placed for adoption with a family which had at least one child already, there was a 50% chance that the eldest child in that family was also adopted. The incidence of previously adopted siblings in an adoptive family decreased the older the child to be adopted was when placed.

CHAPTER 7   A Profile of the Adoption Agency

7.1   Summary

7.2   Key Findings

7.3   Type of Agency involved in the Current Placement

7.4   Inter-Agency Placements

7.5   Payment of Adoption Allowances

7.6   The Stages in the Adoption Process

7.7   The Length of Time from Date of Placement for Adoption to the Date of Panel Placement Recommendation

7.8   The Length of Time from Date of Panel Placement Recommendation/ Agency Decision to the Date of Application to Court

7.9   The Length of Time from Date of Application to Court to the Date the Schedule II Report is lodged with the Court

7.10   The Contested Case

7.1   Summary

In this chapter we look at the agency's involvement in the adoption and freeing for adoption process. First we analyse the type of agency that was involved in the child's current placement, looking for any evidence of regional variation. The proportion of cases involving inter agency placements is examined. The payment of adoption allowances is investigated by area. Finally, we discuss the role of the adoption agency in the adoption and freeing process in terms of its control over the length of time taken to reach our defined stages of the process, both prior to the court process and after it has begun. We should point out that at this stage of analysis we are only interested in ascertaining the time taken to reach each step of the adoption process in order to provide a yardstick in subsequent qualitative investigations. The issue of avoidable delay in the process is not one that can be addressed solely by reference to quantative analysis.

7.2   Key Findings

7.2.1   The majority of agency adoptions involved local authority adoption agencies. Some regional variations were found in the degree of involvement by voluntary agencies in the field of adoption and, to a lesser extent, freeing. (7.3)

7.2.2   Few cases in our sample involved inter-agency placements, with some regional variation being found. (7.4)

7.2.3   Significant regional variations were found in our sample of agency adoption cases in the length of time from the date of the child's current placement to the time the adoption panel recommended the placement as an adoptive one (7.7).

7.2.4   The length of time taken for an application to be lodged with the court varied slightly according to the type of application made. Applications to free a child for adoption took around six months to reach the court from the date the panel placement recommendation had been made. Applications to adopt a child who had not been freed previously took around the same length of time once the placement had been recommended by the panel, but where the child was already freed the time interval was slightly longer—about seven and a half months. Some variation in time was found between the areas according to the type of application being made. Furthermore, the older the child the longer it appeared to take for the application to reach the court once the panel had recommended the placement. (7.8)

7.2.5   Contested adoption applications took over two and a half times as long to reach the court once the panel placement recommendation had been made compared with uncontested adoption applications. No such difference was found between contested and uncontested freeing applications. (7.10)

7.3 Type of Agency Involved in the Current Placement

Using the mini record data, Table 7.3(a) shows a breakdown of the type of agency involved in the current placement by area.

Table 7.3(a)
Type of Agency Involved in the Current Placement by Area (Mini Record)

AGENCY	DEVON		SOMERSET		BIRMINGHAM		WALSALL		LONDON		ALL	
	NO.	(%)	NO.	(%)	NO.	(%)	NO.	(%)	NO.	(%)	NO.	(%)
Local authority	112	(39)	43	(42)	175	(50)	48	(45)	142	(34)	520	(41)
Voluntary	22	(8)	4	(4)	2	(1)	4	(4)	22	(5)	54	(4)
More than one local authority	2	(1)	1	(1)	6	(2)	1	(1)	22	(5)	32	(3)
More than one voluntary	2	(1)	0	–	0	–	0	–	0	–	2	*
Local authority and voluntary	11	(4)	4	(4)	26	(7)	0	–	32	(7)	73	(6)
No agency	126	(44)	48	(47)	98	(28)	49	(46)	194	(46)	515	(41)
N/A—no placement	8	(3)	0	–	34	(10)	0	–	4	(1)	46	(4)
Not recorded	6	(2)	2	(2)	6	(2)	4	(4)	8	(2)	26	(2)
All	**289**	**(100)**	**102**	**(100)**	**347**	**(100)**	**106**	**(100)**	**424**	**(100)**	**1268**	**(100)**

*=less than 1%

From Table 7.3(a) we see that just under half (41%) of the cases in the mini record sample were non-agency placements, that is, adoption applications made in respect of step children, children being placed privately from abroad, and most children being adopted by other relatives.[1] There were fewer such placements in Birmingham than elsewhere in our study areas. Of the cases where agencies were involved, the majority involved local authority adoption agencies. Voluntary agencies on their own accounted for little of the work (4%), the highest propotion being found in Devon (where, amongst others, the Council for Christian Care in Exeter is active). The involvement of voluntary agencies in adoption work will differ from area to area according to the size and activities of the various agencies. It could also depend to a certain extent on the relationship between the local authority and voluntary agencies.

Table 7.3(b) shows a similar breakdown of the type of agency involved in the current placement by area for the court proforma sample.

---

[1]   Foster parents subsequently applying to adopt were included as agency placements.

Table 7.3(b)

Type of Agency Involved in the Current Placement by Area—Agency Adoption Applications (Court Proforma)

	AREA									
	DEVON		SOMERSET		BIRMINGHAM		WALSALL		ALL	
AGENCY	**NO.**	**(%)**	**NO.**	**(%)**	**NO.**	**(%)**	**NO.**	**(%)**	**NO.**	**(%)**
Local authority	100	(72)	48	(83)	129	(83)	43	(90)	315	(80)
Voluntary	22	(16)	4	(8)	2	(1)	2	(4)	30	(8)
More than one local authority	2	(1)	1	(2)	4	(3)	1	(2)	8	(2)
More than one voluntary	2	(1)	0	–	0	–	0	–	2	*
Local authority and voluntary	10	(7)	4	(8)	18	(12)	0	–	32	(8)
Not recorded	2	(1)	0	–	2	(1)	2	(4)	6	(2)
All	**138**	**(100)**	**52**	**(100)**	**155**	**(100)**	**48**	**(100)**	**393**	**(100)**

*=less than 1%

From Table 7.3(b) we see that the majority of agency adoption applications were handled by local authority adoption agencies (80%). Voluntary agencies dealt with only 8% of the adoptions in our sample.

These data confirm our previous findings from the mini record (*ante* at Table 7.3(a)). Furthermore, they show that in Devon the voluntary agencies were involved in a higher proportion of cases (24%) than any of the other areas, the lowest proportion being found in Walsall where only a few (4%) adoption applications involved a voluntary agency at all.

Further investigation using the court proforma data examined the relationship between the type of agency involved in the child's placement with the age of the child at the date of the current placement. We found that voluntary agencies were primarily involved in baby adoptions. This is not surprising, since it is most unlikely that parents would approach a voluntary agency to place a child other than a baby, (although local authorities may approach voluntary agencies for the placement of older children in care). Furthermore, few voluntary agencies run children's homes these days from which older children might be placed.

An examination of the type of agency involved in placement of children who were being freed for adoption revealed that where a placement had been made the majority had been handled by the local authority. Voluntary agencies were seldom involved with the placement of children being freed.

7.4   Inter-Agency Placements

For the purposes of this study we defined an inter-agency placement as one in which more than one agency (whether local authority or voluntary) was involved to some extent in the placement of the child for adoption.[2]

In our mini record sample we found that, in general, few cases (9%) involved an inter-agency placement with a slight variation between the areas, London having the highest proportion (see *ante* Table 7.3(a)). A more detailed examination using the court proforma data (see *ante* Table 7.3(b)) showed that in the case of agency adoption applications (excluding London cases), the highest proportion of cases involving inter-agency placements were found in Birmingham (15%), and the lowest in Walsall (2%). Overall such placements accounted for 10% of the adoption applications and those cases were chiefly concerned with children over 5 years old—children who, almost without exception, had been in local authority care first (see *ante* Part 1 Table 4.4(a)).

Further analysis of these data revealed that just under a quarter of inter-agency placements involved sibling groups (24%). A slightly higher proportion (29%) of inter-agency placements in adoption proceedings involved children with one or more disabilities as defined in Part I, section 3.9.

7.5   Payment of Adoption Allowances

Table 7.5

Payment of Adoption Allowances by Local Authority—Agency Adoption Applications (Court Proforma)

ALLOWANCE PAID	AREA									
	DEVON		SOMERSET		BIRMINGHAM		WALSALL		ALL	
	NO.	(%)	NO.	(%)	NO.	(%)	NO.	(%)	NO.	(%)
Yes	32	(23)	12	(23)	24	(16)	21	(44)	89	(23)
No	44	(32)	15	(29)	103	(66)	18	(38)	180	(46)
Other[1]	4	(3)	0	–	6	(4)	1	(2)	11	(3)
Not known	58	(42)	25	(48)	22	(14)	8	(17)	113	(29)
All	**138**	**(100)**	**52**	**(100)**	**155**	**(100)**	**48**	**(100)**	**393**	**(100)**

[1]   In most cases within this category at the time the Schedule II report was being written the local authority was still considering the application made by the adoptive parents for an adoption allowance.

[2]   Practitioners' views on adoption practice both within and between agencies are described in Part II, Chapter 1 (Organisation of Adoption Work in the Agencies).

An examination of the issue of payment of adoption allowances showed (see Table 7.5) that, where known, an adoption allowance was paid in just under a quarter (23%) of the cases in our court proforma sample. Birmingham appeared to have the highest proportion of cases where no allowance was paid (66%), although these figures should be treated with caution as the information was not recorded in quite a high proportion of cases in the south west.

Whilst practitioners in the Practitioner Study were not specifically asked about their views on adoption allowances, they did express concern at what appeared to be an inconsistent approach by agencies to the financial aspects of adoption work, including adoption allowances. See Part II, Chapter 1 (Organisation of Adoption Work in the Agencies) section 1.3.

7.6   The Stages in the Adoption Process

One of the main aims of the study is to identify the obstacles in the adoption process which may prevent the most beneficial outcome being achieved for all parties concerned, with the minimum of trauma and anxiety. The variation in length of time taken to reach the various steps of the process may provide a clue as to where these obstacles lie. We have already outlined in Part 1, section 3.11 the stages in the adoption process and the reference points that we have elected to use in this study which will allow us to make comparisons. Once again, we must not forget that there are many stages reached and decisions taken by the agency on the future of the child in care prior to being placed for adoption.

We have used the same categorization of routes to adoption as we used in the examination of the age profiles of the child (see Part 1, section 3.12). Thus when examining the variation in the length of time between each stage in the adoption process we have grouped the court proforma data according to the type of application (that is, freeing or agency adoption), and in the case of agency adoption applications whether or not the child has been previously freed).

7.7   The Length of Time from Date of Current Placement to the Date of Panel Placement Recommendation

Initially, we examined the mean length of time (in months) from when the child entered his or her current placement to the date the panel recommended the placement as one for adoption.[3]

---

[3]   See Part 1, section 3.4 for our definiton of the term "date of placement for adoption".

Table 7.7
Mean Length of Time (Months) between Date of Current Placement and Date of Adoption Panel Placement Recommendation by Area—(Court Proforma)

AREA	TYPE OF APPLICATION			
	ADOPTION/PREV. FREED		ADOPTION	
	(months)		(months)	
Devon	5.83	(n=18)	18.53	(n=107)
Somerset	8.37	(n=4)	15.23	(n=43)
Birmingham	1.30	(n=26)	9.75	(n=115)
Walsall	2.51	(n=10)	42.80	(n=30)
All	**3.40**	**(n=58)**	**17.09**	**(n=295)**

[missing cases][1]   [5   (8%)]   [35   (11%)]

[1]   We were not always able to record these dates accurately from the court files, and hence information for some cases is missing.

It appears from Table 7.7 that where a child had already been freed, over three months elapsed from the date of the child's current placement to the time the adoption panel made the placement recommendation. This time span was far less than in cases where the child had not been freed already (just over seventeen months on average). However, there was a wide regional variation in these lengths of time. In cases where the child had already been freed, in Birmingham the time interval was on average just over one month, compared with nearly six months in Devon and over eight months in Somerset, (although in the latter area the number of cases in this sub-sample is very small).

There were also significant regional variations in cases where the child was not already freed. Whereas in Birmingham under ten months had elapsed between the date of the child's current placement and the adoption panel placement recommendation, in Walsall the child had been in his/her current placement for around three and a half years before the panel recommended the placement as one for adoption.[4]

As far as the agency role in freeing a child for adoption is concerned, the first step on this particular route is the agency decision to make the freeing application following the recommendation by the adoption panel. The agency has then to submit the application to court. In adoption proceedings the prospective adoptive parents submit their application to the court.

---

[4]   We have already pointed out in Part 1, section 3.11, that for the majority of cases in our court proforma sample the date of placement for adoption coincided (within a few days), with the date of the panel placement recommendation.

7.8 The Length of Time from Date of Panel Placement Recommendation/Agency Decision to Date of Application to Court

It appears from Table 7.8(a) that once the adoption panel has made the recommendation and approved the adoptive placement (or in the case of freeing, recommended the freeing application to be made), it took on average about five and a half months for the application to reach the court in the case of a straightforward agency adoption. Freeing applications took a little longer (around six months) and, perhaps surprisingly, where the child has already been freed around seven and a half months had elapsed before the adoption application reached the court (and even longer in Birmingham and Somerset, although in the latter area the number in the sub sample was too small to be significant).

Table 7.8(a)

Mean Length of Time (in Months) between Date of Adoption Panel Placement Recommendation/Agency Decision and Date of Application to the Court by Area—(Court Proforma)

AREA	TYPE OF APPLICATION					
	FREEING		ADOPTION/PREV. FREED		ADOPTION	
	(months)		(months)		(months)	
Devon	3.43	(n=15)	6.68	(n=18)	3.37	(n=101)
Somerset	–		10.87	(n=4)	3.93	(n=41)
Birmingham	7.01	(n=66)	9.20	(n=26)	6.99	(n=113)
Walsall	1.95	(n=7)	4.01	(n=10)	9.75	(n=29)
All	**6.00**	**(n=88)**	**7.64**	**(n=58)**	**5.54**	**(n=284)**
[missing cases]	[14	(14%)]	[5	(8%)]	[46	(14%)]

In the case of freeing applications, closer analysis showed that Walsall seemed to be the quickest at lodging the applications in the court (taking just under two months), and Birmingham, taking on average seven months, the slowest. Some regional variation was also found in adoption cases (where the child had not been previously freed), where applications to the court appeared to be a little slower in the Midlands—Walsall and Birmingham (just under ten months and seven months respectively), than in the south west where only three to four months had elapsed between the date of the panel recommendation and the date of application to the court.

When examining these figures for agency adoption cases, one must not forget that the actual application is made by the adoptive parents. As we have pointed out in the summary to this chapter, the length of time that is taken for an adoption application to reach the court is dependent on many factors and is not necessarily indicative of avoidable delay. Furthermore, it is also legally required that the child has been with the adopters for a minimum of thriteen weeks before the order can be made.[5] (Adoption Act 1976 s.13).

Table 7.8(b)
Mean Length of Time (in Months) between Date of Panel Placement Recommendation and Date of Application to the Court by Child's Age at Date of Current Placement (Court Proforma)

	TYPE OF APPLICATION	
AGE OF CHILD AT DATE OF CURRENT PLACEMENT	**ADOPTION/PREVIOUSLY FREED**	**ADOPTION**
	(months)	**(months)**
Up to 1 yr	5.58 (n=20)	3.04 (n=168)
1–5 yrs	8.47 (n=34)	8.96 (n=79)
5–10 yrs	10.87 (n=4)	11.89 (n=27)
10–18 yrs	–	6.18 (n=8)
Not known	–	–7.70 (n=2)
All	**7.64 (n=58)**	**5.54 (n=284)**

[missing cases]   [5   (8%)]   [46   (14%)]

Further investigation was made into the variation in the length of time between the adoption panel placement recommendation and the date the adoption application was lodged with the court, with the age of the child when s/he entered his/her current placment. Table 7.8(b) shows that, in the case of babies who had not been freed for adoption, on average three months had elapsed from the time the adoption panel recommended the adoption palcement until the application was made. Where the baby had been freed the time interval was longer—around five and a half months on average. The data presented in Table 7.8(b) also reveal that the older the child when entering his or her current placement, the longer it appeared to take for the adoption application to reach the court once the adoption panel recommended the placement, with the exception perhaps of children aged ten or over when placed for adoption. The finding could be partly explained by the need for additional observation or settling in time in the case of older children.

---

5   In the case of foster parents subsequently deciding to actually adopt, the child has to have lived with them for a minimum of twelve months prior to the order being made, (Adoption Act 1976 s.13[2]).

7.9   The Length of Time from Date of Application to Court to the Date the Schedule II Report is Lodged with the Court

It is the duty of the adoption agency to supply the court with a Schedule II report detailing information on the child, the birth parents, the prospective adopters (in the case of adoption), together with a description of the agency actions and recommendations to support the application. A Schedule II report should also accompany a freeing application.[6] Where an adoption application has been made the Schedule II report should be lodged with the court within six weeks of receipt of a hearing date.[7]

Unfortunately, in around half the cases in our sample (and in more than half the freeing cases), it was not possible to ascertain from the court records the date that the Schedule II report was lodged. It would therefore be misleading to make any detailed analysis of the interval of time between the date of application and the date the Schedule II report was lodged. Of the cases in the sample where the information was known it appears that overall approximately nine to ten weeks had elapsed from the date of application until the Schedule II report was lodged with the court.

Because of its fundamental importance to the adoption process and the court proceedings in particular, we asked social workers in the Practitioner Study a series of questions concerning the Schedule II Report. This included their views on the time allowed for its completion. Their comments are reported in Part II, Chapter 2 (Schedule II Reports).

7.10   The Contested Case

In some cases the application to adopt or to free for adoption is just one of the final stages in a long contest between birth parents and the local authority. In Part I, section 2.14 we defined a 'contested' case for the purpose of our study. In Part 1, section 3.18 we examined the age profile of children in contested cases and found that contested freeing cases were more likely to involve younger children and contested adoptions were more likely to involve older children.[8]

The data in Table 7.10 show there was little difference between contested and uncontested freeing applications in the time from panel recommendation to make the application to the date the application was lodged with

---

6   Adoption Rules 1984 r.4[4].

7   Adoption Rules 1984 Rule 22.

8   The issue of parental agreement and the effect the withholding of it can have on the progress of a case are discussed in Part II, Chapter 3 (Parental Agreement).

Table 7.10
Mean Length of Time (in Months) between Date of Panel Recommendation and Date Application Lodged with the Court—For Contested and Uncontested Cases (Court Proforma)

AREA	TYPE OF APPLICATION		
	FREEING	**ADOPTION/PREV. FREED**	**ADOPTION**
	(months)	(months)	(months)
Contested	6.31 (n=65)	–	9.95 (n=82)
Uncontested/ not known	5.11 (n=23)	7.64 (n=58)	3.75 (n=202)
All	**6.00 (n=88)**	**7.64 (n=58)**	**5.54 (n=284)**
[missing cases]	[14 (14%)]	[5 (8%)]	[46 (14%)]

the court. On the other hand, contested adoption applications (where the child had not been previously freed), took over two and a half times as long for the application to reach the court from the time the adoption panel made their placement recommendation (nearly ten months), compared with uncontested adoptions (three and three quarter months). It should be remembered that in the case of all freeing applications and contested adoption applications, the legal department of the local authority is likely to be involved in advising and preparing the case alongside the social workers. The involvement of another party with the inherent additional complexities will probably lengthen the time taken for the appliation to reach the court. It is also worth noting perhaps that where the child had already been freed, applications to adopt such children took twice as long to reach the court compared with 'ordinary' uncontested adoption cases.

CHAPTER 8   The Court Proceedings

8.1   Summary

8.2   Key Findings

8.3   The Number of Court Hearings required to reach a Final Order

8.4   The Number of Hearings in Relation to Court Usage

8.5   The Number of Hearings in Relation to Contested Cases

8.6   Length of Court Proceedings

8.7   Length of Court Proceedings in Relation to Type of Application

8.8   Length of Court Proceedings in Relation to Court Usage

8.9   Length of Court Proceedings in Contested and Uncontested Cases

8.10   Length of Court Proceedings in Relation to the Age of the Child

8.11   Length of Time from Date of Application to Date of First Hearing in relation to Area

8.12   Length of Time from Date of Application to Date of First Hearing in Relation to Court Usage

8.13   Length of Time from Date of Application to Date of First Hearing for Contested and Uncontested Cases

8.1   Summary

Information was collected on both the mini record and the court proforma about the court hearings that had taken place. A note was made of each occasion when a hearing had been listed in the court file, including short 'directions hearings' before a Registrar, even where the parties were not present.

Firstly, we examine the number of court hearings that took place before a decision was reached and how this varied according to the type of court, as well as whether the case was contested or not. The length of court proceedings, that is the length of time from the date of application to the date of order, is looked at in relation to the fieldwork area and type of court. We also examine the data to ascertain whether there is evidence to suggest that the length of court proceedings is determined to some extent by whether or not the case is contested and by the age of the child.

The problems created by the system of listing cases is investigated by looking at the time taken from the date the application is lodged to the date of the first hearing. Analysis of this variable by fieldwork area, court usage and whether or not the case is contested is made.

We should once again bear in mind the caveat stated in Part 1, section 7.1 that we are not placing any evaluative judgment on the length of time taken for proceedings to complete in terms of avoidable delay.

8.2   Key Findings

8.2.1   Adoption cases were more likely than freeing cases to reach a decision after one hearing (8.3).

8.2.2   In general, contested freeing proceedings required a greater number of hearings to reach a decision than contested agency adoption proceedings (8.5).

8.2.3   Most uncontested agency adoptions were resolved after one hearing, in contrast to uncontested freeing applications (8.5).

8.2.4   The older the child who was the subject of the adoption application, the more likely it was that the case would require more than one hearing to reach an outcome (8.5).

8.2.5   Freeing cases tended to take longer to dispose of than other types of adoption proceedings (8.6).

8.2.6   Adoption proceedings involving a child already free for adoption in general took a shorter length of time to dispose of than proceedings involving a child who had not been freed (8.7).

8.2.7   Cases that proceeded in the magistrates' court reached a decision sooner than those heard in the higher courts (8.8). One reason for this finding may be because adoption proceedings in the higher courts were more likely to be contested (8.9). Contested cases took longer to dispose of than uncontested cases (8.9).

8.2.8   Freeing cases took longer to reach a first hearing once the application had been made than agency adoption cases. Some regional variations were found in the time taken for cases to reach a first hearing (8.11).

8.2.9   Contested cases took longer to reach a first hearing than uncontested cases (8.13).

8.3   The Number of Court Hearings Required to Reach a Final Order

Data collected on the mini record recorded the number of hearings that had occurred in those cases where a final order was made.

Table 8.3
Number of Hearings to Final Order by Type of Application (Mini Record)

	TYPE OF APPLICATION									
	STEP PARENT		OTHER REL.		NO REL.		FREEING		ALL	
NO. OF HEARINGS	NO.	(%)	NO.	(%)	NO.	(%)	NO.	(%)	NO.	(%)
One	276	(79)	53	(79)	443	(75)	50	(40)	822	(73)
Two	39	(11)	10	(15)	72	(12)	42	(33)	163	(14)
Three	10	(3)	2	(3)	14	(2)	10	(8)	36	(3)
Four	8	(2)	0	–	4	(1)	6	(5)	18	(2)
Five	0	–	0	–	2	*	0	–	2	*
More than five	0	–	0	–	0	–	2	(2)	2	*
Not recorded	2	(1)	0	–	6	(1)	0	–	8	(1)
Not known	14	(4)	2	(3)	47	(8)	16	(13)	79	(7)
All	**349**	**(100)**	**67**	**(100)**	**588**	**(100)**	**126**	**(100)**	**1130**	**(100)**

* =less than 1%

It is apparent from Table 8.3 that freeing cases were less likely to reach a final order after only one hearing—40% compared with 75% of no relation mainstream adoption cases. Moreover, 15% of the freeing cases took three or more hearings to reach a final order, compared with only 5% of the step parent adoptions and 3% of no relation adoptions.

8.4   Number of Hearings in Relation to Court Usage

We next analysed information from the court proforma sample relating to the number of hearings that took place. We divided the agency adoption cases into two categories, those where the child had been freed previously and those where this had not occurred.[1] We have omitted from the following analysis those cases where the child was already free for adoption since we found that, where the information was available, such cases required only one hearing to reach an outcome.

Table 8.4
Number of Hearings to Final Order by Court Usage (Court Proforma)

NO. OF HEARINGS	MAGISTRATES'				COUNTY				HIGH				ALL			
	FREEING		ADOPTION		FREEING		ADOPTION		FREEING		ADOPTION		FREEING		ADOPTION	
	NO.	(%)	NO.	(%)	NO.	(%)	NO.	(%)	NO.	(%)	NO.	(%)	NO.	(%)	NO.	(%)
One	6	(75)	16	(80)	20	(23)	220	(75)	6	(100)	11	(100)	32	(32)	247	(76)
Two	2	(25)	4	(20)	32	(37)	42	(14)	0	–	0	–	34	(34)	46	(14)
Three	0	–	0	–	8	(9)	8	(3)	0	–	0	–	8	(8)	8	(2)
Four	0	–	0	–	10	(12)	2	(1)	0	–	0	–	10	(10)	2	(1)
Five	0	–	0	–	0	–	2	(1)	0	–	0	–	0	–	2	(1)
Eight	0	–	0	–	2	(2)	0	–	0	–	0	–	2	(2)	0	–
Not known	0	–	0	–	14	(16)	20	(7)	0	–	0	–	14	(14)	20	(6)
All[1]	8	(100)	20	(100)	86	(100)	294	(100)	6	(100)	11	(100)	100	(100)	325	(100)

1   In 1% of the adoption sample and 2% of the freeing sample, the proceedings had not yet reached the stage of a hearing.

The data in Table 8.4 show that the majority (76%) of agency adoption applications (excluding cases where the child had been freed previously) was decided after one hearing, irrespective of the type of court to which they were taken. In the county court (where more freeing and adoption cases are heard),[2] it was noticeable that just under a quarter (23%) of freeing applications were disposed of after one hearing, compared with three quarters (75%) of adoption applications.

1   See *ante* Part 1, section 3.12

2   See *ante* Part 1, section 2.5

8.5   Number of Hearings in Relation to Contested Cases

The number of hearings that occurred before a final order was reached in any one case may well be affected by whether or not the case was contested.[3]

From Table 8.5 we see that the vast majority (88%) of uncontested agency adoption applications (excluding cases where the child had been freed previously) were determined after only one hearing, a greater proportion compared with uncontested freeing applications (68%). Nearly a quarter of uncontested freeing cases (24%) still required two hearings before a decision was reached, although some of the first hearings could have been direction hearings.

Table 8.5
Number of Hearings to Final Order According to whether or not the Case was Contested (Court Proforma)

	TYPE OF APPLICATION							
	FREEING				ADOPTION (EXC. PREV. FREED)			
	UNCONTESTED		CONTESTED		UNCONTESTED		CONTESTED	
NUMBER OF HEARINGS	NO.	(%)	NO.	(%)	NO.	(%)	NO.	(%)
None	2	(8)	0	–	2	(1)	3	(3)
One	17	(68)	15	(20)	201	(88)	46	(46)
Two	6	(24)	28	(36)	14	(6)	32	(32)
Three	0	–	8	(10)	4	(2)	4	(4)
Four	0	–	10	(13)	0	–	2	(2)
Five	0	–	0	–	2	(1)	0	–
Eight	0	–	2	(3)	0	–	0	–
Not known	0	–	14	(18)	6	(3)	14	(14)
All	**25**	**(100)**	**77**	**(100)**	**229**	**(100)**	**101**	**(100)**

As far as contested proceedings were concerned, just under half of contested adoption applications (46%) were decided after one hearing, which is more than twice the proportion of contested freeing applications (20%).

Around a quarter of contested freeing applications (26%) reached an outcome only after three or more hearings had taken place, compared with 6% of contested adoption applications.

---

3   See Part I, section 2.14 for definition of a contested case.

A closer examination of the data (excluding that relating to adoption cases where the child had already been freed), revealed that the number of hearings required to reach a final order varied with the age of the child at the date of the current placement. It appeared that the more straightforward baby adoptions were generally decided after only one hearing. (88% of cases involving children under one year old when placed in their current placement were decided after only one hearing). The older the child, the more likely it was that the case would require more than one hearing to decide the outcome, (although all cases concerning children aged ten or over needed only one hearing to reach a decision). As far as freeing proceedings were concerned, just under half (48%) the number of cases involving babies required two or more hearings to reach a decision. This finding indicates that freeing is being used where babies are involved in cases that are different from straightforward adoptions, perhaps where the natural parents are contesting the adoption.[4]

8.6   Length of Court Proceedings

We have already examined (in Part I section 7.7 and on), how the length of time taken to reach different stages in the process of adoption varies according to the area, (which may be related to the use of different agency policies and practices). We also examined the data to ascertain whether or not there were any indications that obstacles to the progress of a case could arise from the time when an application is lodged at court to the date when the final order is made. In addition as we report in Part II, Chapter 5 (Courts Administration), practitioners identified delays which can arise once an application has been submitted to court, thus impeding the progress of the case.

Table 8.6(a) below sets out the mini record data relating to the length of time from the filing of the application to the court to the making of the final order. It should be borne in mind that in the case of no relation adoptions, the child has to be in the care of the applicants for at least 13 weeks before the order can be made.[5] This may influence the length of time taken by the court to process the application.

A clear tendency emerges for freeing cases to take longer than other categories. Although this is not especially marked, it has to be remembered that once the freeing order is made a further application to adopt will follow. This will therefore affect the overall average length of time for those adoption cases in the no relation group that had been preceded by a freeing application. Practitioners were much concerned by the overall length of

---

4   Practitioners' views on the effects on the progress of cases where parental agreement is withheld are described in Part II, Chapter 3 (Parental Agreement).

5   In the case of foster parents subsequently deciding to apply to adopt, the child has to have lived with them for a minimum of 12 months prior to the order being made. (Adoption Act 1976 s. 13[2]).

Table 8.6(a)
Time (in Months) between Date of Application and Date of Order by Type of Application (Mini Record)

Time in months	TYPE OF APPLICATION									
	STEP PARENT		OTHER REL		NO REL		FREEING		ALL	
	NO.	(%)	NO.	(%)	NO.	(%)	NO.	(%)	NO.	(%)
Less than 1 month	2	(1)	1	(1)	5	(1)	0		8	(1)
1 up to 3 months	18	(4)	0	–	66	(11)	6	(4)	90	(7)
3 up to 6 months	156	(37)	24	(29)	317	(52)	38	(25)	535	(42)
6 up to 9 months	70	(17)	16	(20)	74	(12)	25	(17)	185	(15)
9 up to 12 months	44	(10)	12	(15)	33	(5)	20	(13)	109	(9)
12 up to 15 months	24	(6)	4	(5)	27	(4)	16	(11)	71	(6)
15 up to 18 months	14	(3)	3	(4)	21	(3)	9	(6)	47	(4)
18 up to 21 months	5	(1)	2	(2)	2	*	5	(3)	14	(1)
21 up to 24 months	2	(1)	4	(5)	7	(1)	0	–	13	(1)
24 months and over	8	(2)	0	–	7	(1)	3	(2)	18	(1)
Not known/not recorded	83	(20)	15	(18)	51	(8)	28	(19)	178	(14)
All	**426**	**(100)**	**82**	**(100)**	**610**	**(100)**	**150**	**(100)**	**1268**	**(100)**

* =less than 1%

time taken to complete the process of adoption in cases where the child is first the subject of a freeing application. Indeed, in some agencies it influenced their decision whether or not to use freeing, as we report in Part II, Chapter 8 (The Legal Process) section 8.3.2.

Figure 9 illustrates graphically the difference in the time intervals between date of application and date of order for each type of case. After six months had elapsed from the date of application, around 30% of freeing cases had completed compared with about 45% of step parent adoptions and about 65% of no relation adoptions. After twelve months the percentage of freeing cases completed (just below 70%) was still less than the percentage of step parent adoptions (just over 80%) and no relation adoptions (85%).

An examination using the mini record data of the mean time taken from the date of application to the date of the order for each type of application (see Table 8.6(b)) showed that freeing cases took over nine months to complete compared with about six months for no relation adoption.

It should be borne in mind when interpreting the data given in Table 8.6(b) above that they included information from all three types of court and they do not necessarily reflect the management of adoption cases by any one type of court. Nevertheless, it will be seen that there were considerable variations between areas in the time taken to complete cases.

Figure 9:
Length of time from application to order for each type of application (mini record)

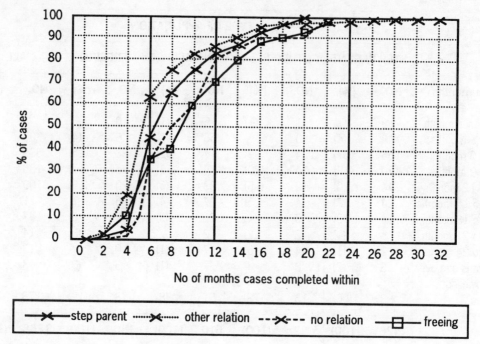

Table 8.6(b)

Mean Time (in Months) between Date of Application and Date of Order for Each Type of Application by Area (Mini Record)

AREA	STEP PARENT (months)		OTHER RELATION (months)		NO RELATION (months)		FREEING (months)	
			TYPE OF APPLICATION					
Devon	6.90	(n=66)	11.15	(n=9)	5.73	(n=140)	10.42	(n=19)
Somerset	6.68	(n=40)	–		5.59	(n=50)	–	
Birmingham	8.14	(n=77)	7.50	(n=14)	4.93	(n=158)	7.53	(n=64)
Walsall	4.79	(n=38)	6.17	(n=14)	5.49	(n=40)	18.04	(n=5)
London	9.06	(n=120)	10.20	(n=28)	8.32	(n=170)	10.70	(n=34)
All[1]	**7.68**	**(n=341)**	**8.88**	**(n=65)**	**6.26**	**(n=558)**	**9.29**	**(n=122)**

1   In 182 cases (14%) some of the information was missing.

As far as freeing cases were concerned, applications made in Birmingham, an area which made relatively high use of freeing, (see *ante* Part I, section 2.3), were dealt with more quickly (an average of seven and a half months) than in nearby Walsall, although only five such cases were sampled in Walsall. No relation adoptions were completed in the shortest time in Birmingham (just under five months), and took longest in London (nearly nine months).

8.7   Length of Court Proceedings in Relation to Type of Application

Further investigation into the length of time between the date of application and date of order was carried out, this time using the court proforma data. For the purpose of this analysis, we once again sub-divided the agency adoption applications according to whether or not the child had been previously freed.[6]

Table 8.7
Mean Time (in Months) between Date of Application and Date of Order by Area (Court Proforma)

AREA	TYPE OF APPLICATION					
	FREEING		**ADOPT./PREV. FREED**		**ADOPTION**	
	(months)		(months)		(months)	
Devon	10.42	(n=19)	3.56	(n=21)	5.70	(n=107)
Somerset	–		4.10	(n=4)	5.53	(n=44)
Birmingham	7.10	(n=58)[1]	2.98	(n=28)	5.31	(n=125)
Walsall	18.04	(n=5)	3.57	(n=10)	5.83	(n=35)
All[1]	**8.53**	**(n=82)**	**3.34**	**(n=63)**	**5.53**	**(n=311)**
[Missing cases]	[20 (20%)]		[0]		[19 (6%)]	

1   There is a slight variation between this figure and that shown for Birmingham in Table 8.6(b) because some cases were missing from the court proforma sample.

Overall, the data in Table 8.7 support the findings from the mini record survey that freeing cases took longer to complete than adoption cases. The main point that emerges from the table above is that if a child had already been freed it took less time for the adoption application to be decided (just over three months on average) compared with the application to adopt a child who was not already freed which took about five and a half months on average. Indeed, closer examination showed that no such adoption application where the child had been previously freed took over six months to complete. Overall our findings show however that by the time a child who has been freed previously is adopted, s/he will have spent nearly a year involved in court proceedings relating to both the adoption and the freeing before his/her future is secured.

6   See Part I, section 3.12

8.8 Length of Court Proceedings in Relation to Court Usage

Another important variable to be considered when looking at the variation in the length of time cases take to complete is the type of court to which the application has been made.

Table 8.8
Mean Time (in Months) between Date of Application and Date of Order by Court Usage (Court Proforma)

	TYPE OF APPLICATION					
TYPE OF COURT	**FREEING**		**ADOPT./PREV. FREED**		**ADOPTION**	
	(months)		**(months)**		**(months)**	
Magistrates'	4.05	(n=8)	2.12	(n=12)	3.91	(n=20)
County	8.50	(n=68)	3.61	(n=50)	5.18	(n=280)
High	14.94	(n=6)	4.37	(n=1)	17.35	(n=11)
All	**8.53**	**(n=82)**	**3.34**	**(n=63)**	**5.53**	**(n=311)**
[Missing cases]	[20 (20%)]		[0]		[19 (6%)]	

Table 8.8 shows that all cases that proceeded in the magistrates' court reached a decision sooner than those heard in the other two courts. In cases where the child had been previously freed, the difference in the time from application to order was only a matter of a couple of months between the magistrates' court and the High Court. On the other hand, freeing cases appeared in general to take just under one year longer to complete if heard in the High Court rather than the magistrates' court, and six months longer than the county court. Adoption applications where the child had not been previously freed that were heard in the High Court took on average about seventeen months before a decision was reached, that is around a year longer than those heard in the magistrates' court and the county court. This finding however begs the question as to whether or not the cases appear to be taking longer in the higher courts (and in particular the High Court) due to the court process itself, or whether the magistrates' court is dealing with a different type of case from the other two courts[7] (excluding perhaps cases where the child is previously freed). Despite their criticisms of the county court, a strong preference for that forum for adoption emerged from our interviews with practitioners (see Part II, Chapter 6—The Court Hearing).

7 Indeed see Re PB (A Minor) [1985] FLR 394 where Sheldon J commented that magistrates' courts should not hear contested adoption cases.

8.9 Length of Court Proceedings in Contested and Uncontested Cases

Closer analysis of our data showed that the magistrates' courts dealt only with uncontested cases (both freeing and adoption), whereas the county court and High Court heard only a small proportion of uncontested freeing cases (18% and 17% respectively). In the case of adoption applications (where the child had not been freed previously), 70% of the cases taken to the county court were uncontested, compared with under a quarter (21%) of High Court cases. One reason why cases appeared to take longer to complete in the higher courts may be because those cases were more likely to be contested. The data in Table 8.9 shows that for both freeing and adoption (where the child had not been previously freed), contested cases took longer to complete than uncontested cases. A contested freeing case took on average about ten months to complete, which was around twice as long as an uncontested freeing case. A contested adoption application (where the child was not previously freed) in general reached a final order about eight months after the application had been made, compared with four and a half months for an uncontested adoption application.

Table 8.9
Mean Time (in Months) between Date of Application and Date of Order According to whether the Case was Contested or not (Court Proforma)

	TYPE OF APPLICATION					
	FREEING		**ADOPT./PREV. FREED**		**ADOPTION**	
	(months)		(months)		(months)	
Contested	9.68	(n=63)	–		7.94	(n=94)
Uncontested/not known	4.73	(n=19)	3.33	(n=63)	4.49	(n=217)
All	**8.53**	**(n=82)**	**3.34**	**(n=63)**	**5.53**	**(n=311)**

[Missing cases]   [20 (20%)]   [0]   [19 (6%)]

8.10 Length of Court Proceedings in Relation to Age of Child at Date of Current Placement

Finally, in the case of adoption applications, we decided to look at the variation in the length of time from application to order according to the age of the child when s/he entered the current placement.

We found no significant pattern emerging from the data, except perhaps that adoption proceedings took somewhat longer to complete in cases involving children who had not been freed and were aged between one and ten years when entering their current placement. For these children, the length of court proceedings may be determined by a number of other factors—for instance, whether or not the case was contested.

8.11 Length of Time from Application to First Hearing in Relation to Area

One potential source of delay in the court process may lie in the procedure for listing cases for a hearing once the application has been received by the court.

We can see from Table 8.11 that overall, freeing cases took longer to reach a first hearing once the application had been made—just over six months— compared with under five months for adoption cases where the child had not been freed, and an even shorter length of time—just over three months—where the child had already been freed for adoption. When examined regionally, the data revealed that, in the case of freeing applications, Birmingham was quickest at listing the case for a first hearing (around five and a half months on average), compared with nearly seven months in Walsall and somewhat longer in Devon (about eight and a half months). There was little regional variation in the case of adoption applications whether or not the child had been previously freed, although once again Birmingham appeared to be slightly quicker than in the other areas of study.

Table 8.11
Mean Time (in Months) between Date of Application and Date of First Hearing—by Area (Court Proforma)

AREA	TYPE OF APPLICATION					
	FREEING		ADOPT./PREV. FREED		ADOPTION	
	(months)		(months)		(months)	
Devon	8.61	(n=17)	3.56	(n=19)	5.13	(n=101)
Somerset	–	–	4.10	(n=4)	5.07	(n=40)
Birmingham	5.56	(n=62)	2.98	(n=28)	4.40	(n=115)
Walsall	6.82	(n=7)	3.57	(n=10)	5.61	(n=35)
All	**6.26**	**(n=86)**	**3.33**	**(n=61)**	**4.89**	**(n=291)**

[Missing cases]	[16 (16%)]	[2 (3%)]	[39 (12%)]

To summarise the findings from Table 8.11, it appears that freeing cases took longer to reach a first hearing once the application had been made than agency adoption cases. Furthermore, it seems that cases were listed for a hearing in Birmingham earlier than in the other areas of our study.

Practitioners were concerned about the time taken waiting for a court hearing date. Amongst the reasons they suggested for delays occurring in the progress of cases through the courts, listing was a prominent one. They were particularly concerned about this problem in the High Court. We report their views about this issue in Part II, Chapter 5 (Courts Administration) section 5.3.

8.12 Length of Time from Application to First Hearing in Relation to Court Usage

We have already found (see *ante* Part I, section 8.5), that cases in magistrates' courts reached a final decision earlier than cases heard in the other two types of courts. One may thus expect to find that the time between the application and first hearing was shorter in the magistrates' courts than the other two courts.

Table 8.12
Mean Time (in Months) between Date of Application to Date of First Hearing—by Type of Court (Court Proforma)

COURT	TYPE OF APPLICATION					
	FREEING		ADOPT./PREV. FREED		ADOPTION	
	(months)		(months)		(months)	
Magistrates'	3.82	(n=8)	2.12	(n=12)	3.69	(n=20)
County	5.81	(n=72)	3.61	(n=48)	4.46	(n=260)
High	14.94	(n=6)	4.37	(n=1)	17.35	(n=11)
All	**6.26**	**(n=86)**	**3.33**	**(n=61)**	**4.89**	**(n=291)**
[Missing cases]	[16 (16%)]		[2 (3%)]		[39 (12%)]	

The data presented in Table 8.12 support this prediction. Where the child had already been freed, just over two months had elapsed before an adoption application was heard in the magistrates' court, compared with around three and a half months for freeing and adoption cases. In the county court, freeing cases took the longest to reach a first hearing—just under six months on average—compared with about three and a half months in adoption cases where the child had already been freed and about four and a half months for the other agency adoptions. Although the number of cases heard in the High Court were small, it is worth noting that freeing cases heard in that court took on average nearly fifteen months to reach a first hearing, and adoption cases (where the child had not been freed), even longer (over seventeen months).

8.13 Length of Time from Application to First Hearing for Contested and Uncontested Cases[8]

In terms of whether or not a contested case took longer to reach a first hearing than an uncontested case, the data in Table 8.13 confirm this was the case for all types of application. A contested freeing application took on average about two months longer to reach a court hearing than an uncontested freeing application. Similarly, a contested adoption application took seven months to reach a first hearing, compared with four months for an uncontested case. One suggestion as to why such a difference should be found between contested and uncontested cases may be that in contested case more documentation, for example GAL reports, have to be filed with the court before the hearing can take place. Social workers and solicitors interviewed in the Practitioner Study identified possible reasons; for instance, the additional work involved in a case where parental agreement is withheld (Chapter 3—Parental Agreement); problems created for solicitors who have no automatic right of access to Schedule II Reports and GAL Reports (Chapter 4—Legal Advice and Practice) section 4.3 and 4.4; delays involved while legal aid applications are processed (Chapter 5—Courts Administration).

Table 8.13

Mean Time (in Months) between Date of Application and Date of First Hearing According to whether the Case was Contested or not (Court Proforma)

	TYPE OF APPLICATION					
	FREEING		ADOPT./PREV. FREED		ADOPTION	
	(months)		(months)		(months)	
Contested	6.74	(n=67)	–		7.06	(n=82)
Uncontested/not known	4.59	(n=19)	3.33	(n=61)	4.04	(n=209)
All	**6.26**	**(n=86)**	**3.33**	**(n=61)**	**4.89**	**(n=291)**
[Missing cases]	[16 (16%)]		[2 (3%)]		[39 (12%)]	

---

[8]   See Part 1, section 2.14 for our definition of a contested case.

CHAPTER 9   An Overview of the Adoption Process

9.1   Summary

9.2   Length of Time from Date of Placement for Adoption to Date of Order

9.3   Length of Time from Date of Current Placement to Date of Order

9.1   Summary

We have found in the previous chapters (Part I, Chapters 7 and 8), that various factors appear to influence the time that cases take to reach each stage within the adoption process until a decision is reached by the court.

Social workers and solicitors whom we interviewed in the Practitioner Study expressed much concern about the time taken to complete the various stages involved in the adoption process. They were particularly worried by what many regarded as the unacceptable length of time taken to process freeing applications and the implications of this for the child. Their views are reported throughout Part II which follows.

Our evidence suggests that the areas within our study have developed different practices regarding the placement of children for adoption. In one area, children, particularly pre-school and older, once identified as suitable for adoption, were initially placed with long term foster parents with a view to adoption. Those children might therefore remain in the same placement for several years before the adoption panel recommended the placement as an adoptive one, following which an application to the court might be made by the prospective adopters. In other areas, the policy appeared to be more rapid in that once the child had been identified as suitable for adoption, the adoption placement and panel recommendation were made as soon as suitable adoptive parents were found.

Regional variation was found in the length of time taken for the application to reach the court once the Adoption Panel had recommended the placement or, in the case of freeing, recommended the application be made. The age of the child and whether or not the case was likely to be contested seemed to have some bearing on the speed with which the application was made to the court. It is also relevant to bear in mind that babies were rarely found in contested adoption cases. On the other hand, quite a high proportion of contested freeing cases involved babies—a finding that contradicts the original predictions of the Houghton Committee (1972).[1] In the case of adoption, the application is of course made by the adoptive parents and not by the agency, although the parents may well be following their guidance.

Once the application has been lodged with the court, the adoption agency and the court have to work in tandem to a certain extent. For instance, it is the duty of the adoption agency to submit the Schedule II report. At the same time, the court has to list the case for a hearing. We found that the time taken before the case reached a first hearing varied according to area, as well as to the type of court and whether or not the case was likely to be contested.

---

[1]   See Part I, section 2.13 and for further discussion see Lowe (1991), Report of the Research into the Use and Practice of the Freeing for Adoption Provisions (Chapter 3).

In the following two sections we examine the overall length of time taken to complete the process of adoption both from the date of placement for adoption to the date of order and from the date the child entered his or her current placement to the date of the order.

9.2   Length of Time from Date of Placement for Adoption to Date of Order

Looking at the process of adoption as a whole in Table 9.2(a), we see that overall roughly a third (35%) of agency adoption cases took up to six months from the date the child was placed for adoption until the adoption order was made. Broken down by area, the data reveal that whereas nearly half (48%) of adoption cases in Somerset had been concluded within that time span, in Birmingham the proportion of cases was somewhat lower (29%). These differences in the disposal rate of cases may be explained in part by the fact that, for instance, Somerset had the lowest proportion of uncontested cases within the fieldwork areas, (see *ante* Part I section 2.15). Approximately 70% of all the agency adoption cases had been concluded within a year of the child being placed for adoption.

At the other end of the time scale, Table 9.2(a) shows that, compared to other areas, Walsall had a high proportion of cases—one in eight—where

Table 9.2(a)
Length of Time from Date of Placement for Adoption to Date of Order by Area—Agency Adoption Applications (Court Proforma)

LENGTH OF TIME	AREA									
	DEVON		SOMERSET		BIRMINGHAM		WALSALL		TOTAL	
	NO.	(%)	NO.	(%)	NO.	(%)	NO.	(%)	NO.	(%)
Up to 3 months	4	(3)	2	(4)	0	–	0	–	6	(2)
3 to 6 months	42	(31)	22	(44)	44	(29)	18	(40)	126	(33)
6 to 9 months	38	(28)	10	(20)	28	(18)	8	(18)	84	(22)
9 to 12 months	19	(14)	0	–	26	(17)	6	(13)	51	(13)
12 to 18 months	11	(8)	3	(6)	22	(14)	2	(4)	38	(10)
18 to 24 months	5	(4)	7	(14)	14	(9)	2	(4)	28	(7)
2 to 3 years	13	(9)	6	(12)	13	(8)	3	(7)	35	(9)
3 to 5 years	0	–	0	–	4	(3)	4	(9)	8	(2)
5 to 10 years	0	–	0	–	2	(1)	2	(4)	4	(1)
10 years +	4	(3)	0	–	0	–	0	–	4	(1)
All[1]	136	(100)	50	(100)	153	(100)	45	(100)	384	(100)

* =less than 1%

1   In 2 cases where a final order had been made the information was not available from the records.

the child was in an adoption placement for three years or more before the adoption order was made.

Table 9.2(b) shows the length of time from date of placement for adoption to the date of the order in relation to the age of the child at the date s/he was placed for adoption.

Just over half (56%) of babies placed for adoption were adopted within six months of being placed. In only a few cases involving babies (5%) did the adoption process take longer than a year to complete. However the same is not true for children over 1 year old. Only 14% of children in the age group 1–5 years and 8% in the age group 5–10 years had been adopted within six months of being placed for adoption. A higher proportion (33%) of children aged 10 years and over had been adopted within six months of being placed. Children for whom two years or more had elapsed from the date of placement for adoption to the adoption order fell either in the 5–10 years old age group (40%) or the 1–5 years age group (28%).

Table 9.2(b)
Length of Time from Date of Placement for Adoption to Date of Order by Age of Child at Date of Placement for Adoption—Agency Adoption Applications (Court Proforma)

	AGE OF CHILD AT DATE OF PLACEMENT FOR ADOPTION									
LENGTH OF TIME	**UP to 1 YR**		**1–5 YRS**		**5–10 YRS**		**10–18 YRS**		**TOTAL**	
	NO.	**(%)**	**NO.**	**(%)**	**NO.**	**(%)**	**NO.**	**(%)**	**NO.**	**(%)**
Up to 3 months	0	–	2	(2)	4	(8)	0	–	6	(2)
3 to 6 months	100	(56)	14	(12)	0	–	12	(33)	126	(33)
6 to 9 months	58	(32)	14	(12)	4	(8)	8	(22)	84	(22)
9 to 12 months	12	(7)	16	(14)	9	(17)	14	(39)	51	(13)
12 to 18 months	6	(3)	26	(23)	6	(11)	0	–	38	(10)
18 to 24 months	4	(2)	13	(11)	9	(17)	2	(6)	28	(7)
2 to 3 years	0	–	18	(16)	17	(32)	0	–	35	(9)
3 to 5 years	0	–	4	(4)	4	(8)	0	–	8	(2)
5 to 10 years	0	–	4	(4)	0	–	0	–	4	(1)
10 years +	0	–	4	(4)	0	–	0	–	4	(1)
All[1]	**180**	**(100)**	**115**	**(100)**	**53**	**(100)**	**36**	**(100)**	**384**	**(100)**

1   In two cases where a final order had been made the information was not available from the records.

9.3 Length of Time from Date of Current Placement to Date of Order

A closer examination of data, this time looking at the length of time from the date that the current placement (whatever its original purpose) began to the date of order, revealed that Walsall was well behind the other three areas in terms of the proportion of cases completed.

Table 9.3(a)
Time between Date of Current Placement and Date of Order by Area—Agency Adoption Applications (Court Proforma)

LENGTH OF TIME	DEVON		SOMERSET		BIRMINGHAM		WALSALL		TOTAL	
	NO.	(%)	NO.	(%)	NO.	(%)	NO.	(%)	NO.	(%)
From 3 up to 6 months	38	(28)	20	(40)	44	(29)	12	(27)	114	(30)
6 to 9 months	38	(28)	6	(12)	22	(14)	8	(18)	74	(19)
9 to 12 months	6	(5)	0	–	14	(9)	0	–	20	(5)
12 to 18 months	8	(6)	8	(16)	24	(16)	4	(9)	44	(11)
18 to 24 months	8	(6)	2	(4)	8	(5)	0	–	18	(5)
2 to 3 years	14	(10)	8	(16)	14	(9)	4	(9)	40	(10)
3 to 5 years	5	(4)	0	–	11	(7)	1	(2)	17	(4)
5 to 10 years	5	(4)	4	(8)	16	(10)	12	(25)	37	(10)
10 years +	12	(9)	2	(4)	0	–	4	(9)	18	(5)
All[1]	**134**	**(100)**	**50**	**(100)**	**153**	**(100)**	**45**	**(100)**	**382**	**(100)**

1   In four cases where a final order had been made the information was not available from the records.

From the above table (Table 9.3(a)), we can see that Somerset had the highest proportion of cases (40%), where less than six months had elapsed from the date of current placement to the final order, compared with only just over a quarter of cases in Walsall, Devon and Birmingham (27%, 28% and 29% respectively). When analysing the data in terms of percentages of cases reaching a final order within a year of the child's current placement, Walsall was a little behind (45%), compared with just over half the cases (52%) in both Somerset and Birmingham and a higher proportion of cases (61%) in Devon.

At the other end of the scale, Table 9.3(a) shows that around a third of the cases (36%) in Walsall took three years or more from the date of current placement of the child to the date of the final order, roughly twice as many cases as in the other three areas. These findings again add power to the suggestion that a different practice in adoption is perhaps being used in Walsall compared with the areas of Somerset, Devon and Birmingham, that is, in Walsall the child may have been placed initially with long term foster parents, perhaps with a view to adoption, for some years before a final decision on adoption was made.

Table 9.3(a) illustrates the relationship between the time from the date of the child's current placement to the date of the adoption order with the age of the child at the *date of the order*. In the case of babies being adopted for over two thirds of the sample (69%) the baby had been adopted within six months of entering the current placement. For children over 1 year old the time in placement before an adoption order was made much longer on the

Table 9.3(b)
Time between Date of Current Placement and Date of Order by Age of Child at Date of Order—Agency Adoption Applications (Court Proforma)

LENGTH OF TIME	AGE OF CHILD AT DATE OF ORDER									
	UP to 1 YR		1–5 YRS		5–10 YRS		10–18 YRS		TOTAL	
	NO.	(%)	NO.	(%)	NO.	(%)	NO.	(%)	NO.	(%)
From 3 up to 6 months	94	(69)	20	(15)	0	–	0	–	114	(30)
6 up to 9 months	40	(29)	28	(22)	4	(6)	2	(4)	74	(19)
9 up to 12 months	2	(1)	16	(12)	2	(3)	0	–	20	(5)
12 up to 18 months	0	–	38	(29)	6	(9)	0	–	44	(12)
18 up to 24 months	0	–	10	(8)	8	(12)	0	–	18	(5)
2 up to 3 years	0	–	12	(9)	22	(32)	6	(13)	40	(10)
3 up to 5 years	0	–	6	(5)	11	(16)	0	–	17	(4)
5 up to 10 years	0	–	0	–	15	(22)	22	(46)	37	(10)
10 years +	0	–	0	–	0	–	18	(38)	18	(5)
All[1]	136	(100)	130	(100)	68	(100)	48	(100)	382	(100)

1   In four cases where a final order had been made the information was not available from the records.

whole. Only 15% of children aged 1–5 years old and none over the age of 5 years were adopted within six months of entering their current placement. It seemed that the older the child when adopted the longer s/he had been in his/her adoption placement before the order was made.

PART II

The Practitioner Study

Introduction

The findings presented in this part of the report arise from the second phase of the project, the Practitioner Study. It sought to establish the views of social workers who had written the Schedule II report and of solicitors who had been involved in a sample of cases drawn from the Court Record Survey. These concerned the adoption process, the law relating to it and identifying obstacles which they considered might make the achievement of adoption unnecessarily problematic.

The Sample

Given the time and resources available, the researchers aimed to conduct 80 interviews with practitioners—two thirds with social workers and one third with solicitors.

The sampling frame was devised by first dividing the 258 cases from the court proforma sample into four categories:

(i)   South West/children up to 1 year of age;

(ii)   South West/children over 1 year;

(iii)   Midlands/children up to 1 year;

(iv)   Midlands/children over 1 year.

The age range was split in this way to ensure that we met the Department of Health's request that children under one year of age were well represented. A stratified systematic sample was taken. This produced 62 social work cases and 28 involving solicitors. However as the response rate from solicitors was low all solicitors were included in the sample.

(a)   Social workers

52 interviews were conducted with social workers covering 57 cases. (In a few instances one social worker was involved with more than one case in the sample). In 67% of the cases the task of writing a Schedule II report involved more than one social worker. In 39% of these both or all the social workers involved were interviewed.

The cases were located in:

		%
Devon	23	40
Somerset	5	9
Birmingham	26	46
Walsall	2	3
Other	1	2
	57	**100**

79% worked for local authority adoption agencies; 19% for voluntary adoption agencies and 2% for both local authority **and** voluntary agencies.

(b)   Solicitors

24 interviews were conducted with solicitors in private practice concerning 28 cases in all. In four instances the solicitor we saw dealt with more than one case in our sample.

The cases were located in:

		%
Devon	12	43
Somerset	3	11
Birmingham	8	29
Walsall	4	14
Other	1	3
	28	100

Over half the solicitors (60%) acted for the prospective adopters; 14% acted for the birth mother, 7% for the birth father and 11% for both birth parents.

In addition, four local authority solicitors were interviewed: two in the South West and two in the Midlands. A third in the Midlands completed a questionnaire herself rather than by interview.

Methodology[1]

Questionnaires were designed and tested with the help of solicitors and social workers in Avon, Gloucestershire and Wiltshire. The questionnaires used in the interviews are given in Appendix D (social workers) and Appendix E (solicitors).

On the day of the interview we explained more about the research and its purpose, answering any queries the interviewee had. We also assured them again that when we compiled our report their identity would not be disclosed.

We then asked if they would be willing for the interview to be tape recorded, explaining that this would not only speed the flow of the interview, but would also assist us in making an accurate record of what they had said. They were assured that the interviews would be erased once they had been transcribed. We also offered to turn off the tape recording if at any point during the interview they did not want what they were saying to be recorded. All were willing to be tape recorded.

---

[1]   This account of the methodology has been kept brief at the request of the Department of Health.

Coding sheets were designed so that the responses to some questions could be quantified. A verbatim record was also made especially of those answers which could not be coded and which produced unusual or interesting views which were well expressed and of special relevance to the issues with which the research was concerned. These transcriptions were gathered together into 'books' and it is from these that the quotes used in the report which follows have been taken.

The Findings

In considering the material from the practitioner interviews, we have endeavoured to identify: (i) those areas of the process which might act as some kind of obstacle to the process of cases along the pathway to adoption from the time when it is agreed that adoption is the preferred plan for the child through to the final hearing; (ii) any issues related to the wider debate on adoption generally about which there was strong feeling; and (iii) report the views expressed about adoption law and process current at the time of the interviews.

It should be remembered that the views expressed are restricted to social workers and solicitors. It should also be borne in mind that any views the practitioners express about what they considered to be the perceptions of the birth parents, adopters and children concerning the adoption process are at best second hand. Our projected study on the consumer view will endeavour to report these views first hand.

CHAPTER 1 Organisation of Adoption Work in the Agencies

1.1   Introduction

1.2   Establishing Priorities

1.3   Inconsistent and Uncoordinated Policies and Practices Within and Between Agencies

1.4   The Issue of Specialization

1.5   Specialist Supervision and Support

1.6   Comment

1.1   Introduction

Interviews with adoption agency social workers revealed that there were a number of interacting problem areas concerning agencies' organisation of adoption work which were viewed as potential obstacles to the adoption process:

(i)   establishing priorities;

(ii)   inconsistent and uncoordinated policies and practices within and between agencies;

(iii)   problems arising from a lack of specialization:

(a) in respect of individual social workers, including supervisors;
(b) within agencies.

Although it was not possible, given the limitations of the study, to establish precisely where these problems occurred most frequently and acutely, the great majority of the social workers (85%) reported experiencing organisational problems of one kind or another. Thirteen per cent said there were no problems arising from the way the adoption work was organized. The remaining 2% did not know.

To some extent this view was reinforced by the solicitors. When we asked them what they saw as the main problem areas of adoption, over a quarter (28%) mentioned agency-related difficulties.

1.2   Establishing Priorities

A number of local authority social workers said they experienced difficulty in giving sufficient priority to adoption work, which tended to take second place to the potentially more crisis-laden part of their case load, for example, child abuse work which requires immediate attention. Several social workers thought that adoption work suffered as a result. As one in the West Country explained, although adoption was *"tremendously important"*, it was also *"planned, focused work"* and was therefore *"upset completely"* by high priority child abuse work. Another in the Midlands said that once a child had been placed in care, *"they were then safe technically"* so social workers could *"pick up the next child child abuse referral"*.

One of the social workers in the South West with a general case load put the matter this way:

> "Something may not be more important than adoption but it may be more immediate. In the scheme of things there may be a case which is less important—perhaps arranging holiday care for elderly people—but it's immediate. There are tremendous pressures which district staff have to cope with. Adoption can always wait for

another day. I know children who are waiting for adoption—the children who wait syndrome—and they are still there. And that's not a criticism of managers. I've been a team leader in a district office and I've had to say 'that adoption will have to wait'.

She went on to comment:

"The thing about generic social work as well is that I don't think adoption is everybody's cup of tea. People who want to do adoption work get torn in shreds by other aspects of departmental responsibilities which get in the way. It's a difficult enough task arranging adoption without the weight and cumbersomeness of the department behind you."

Another from the Midlands suggested that it was largely a matter of the way the organisation's workload was managed. There was no overall system in her area and social workers were left to work out their own priorities. She said that although she gave adoption work higher priority than say, supervision orders, lack of time was still a problem.

More positively, a social worker in the West Country explained how the priority issue was dealt with in her area, with a view to achieving more consistent agency practice:

"It's a matter of organising the work and here we have a case load weighting system, so you have to ask for enough space on your case load for it really and I've always been able to get that. . . . Basically each case gets a number of points. They get points for meetings and duties and there's a fairly objective scoring system. So basically when your case load has reached the total which is 42 then you don't get any more cases. The points are scored on things like if you visit weekly you get a point; if there's a child in care you get an extra point; if it's a complex family case you get an extra point for that and so on. You decide on supervision with your supervisor if it's a complex family case. It works quite well. It enables me to put say the first five points an adoption case might be taking me and if there are times when it gets busier you just put up more points and it stops you from being loaded with new work when you need the space."

1.3 Inconsistent and Uncoordinated Policies and Practices Within and between Agencies

Many of the problems the individual case workers experience arise from a lack of a standard or coordinated approach to adoption work within their own local authority. This problem can be exacerbated in the larger authorities which are split into areas and operate on the 'path system', with considerable delegation of responsibility for organization and practice. For example, we were told by one social worker that whilst she felt that in her authority the **principles** upon which adoption work was organised were basically sound, each team in the four areas into which the authority was divided developed and practised its own idiosyncratic approach. She felt this problem could have been overcome if there had been one overall policy for the authority with good communication between each of the areas. In this way each area would have been aware of the needs of the others, resulting in more effective use of resources overall.

Another explained the frustrations such a fragmented approach can cause:

> "I am the only social worker in this (maternity) hospital. There is short term crisis work. Adoption is very long term work. Although as a department you would expect (local authority) to have a policy on this, you would be surprised how much things differ from one district to another as if you are working for a different local authority. For instance, a colleague of mine at X Maternity Hospital is not able to see her adoptions through. She begins to counsel mother during pregnancy. As soon as the child is born she has to pass it on to a new social worker in Area Office who doesn't know anything about her case and has to start afresh. It doesn't provide continuity. The natural mother goes through this heartsearching and during the most critical period she has to face a new social worker. That doesn't happen with me. If my Team Leader was to tell me that I wasn't able to see my adoptions through I would kick and make a fuss because I think it's just so unfair to clients. And also it gives you more satisfaction if you are able to see a piece of work through and look forward to the placement than leave it in mid-air."

A local authority solicitor in the West Country described similar problems, explaining that two of the four districts in his local authority ran along the same lines, whilst a third was run *"almost as if it was in a different county"*. Not only were there differences in procedure but, as he perceived it, internal procedures were interpreted differently too. He felt that planning for children in care suffered as a result, causing problems for the children. He also thought they tended to *"languish in care"* more in one district than in the others.

This uncoordinated approach can have an adverse effect on various aspects of adoption work. For instance, in one district of a particular authority an acute problem has arisen over the recruitment of adopters. One social worker in this district said that because of the priority given to child abuse work, the recruiting and vetting of prospective adopters was taking second place. A new scheme had been introduced in an attempt to overcome this problem: each of the four districts in her authority had a target quota of different types of adopter which it must meet each year. However, she anticipated difficulties in this approach:

"It may be that an area that has a large, middle class private occupied housing stock is going to find it easier to find good prospective adopters than one of the districts that has one of the less popular council housing areas that takes up most of their district because most of those properties are occupied by single parents with financial problems and you are not likely to find many prospective adopters among those.

I don't think it will be possible to meet the quotas so that is an unrealistic response to the problem of getting enough adopters. It doesn't seem an appropriate response. It could be resolved in two ways really; either in those districts where they are likely to recruit more prospective adopters (they) should have extra resources to do that and less in the areas where they are less likely to recruit from; or that there should be a central area-wide recruiting group—a specialist who would first do adoption vetting for the area."

A social worker from another district in the same local authority thought that some progress was being made in the recruitment of adopters. However, she felt that the success of the recruitment system depended to some extent on goodwill and a *"spirit of compositeness"* operating between the districts. She went on to explain that:

". . . It's a very time consuming piece of work to vet and recruit prospective adopters and if a district office invests a lot of time in it, then that district gets no return from that because it's highly unlikely that a child from that district will be placed there. So you are actually spending a lot of time, a lot of your very valuable resources to produce a resource for another district. . . ."

If problems are created by a lack of co-ordination within an agency, it is hardly surprising that these can be intensified when more than one agency is involved in a case, since one local authority may well have different priorities from another. If a voluntary agency is involved, priorities are likely to be different again.[1] A West Country social worker described her experience of inter-agency adoption:

"Serious delays arise with inter-agency adoptions where we are supervising on behalf of another authority. It's bloody difficult because it's out of sight out of mind for the home authority and then if you've got to get them to agree adoption allowances or some new quirk comes in—blue eyed children have to be adopted by blue eyed parents—you are snookered. Local authorities have these zany policies from time to time and you can find then that they throw a spanner in the works for a child. Seriously, sorting our permanency issues for inter-agency placements is pretty difficult and usually

---

[1]   See Part I, section 7.4 of the Court Record Survey for an analysis by area of the proportion of cases in our sample that involved an inter-agency placement.

involves very substantial delays unless you are very vigorous—it's letters to the Director and if you haven't heard in a fortnight it's a letter to the Director again, that sort of thing to actually get them off their butts and moving on the case."

A social worker in the Midlands said there was no *"overall linking in of information between local authorities"*. What could be a priority for her authority might not be perceived in the same way by another.

The financial aspects of adoption work is another area in which inconsistencies occur. This can cause several difficulties, for example, over the differential rates in adoption allowances.[2] A social worker in the Midlands was hampered by financial restrictions in her efforts to elicit the help of a voluntary agency in finding a family for a child who was difficult to place. At the time of the interview she was trying to identify a placement for a child in London, but her authority's maximum enhanced allowance was less than the average allowance offered by London authorities, and that restriction was playing *"quite an important role"* in her handling of the case.

A voluntary agency social worker told us that while some authorities automatically paid a fostering allowance and then an adoption allowance if it was needed, others had to be convinced that adopters needed an adoption allowance.

Local authorities also differ in the extent to which they provide post adoption support. A worker in another voluntary agency described her experience of the problem:

> "You are placing children from one care authority into another care authority and very often the host authority is very reluctant to pick up the tab in on-going support after the order is made. The local authority who placed wants to wash their hands of them completely. So in terms of the Adoption Act where there is a duty on local authorities to provide post-adoption support, it's something that the vast majority of local authorities have not taken on board seriously. Most of them have done nothing about it and have got no long-term commitment at all to families where we are placing very very abused children and we know that there are going to be on-going problems after the order is made."

Local authorities vary, too, in their policy concerning the payment of legal costs for adoption. For instance, some require all prospective adopters to apply for legal aid in contested cases but make it clear that if the application is unsuccessful they will then meet the costs. If the Law Society has knowledge of such a policy it will be unlikely to grant an application and much time will have been wasted as a result. (We discuss this further in Part II, Chapter Four).

---

[2]   An examination of the payment of adoption allowances by local authority areas from the court proforma sample of cases in our Court Record Survey is made in Part I, section 7.5.

1.4   The Issue of Specialisation

The issue of whether or not adoption work should be regarded and organized as specialist work both for individual social workers and for the local
authority adoption agencies emerged as one of the major concerns of the
social workers. In an attempt to ascertain whether adoption was regarded
by local authority agencies as case work more appropriately undertaken by
specialist workers, we had intended to ask each social worker we saw to
describe the basis on which they undertook adoption work and how and
why it was allocated to them. However, it became clear from our "test"
interviews that there was no straightforward answer to these questions.
The researchers found the responses confusing. Rather than run the risk of
misrepresenting the arrangements being described, we decided merely to
establish how experienced the social workers we interviewed were, and
what proportion of their current workload was spent on adoption.

Table 1.1
No. of years spent working as a social worker

	No.	(%)
Up to 5 years	4	(8)
6 up to 10 years	11	(20)
11 up to 15 years	15	(29)
16 up to 20 years	15	(29)
21 up to 30 years	7	(14)
ALL	**52**	**(100)**

Table 1.2
No. of years spent working in child care field

	No.	(%)
Up to 5 years	8	(16)
6 up to 10 years	12	(23)
11 up to 15 years	14	(28)
16 up to 20 years	13	(25)
21 up to 30 years	5	(8)
ALL	**52**	**(100)**

It will be seen that the social workers in our sample were experienced in
both general social work and in child care. Nevertheless, it does not follow
from this that they were necessarily experienced in adoption work. In an
attempt to establish what proportion of their work time was spent on
actual adoption work, we asked them how much of it had been allocated to
adoption work in the twelve months preceding the interview. Table 1.3
below shows their response.

Table 1.3
Proportion of workload spent on adoption in twelve months preceding interview

	Local authority Adoption Agency Social Worker	Voluntary Adoption Agency Social Worker	All	(%)
None	7	–	7	(13)
Less than ¼	16	–	16	(31)
¼ to ½	7	2	9	(18)
½ to ¾	8	–	8	(15)
More than ¾	4	3	7	(13)
All	1	3	4	(8)
DK	1	–	1	(2)
ALL	**44**	**8**	**52**	**(100)**

[NB—table indicates the number of local authority social workers and voluntary agency social workers in each category where appropriate]

From these figures it does not seem unreasonable to conclude that for half the local authority social workers in our sample, adoption work could not be regarded as a specialized activity since less than a quarter of their overall work time involved adoption work.

Many of the social workers expressed concern about the level or lack of specialisation in adoption work. A social worker in the West Country said that although in his authority adoption work was supposed to be undertaken by senior practitioners, in practice all child care social workers could be involved. He felt that was at least preferable to involving social workers who undertake general case work.

This was echoed by a social worker in the Midlands who pointed out that it was difficult for social workers *"to be good at all aspects of social work"*. She said that social workers *"on general service"* needed to have knowledge about a lot of things. Because of the amount of legislation involved, not everybody could be familiar with every aspect of it. She felt that sometimes social workers were *"left just to flap in the wind"*. A typical general view seemed to be:

> ". . . that people who are doing it all the time and are interested in it will give a better service than those who are sort of dabbling, doing one here, one there."

Another Midlands social worker expressed concern at the apparent decline in the number of social workers experienced in adoption work:

> "There is a worry that the numbers of workers actually experienced in adoption do seem to be dropping. There are very few people in each team who have a good, solid grounding in adoption work. A lot of the more experienced ones have moved away so there's a gentle loss, a bleeding away which is worrying particularly for the

young child under three's adoption, which needs a great deal of care. We seem to be losing that expertise. Also the people who are being recruited into homefinding often don't have a background other than general child care."

Social workers suggested that specialist adoption workers in local authorities offered the consumer a better deal, although there were some who saw disadvantages in specialisation. For example, one suggested that specialists could lose touch with the day to day pressures and stresses of *"frontline work"*.

We were told of one local authority in the West Country, which had appointed specialists to undertake adoption work in the smaller areas in the country but had found they had no-one to fall back on if the specialist was away or sick.

One social worker in the South West who worked part of the week for the local authority and the rest for a voluntary agency clearly saw great advantages in working in a specialist agency.

> "Having a foot in both camps I can particularly see the advantages of a small independent agency where I'm not bogged down with a lot of bureaucracy and a plethora of forms which the local authority has. We have a big fat book on adoption procedure in the local authority and quite honestly—and I'm quite an experienced adoption worker—I find it very confusing. . . ."

However, she thought that a possible shortcoming of working in her voluntary agency was that it did not handle children in care, and there could be a risk that specialist adoption agency staff would not fully appreciate what was involved in crisis child care work.

Several practitioners advocated the development of specialist adoption agencies outside the local authority domain. As one local authority social worker in the South West said:

> "I'm a great believer that in lots of ways adoption work should be hived off to people like NCH, Barnardos or someone like that—we would say this is the adoption aspect of our work. We need so many homefinding places; we have these children now ready. I think ideally it should be part of our work—it gives that completeness and roundness—but from the clients' point of view I really think they'd get a better service."

And another from the Midlands remarked:

> "I would like to see voluntary agencies like NCH continue doing adoption work. I would like to see voluntary agencies offering a specialist service on behalf of local authorities because perhaps that's the only way they will have a protected specialist service which isn't going to be eaten away by the call of other crises or imperatives."

1.5   Specialist Supervision and Support

We wanted to find out if the social workers we saw were supervised in their adoption work and, if so, whether they considered their supervisor to have sufficient experience and specailist knowledge of adoption. Just over half (51%) confirmed that their adoption work was supervised, but 13% said their work was not supervised. The remaining 6% were themselves supervisors.

Of those who were supervised, 50% considered their supervisor to have specialised knowledge of adoption but 31% did not. It was clear that some social workers felt they were thrown in at the deep end with little support:

> "My first lot of adoptions I did almost unsupervised. I had no knowledge and no course training or anything—I mean, it was extremely frightening for me. It was dreadful. . . . I think it was a very unfortunate thing that the person who was trying to supervise really wasn't perhaps able to carry out that role . . . I was told by someone that you can't do adoption work for 18 months. One of my very first cases was an adoption that I picked up when I first started."

Yet lack of experienced adoption supervision does not necessarily imply a lack of alternative expert support. Thus when we asked the social workers if there was someone whom they could consult if they needed advice and support in their adoption work, virtually all (98%) replied that there was. The people with specialist knowledge on adoption whom they were most likely to consult were child care advisers, team leaders and other colleagues in their agency. Back-up and support from practitioners with specialist knowledge therefore appeared to be fairly readily available to the social workers whom we interviewed, though for the majority this was much less likely to come from their supervisor. One of the less experienced in adoption described her position thus:

> "My last adoption case was three or four years ago now and with all due respect to my team manager then, he didn't know too much about adoption—probably even less than I do—because general services don't deal with adoption very often the way the department is organised. And although I'd been doing the job for several years, I still needed somebody to guide me on what I was doing. Fortunately with the specialist teams I think they do provide some element of that. Although they can advise you, they are not your supervising officer. You are conscious of the importance of it all and if it's something that you don't have experience of or have experience of on a regular basis you do kind of think 'what the hell have I got to do next? What's the next stage?'"

1.6 Comment

In the light of these findings, it seems to us there are five outstanding policy questions:

(i)   Can local authority adoption agencies give adoption greater priority in their overall work?

(ii)   How can the problems of inconsistent and uncoordinated approaches of adoption work practice both within and between agencies be reduced?

(iii)   Can a more consistent approach to financial matters concerning adoption be developed, for example in relation to adoption allowances, applications for legal aid, etc.?

(iv)   Would adoption work be better undertaken by "specialist" adoption workers rather than by social workers who may have a general child-related case load?

(v)   Would the organisational problems which have been considered be overcome if adoption work was undertaken only by specialist agencies?

CHAPTER 2   Schedule II Reports

2.1   Introduction

2.2   Social Workers' Level of Experience

2.3   Sources of Information

2.4   The Relevance of the Schedule II Report

2.5   Format

2.6   Time Allowed for Completion of Schedule II Reports

2.7   Should Schedule II Reports Be Lodged at the Court when the Application is Submitted?

2.8   Comment

2.1   Introduction

Schedule II reports are a key information resource in the freeing and/or adoption process. A freeing application must be submitted to court accompanied by the Schedule II report, (Adoption rules 1984, rule 4[4]). In adoption, the adoption agency is required to submit the Schedule II report within six weeks of the receipt of the notice of hearing, (Adoption Rules 1984, rule 22). Until the Schedule II has been completed, the reporting officer and/or guardian ad litem is/are unable to proceed with their own investigation.

Matters to be covered in the report are outlined in Schedule II to the Adoption Rules and inform social workers about the items of information the court requires in the report. It covers details concerning the child, including his/her care history where appropriate; the birth parents; prospective adoptive parents, and actions of the local authority. At present the same format is used for adoptions by step-parents or other relatives, no relation adoptions and freeing applications, whatever the age of the child concerned.

The Schedule II report is intended to act as an independent unbiased report which presents all the factual information the court is likely to require to enable it to reach a decision about the application. Its purpose is not a justification of the local authority's action although, as we have said, the agency is required to describe its actions in the report. Because of its fundamental importance in the adoption process we asked social workers a series of questions about it (see questionnaire in Appendix D).

From their response, several problems emerged. They concerned:

(i)   practitioners' level of experience;

(ii)   sources of information;

(iii)   relevance of the Schedule II report to all types of adoption;

(iv)   the guidelines;

(v)   the time allowed to prepare the report;

(vi)   the timing of the submission of the Schedule II report.

Given the parameters of the research drawn by the Department of Health which, as we explained in the Preface, excluded guardians ad litem and reporting officers from inclusion in the practitioner interviews, we are not able to explore the relationship between their reports and the Schedule II reports, an issue of major importance which needs to be investigated in considering any possible streamlining of the adoption process.

2.2   Social Workers' Level of Experience

As we reported in the previous chapter, many social workers were concerned by their lack of specialist knowledge of adoption. This anxiety emerged again when social workers talked about the preparation of Schedule II reports.

In order to gauge something of the frequency with which they compiled Schedule II reports, we asked social workers to estimate how many they had prepared in the 12 months preceding the interview. Table 2.1 shows their response:

Table 2.1
How many Schedule II reports social worker prepared in the 12 months preceding the interview

	No.	(%)
None	14	(27)
One	8	(15)
Two	3	(6)
Three	7	(13)
Four	6	(12)
Five	3	(6)
Six	7	(13)
Eight	1	(2)
Ten	2	(4)
N/A—not in same job	1	(2)
All	**52**	**(100)**

Just over a quarter (27%) had prepared none, whilst at the other end of the scale a quarter had prepared between five and ten. This left just under half (46%) who had prepared as few as one but as many as four. From these figures it is clear that only a quarter of the social workers in our sample prepared Schedule II reports with any frequency in the year preceding the interviews, whilst almost a half (48%) had prepared none or no more than one or two.

Further analysis of this information suggests that the social workers in the voluntary agencies prepare proportionately more Schedule II reports than those in local authority agencies. They prepared 25% of the total number of reports completed (144), but represent only 16% of the total number of social workers in our interview sample. However, it should be remembered that, as we showed in Part II, Chapter One, social workers in voluntary agencies overall spend more time on adoption work than those in local authority agencies.

This apparent lack of practice must make the task more difficult and time-consuming for those social workers who prepare the reports infrequently. As one said:

> "Obviously if it's a while since you've written one because you are not doing it every week, and you've forgotten exactly how it flows, you find yourself saying—oh help—I've got to put that in later on. And some things you repeatedly have to look up to remember what they actually mean. I think it's difficult for area workers, too, who do them less frequently than we do."

It can have implications, too, for those social workers who act in a supervisory role, since some of them reported having to rewrite reports. If they were prepared by area workers for instance some supervisors would *"quietly rewrite large pieces of them to make them more intelligible"*. this was often because the social workers who had prepared them in the first instance were not used to them and would inevitably miss things. In an already over-stretched service, the burden on more experienced social workers of having to rewrite reports which will already have taken up much time for the original social worker may be unjustifiable and suggests inefficient use of resources in the organisation. In our view it again points to a need for a more specialist or re-structured approach to adoption work and how it is organised in the local authority agencies.

2.3 Sources of Information

In many instances, social workers look to the case files for much of the information they require when preparing the report, although they also have to go outside these to complete the process. We asked them if they usually found the information contained in the case files sufficient. Nearly two thirds (64%) said it was; a further 13% said it was sometimes but not always; a further 2% said it was but not in step parent cases; 19% said it was not sufficient and the remaining 2% felt unable to judge.

Although for the vast majority the information on the files was sufficient, problems could arise. For instance, if one social worker takes the case over from someone else then the information could be, as one put it, *"here, there and everywhere"* and *"a nightmare to sort out."* Also, some information on the files might need updating with the passage of time. One social worker cited the income of the prospective adopters as an example of this. Some information can be missing from the files, for example, details of care orders.

As for seeking further information from outside sources, the majority of social workers (60%) said they usually did so. The main sources to which they were most likely to turn were the birth family; other professionals such as GPs, and other local authority social services departments.

We also asked—in relation to the specific case with which the social worker had been involved in our Court Record Survey—whether any problems arose in obtaining information about the birth mother, the birth father and the child. Of these, obtaining information about the birth father proved the most difficult for nearly half the social workers, whilst no problems were encountered for over a half where the birth mother was concerned. Few expressed difficulty in obtaining the necessary information about the child.

Obtaining information about putative fathers can be very difficult. Sometimes the birth mother will be reluctant to reveal his identity. However, even if it is known, tracing him can often be a lengthy and not altogether produtive exercise. Many likened it to "*detective work*" requiring great care and diplomacy. For instance, a social worker who successfully traced a putative father reported that his family had no idea he had fathered a child.

Amongst a range of idiosyncratic problems which arose was one described here:

> "I was able to go and visit the putative father in prison. The only problem is that you have to be accompanied by a prison officer which could restrict what he might have to say. If he's got a tough image in the prison he doesn't want to be seen to be sensitive about his child, which is why I say he was different when he came out—he had a different view. They couldn't let me see him on his own because of his violent nature and the fact he'd said he wasn't going to co-operate originally and wouldn't see me. But eventually after I'd written several letters he did agree to see me. I had mixed feelings about the need for someone else to be present because I wanted to be protected but I also wanted to get the right information."

Social workers reported some differences between judges concerning the amount of effort that should be made to search for and contact putative fathers. Some tend to adjourn proceedings so that further investigations can be made, even though in many instances the agency will have gone to what it might regard as considerable and thorough lengths already which they will have fully described in the report. The progress of a case can be delayed by several months if the judge insists that additional investigations be made. (We discuss the adjudication process in part II, Chapter Seven).

Sometimes the family will have been well-known to social services, often for some considerable time. In those circumstances a lot of information is likely to be available, but problems can arise when the birth parents are reluctant to co-operate for one reason or another. A social worker in the Midlands explained:

> "Two areas—mum just wanted to forget it and didn't want to give you any details. Quite often in a few of my cases the children who had been placed for adoption were taken from the parents because of abuse and therefore to get information from the birth parents was

almost impossible because they hadn't wanted to give the child for adoption. A lot of questions relate to their own family life and they weren't prepared to co-operate with that."

Another felt that much depended on the way the social worker approached the birth parents, even in contested cases:

"There's never any doubt that these children are cared for, whatever the circumstances. It's very rare we find the child isn't loved by the birth family and we can say 'you can help the child in the future. Maybe it's not your fault that you're in this position now, but it's also not the child's and if you want them to grow up into healthy adults you can provide this information. No one else can provide it. The child will know you provided it so it's important for you to help now. You are still responsible for him. You are still his birth mother'. People will co-operate if you put it to them like that."

2.4   The Relevance of the Schedule II Report

The majority of the social workers saw the main purpose of the Schedule II report as being to provide the court/judge with sufficient information. Amongst the other purposes they mentioned, the predominant ones were: providing a statement of the background of the case; providing a statement in support of the recommended plan for the child. Some also mentioned that it could be made available to the adoptee once s/he reached the age of eighteen.

Whilst just over half the social workers (54%) felt that the information required was *"about right"*, they had some criticisms to make, joining the 40% who felt there were *"problem areas"*. Many of these concerned the relevance of the report, an issue of fundamental importance. (The remaining 6% either felt it was not right at all or did not know.)

2.4.1   Is the Schedule II report relevant for all types of adoption?

As we have already explained, at present the same format is used for all types of adoption: baby adoptions; older children; hard to place or special needs children; relation and no relation adoptions; step parent adoptions. It is also used for freeing applications.

Many of the social workers felt that it was not appropriate for all types of adoption. For instance, this social worker in Somerset, who thought it inappropriate for baby adoptions, replicated the views of many more when she said:

"Really the Schedule II report is more relevant for older children. Some of the information required is not relevant for babies. In the conclusions they are wanting a fuller background picture and there often isn't a fuller background picture with babies, unless we repeat it all over again. The effect on the mother if we are following her wishes, it's not really relevant to straightforward baby cases."

Many who questioned the relevance of the Schedule II report suggested that each type of adoption needed a report which was adapted appropriately to meet its particular needs. For instance, frustration with what was sometimes felt to be the rigid bureaucratic formality of the task is described in this comment:

"I think it's horrendous. It's a blunderbuss procedure. It's bureaucratic. It doesn't make any distinction between agency adoptions where children are being placed with non-relatives and step-parent adoptions. Some of it is very tedious and repetitive. . . .

If you are doing a step-parent adoption you have to have a physical description and personality profile of the natural mother—and that seems a bit senseless. The child is actually going to be brought up by their own parent and I can't see the need for having a separate record of information when their circumstances are not so different from other children. I'd have a different Schedule II for step-parents. With non-related adoptions I think the Schedule II makes more sense."

2.4.2   Is the Schedule II report relevant to the audience it addresses?

As we have said it is the court which requires that the Schedule II report be provided. However, in the light of many of the comments made by practitioners we question whether the court is absolutely clear about what it requires and whether its needs are met by the Schedule II report. A social worker in the South West put it succinctly when he said:

"I can just recall remarks made by judges who are frustrated and annoyed at having to plough through something which they regard as tedious and irrelevant information."

One social worker spoke for many when she said that she felt that the information was provided *"because it's in the Schedule rather than because the court needs it or it needs to be recorded."* Another was more expansive:

"I wonder about the validity of some of it, I must admit. I think part of my problem comes from different perceptions from different judges about what this information is for. I'm not sure the courts have a very clear idea of what some of the information is for. They are quite difficult things to write because of the fairly unclear messages I've come across. Members of the legal profession want a very short, concise and clipped answer to a question. I've come across others who want it to flow and to be narrative. Without knowing the audience to which you are writing it is sometimes quite difficult to know whether to keep it on a clinical and short basis or whether to try and make it flow as a story of the family. Given the guidelines (a b c d e etc.) you can write it in a very disjointed fashion and assume that somebody is going to read the questions and then the answers."

As we said earlier, many social workers saw one of the main purposes of the Schedule II report as a document that could provide the adoptee at eighteen plus with insight into their background and how and why the adoption came about. A West Country social worker thinks it is important to bear this in mind when preparing the report:

"It's a report for the court as much as for the child and the would-be adoptive parents. So we're talking about style rather than about area. I find that difficult to answer. Part of me would say, well, I don't think these areas are necessarily appropriate or applicable. Having said that, I am mindful of the fact that's my view and that the would-be adopters and children trying to search for their origins want as much as possible. What may not seem significant to me is to them: the fact that their original mother had green eyes and worked in Woolworths as a cashier at weekends so I think you've got to put it all in. It's got to be of some value and if it isn't, well it's not necessarily wasted."

2.5   Format

Much criticism was levelled at the present 'a to z' format outlined in the Guidelines, (see Rules 4[4], 22[1] or 22[2] of the Adoption Rules 1984), which explains the information to be provided under each letter. In many Schedule II Reports, the social worker gives the 'answer' but provides no indication of the 'question'. This can prove very difficult if the writer puts, for example, "(q) not applicable". Without the guidelines the reader will not be able to work out what it is that is "not applicable". Indeed, the researchers experienced this problem for themselves at firsthand during the court record study, and it was only after reading several Schedule II reports that the format became sufficiently familiar for us to remember to what the writer was referring. Unless the judges and magistrates have a copy of the guidelines to hand, the Schedule II report could present something of a challenge to them.

A Devon social worker developed the point:

"I think what's required is fairly comprehensive. The way that that's interpreted is variable. I don't think there's anything missing, but I do see Schedule II reports where they will go through giving two or three word answers under each heading and instead of making a report that flows they'll put down "a) yes. b) not for some time." So there's a fair amount of scope for making a bad job of it even with the format that we've got. I can't really identify any great gaps in that except possibly that so much comes down to the enthusiasm with which you attack the task. What I tend to find in reading those that others have written is that all the details are there but they don't give you a very coherent, overall picture or flavour of what the case is all about. You have to read it through from beginning to end before you understand why they are planning adoption for this child and then you have to read it a second time to pick up the detail. I don't know how that could be addressed in the format. Quite often I say to social workers "stick in another paragraph at the beginning which just says this child is two years old and . . ." and then the person can read on, having got the framework. I don't think there's too much in it bearing in mind its purpose. I think some social workers tend to view the adoption panel as a bureaucratic obstacle and might view the courts in the same way—and think it's only got to be rubber-stamped and don't inform the court sufficiently."

She hints at a style many others said they would prefer, i.e. a more narrative approach which would help those who are required to read it to understand it, especially the judges and magistrates.

Another was concerned that a narrative style would go against a recent BAAF practice note. Despite this, she felt that approach would be *"more professional"*. Many of the misgivings which were voiced by practitioners are encapsulated by this social worker in the Midlands:

"Sometimes I feel that however many spaces and paragraphs there are to write in you never quite say what you really want to say. I suppose I take the line that I'll make a hole for it somewhere and put it in. But somehow occasionally it doesn't seem to capture the spirit of what you are trying to say. It comes out as a very pedantic, soulless piece of writing if you're not careful. Some of it is very precise, very dry and then you find yourself likely to burst into florid prose which looks very strange. I find it restricts the flow of what you are trying to say. I feel I could write a report which contains everything that the Schedule II asks for and it would be much more readable. I feel quite sorry for judges having to plough through them. They must be so boring to read. The risk is that if you don't follow some guidelines, particularly when you've got people writing them who are not used to them, you are going to have things missed. I would like to think there was a middle way, but I don't know what it is. I certainly worry about the way they are written. . . . I feel a report should read like a story with information to know what's going on. If in answer to a question you put down "British", well you can guess it's a question about nationality but it reads better if you can say "so and so is of British nationality", and equally if someone is reading it in years to come when we are all dead and gone."

Clearly some local authorities have overcome the problem of the "abc format", since one social worker told us that when she was involved in interagency adoptions she had come across some who produced their own printed forms which incorporated all the questions.

Another major criticism was that in its present format the report tended to be repetitious. Sections on birth parents, why the local authority had opted for a particular plan for a child and conclusions were all singled out as being particularly vulnerable to repetition. For instance:

> "I always struggle with the conclusions because I feel if I've done the first part properly then in actual fact I've already said what there is to be said and to attempt to put in different words, to attempt to do the conclusion I feel I'm repeating myself."

Another said she felt it was a very clumsy report to write because one had to *"keep going backwards and forwards"* in the sense that information that had been given in one section had to be put in again several times further on.

In considering the information that was requested, one social worker suggested that it was up to each social worker to decide how they dealt with it. She went on:

> "It is up to social workers how they elaborate on things requested. As a black person there is an issue for me in terms of how it can be stated in certain respects. I feel there should be more to do with the racial, cultural and religious dimension. Even though it's mentioned, I think social workers can actually get away without detailing more. For example, under 'child' it's got personality and religion. Religion? What does that mean? I think there needs to be a more elaborate way of getting information that social workers have to think about the implications of religion and not just say 'Sikh' or 'Muslim' or 'Pentecostal' or whatever."

But another dealt with this in a different way since she had decided that judges did not need to know **all** the details about occupation, accommodation and marital status. She simply left some out! this comment suggests that the social worker did not fully understand that the purpose of the report is to provide the court with all the factual information concerning the case. It may well reflect the fact that she had not been trained for the task. It also raises questions about the quality of her supervision.

The frustrations engendered by the repetitive aspects of the report were made all the worse because some of the information provided in the Schedule II report is in any case a duplication of information already provided for the Adoption Panel, for example on BAAF Forms F (which concerns the adoptive parents), and E (which concerns the birth parents and child) although, of course, BAAF Forms E and F are not submitted to the court. This led one practitioner to plead for *"universal forms which would serve several functions."*

Clearly, from what the practitioners have said, there is ample scope for refinement in the present Schedule II and for improvements to be made in the guidelines.

This might help to overcome additional problems which can arise when more than one social worker is involved in compiling the Schedule II report, for instance in an inter-agency adoption where one social worker might be in a local authority agency and the other in a voluntary agency. One may be responsible for providing the information about the prospective adopter, whilst another will provide it for the child, its birth family and actions of the local authority. Given the variations in approach in compiling the Schedule II report, it is hardly surprising that these problems are exacerbated when two or more social workers are involved, especially if they are in different local authorities or different types of agency. Some of the social workers in the voluntary agencies, apart from commenting on the differences in stylistic approach and so on, mentioned that they had sometimes experienced delay in completion of Schedule II reports if the other part of it was being written by a local authority social worker. They acknowledged that this was probably because s/he was subject to so many other pressures that the Schedule II report could not always be given the priority they felt it deserved.

2.6   Time Allowed for Completion of Schedule II Reports

The adoption agency is usually required to submit the Schedule II report to the court within six weeks of the receipt of the notice of hearing (Rule 22, Adoption Rules 1984). Neither the reporting officer nor, where appropriate, the guardian ad litem, can proceed with their own enquiries until they have received the Schedule II report. Any delays in its submission consequently have a knock-on effect. In an attempt to ascertain whether or not social workers thought the six week period a realistic one we asked: "In adoption cases do you think sufficient time is allowed for the preparation of the report?" Their response is shown in Table 2.2 below.

Table 2.2
Whether sufficient time is allowed for preparation of Schedule II Report

	No.	(%)
Yes	28	(54)
No	10	(19)
Yes, but not for step-parent adoptions	5	(10)
Sometimes but not always	8	(15)
Other	1	(2)
All	**52**	**(100)**

Clearly the majority thought the time allowed was usually sufficient. Those who thought the time insufficient related the reasons to: delays caused within their own agency; step parent adoptions where they had to *"start from scratch"*; complexity of the case; delays related to birth parents; delays caused by another agency, and delays caused by the court.

Many of those who said the time allowed was sufficient, pointed out that much of the information that was required was readily available anyway, and it was just a question of transferring it to the Schedule II. Others said that social workers should be able to organise their adoption work so that the Schedule II report was completed in good time, since the plan for the child would have been known long before the application was lodged. However, as we have already shown in Part II, Chapter One, this can be a problem for social workers in local authorities with a general case load. A social worker in a voluntary agency said:

> "If you give people six months to do it, they'll still do it at the last minute. My practice is to lodge the Schedule IIs with the application. I don't even allow myself six weeks. Everyone knows they've got to do Schedule IIs. I think there's enough time."

However, for a local authority social worker in the West Country it was clearly not so *"simple"*, because he said:

> "Currently we ask for in the region of three to four months which on the whole is sufficient. Lately the court tends to fix a date which is three months hence and that means that the Schedule II is ready in that time."

He went on to say that some Schedule IIs were *"relatively easy, very straightforward"*, whilst others were more complex. Clearly, the former could be completed more quickly than the latter. Perhaps there is a case here for an acknowledgement of this by the court, which might consider some flexibility in the time allocated for submission of the report depending upon the degree of complexity of the case.

Several practitioners said that delays could occur, not because they had been slow in writing the report, but because once they were completed they had to wait for them to be typed. We asked social workers if they had any difficulty in obtaining adequate administrative/secretarial assistance for their adoption work. Whilst the majority (58%) had no such problem, 40% did experience difficulty. The main effect of this was to delay cases and result in social workers having to use their time inappropriately. For instance, in one area in the Midlands a social worker reported:

> "All typing is done in a central pool. It's in the office here and if they're very busy—and they always are—you have to wait an awful long time for what you want. Having said that, Schedules are seen as high on their list of priorities."

A social worker in another area of the Midlands did not fare quite so well, since she explained that she sometimes had to *"wait weeks for a report."*

Things were no better in an area in the South West:

> "It's a major headache for social workers. It adds to the general workload. It means that social workers are spending a lot of time doing clerical tasks which divert their energy and their attention from planned work particularly. When social workers are forced to prioritise it's the crises that get the priority and some of the cases that come through the adoption panel here display that once the child is safely placed with the foster parents all sense of urgency goes out of the situation. I think an awful lot of social workers' time goes on basic administrative tasks . . ."

We asked the solicitors we interviewed whether they had experienced any delays in freeing and adoption cases and what the causes might be. Several mentioned that they had to wait for Schedule II reports. (Solicitors, of course, do not have an automatic right to see the Schedule II reports, an issue considered later in Part II, Chapter Four).

A Walsall solicitor spoke for many when he said:

> "Sometimes the Local Authorities take ages to prepare Schedule II reports which can sometimes be a bit annoying, because you have to wait for information to start it going . . ."

This is another area in which local authorities clearly face organisational difficulties where adoption work is concerned. Where there is a problem about clerical assistance it must affect all aspects of adoption work.

In the sample of cases from the Court Record Survey we had hoped we would find some indication of the time scale involved between submission of the adoption application to the court and lodging of the Schedule II report. Unfortunately, as we have already stated in Part I of this report, at section 7.9, a detailed analysis was not possible because in about half the cases the relevant dates were not available from the records.

2.7   Should Schedule II Reports be Lodged at the Court when the Application is Submitted?

We asked both social workers and solicitors in private practice if they thought it would improve the process in any way if applications to adopt had to be submitted to court accompanied by the Schedule II report (as happens with freeing for adoption applications). The social workers were more sceptical than the solicitors in their response, being more or less evenly split for and against, whereas the majority of solicitors (58%) thought it would improve the process.

Amongst the social workers who could see advantages in such a system, one in the Midlands explained:

> "We do that sometimes if it's possible, partly because it speeds things up but also because it's sometimes quite difficult well after the event of placing a child to get area workers sufficiently galvanised to do their bit of the Schedule II. I think there's a quite natural reaction that once a child is placed everyone can breath a sigh of relief. The area worker in particular goes off and does more urgent things. If it could be more tightly tied to placement and early stages of placement we'd be likely to spend less time running round after the area worker saying please can you write this bit or that bit."

Others were more sceptical. For instance, one suggested that the social workers would then become "*the stumbling block*" since the prospective adopters would have to postpone submitting their application until the social worker got round to completing the report.

A solicitor in the South West could see aditional advantages both for the court and for his clients:

> "Yes, it would give the court perhaps an idea about whether the case is likely to be a long one or contested or what. And also if we had the full facts that the local authority were relying on at the time we were served with the summons or the application, then we'd be in a position to advise the client accordingly. Generally I feel that there's no reason for that to be kept back. If you've got a case then state it at the time you issue your application."

But another feared delays could be increased:

> "Without the teeth to ensure that the Schedule II has to be produced, all that you are doing is making the delay longer before the application's made and shorter afterwards, rather than the other way round. I suppose that it's very simple as far as I'm concerned. I can simply give notice, bash off the application—that's all I have to do. If I had to try to get the report in first—unless there was some sanction if they didn't produce the report in six months I'm rather worse off. I think the court have got better teeth to say 'where is it?' than I have."

2.8   Comment

There is no doubt that preparation of the Schedule II report is a time-consuming task often made more difficult depending on the degree of the complexity of the case. For those social workers who have little and infrequent experience of adoption work it is all the more time-consuming because of unfamiliarity and the constant need for checks and possible assistance from colleagues and supervisors. Even for those with experience it can prove a lengthy task.

Given their comments on its format, it is clear that many social workers also find it a tedious task which involves a certain amount of duplication. They also question the Schedule's relevance to all types of adoption. Its completion can involve the social worker in a fair amount of detective work. That they need to be diplomats too is shown in many of the comments, particularly those concerning the extraction of information from and about the birth parents. Finding the time for all this and working out some kind of priority must be especially hard for those social workers with a generic case load. A re-examination of the information the court requires together with some kind of refinement to the Schedule itself to eliminate repetition and duplication of work would seem advisable. In this way the delays which occur could well be reduced.

Accordingly, we suggest that the Department of Health and the Adoption Law Review should now consider the following questions:

(i)   Is it time for a fundamental reappraisal of the purpose of Schedule II reports, given that adoption agencies now mostly prepare detailed background information for the Adoption Panel using the BAAF Forms E and F, and that the courts will receive a report from either a reporting officer or guardian ad litem? In other words, is it really necessary to have **three** background reports? Could not the process be simplified by either amalgamating the Schedule II report with the initial report to the Panel, or eliminating it altogether?

(ii)   What real use do the courts make of Schedule II reports? Are they central to the decision making process, or merely supplementary to the report of the reporting officer and/or guardian ad litem?

(iii)   If it is considered necessary to retain Schedule II reports, are they required in **all** types of adoption? For example, are they really essential for uncontested baby adoptions or step-parent adoptions? Should the format at least be adapted to the particular requirements of step-parent adoptions, no relation adoptions, baby adoptions, older child adoptions, adoption of children with special needs?

(iv)   Should the current format of Schedule II reports be altered to allow for a more flexible narrative style? Do the current categories of required information need to be reconsidered and simplified in order to reduce repetition?

(v)   What can be done to speed up and simplify the preparation of Schedule reports?

(vi)   Is sufficient time allowed by the court for completion of the Schedule II Report? Should there be variations in the length of time allowed depending on the type of adoption and complexity of the case?

CHAPTER 3   Parental Agreement

3.1   Introduction

3.2   The Practitioner View

3.3   Comment

3.1　Introduction

(a)　The Process

An application to adopt may or may not be made with the agreement of the birth parent(s) (s. 16(1), Adoption Act 1976). Similarly an application to free may be made with or without the birth parent(s)' consent (s. 14(1), Children Act 1975). The agreement or consent of the father is not required if the child is illegitimate, though the court must be satisfied that the putative father is unlikely to apply for a custody order under s. 9, Guardianship of Minors Act 1971.

If an application is lodged **with** agreement/consent, the court will then appoint a reporting officer. S/he will visit the birth parent(s) to explain the implications of adoption or freeing and, if the birth parent(s) is/are satisfied the reporting officer will then ask her/them to sign a form giving her/their agreement or consent. The reporting officer will then submit the form and a brief report to the court (Adoption Rules 1984, rule 5). In those cases where an application is lodged **without** the birth parent(s)' agreement or consent, a guardian ad litem is appointed by the court. S/he will investigate the circumstances of the case and report her findings and conclusions to the court (Adoption Rules 1984, rule 6). An application to dispense with parental agreement will also have to be lodged with the court together with a Statement of Facts which sets out the facts and sequence of events. This is usually prepared by the applicants' solicitor, but sometimes by the adoption agency social worker. If agreement or consent continues to be withheld, affidavit evidence may also be required before the case proceeds to the final hearing. If agreement or consent is still withheld at the hearing the court may then dispense with it where it considers that it is being withheld unreasonably (Children Act 1975, s. 12).

(b)　The problem of defining a contested adoption

In our Court Record Survey (see Part I, section 2.11) we showed that in the mini record sample it appeared that the majority of each type of adoption application was made with the agreement of the birth mother. In freeing the reverse was true; 67% appeared to withhold their consent at the time the application was made (see Table 2.11). We also tried to ascertain how many cases in the same sample were actually contested at the final hearing (see Part I, section 2.12). However, in nearly half the records we examined (41%) the information about the hearing was just not sufficient for us to state with certainty whether or not it was contested. From the information we did have it would appear that freeing applications are more likely to be contested at the final hearing than no-relation adoptions (see Table 2.12, in Part I of the Report). Due to the lack of information concerning the nature of the final hearing we were thus unable to make a reliable analysis of birth mothers who had changed their mind about agreement/consent during the course of proceedings.

Many of the practitioners we interviewed had knowledge of cases where the birth mother, who at the outset agreed or consented to the application, later changed her mind. They also reported instances where the reverse was true: mothers who withheld their agreement/consent initially but changed their mind as the case proceeded. We were also told of some cases where the birth mother had changed her mind backwards and forwards several times before the final hearing, some even waivering at the door of the court on the day of the final hearing.

The implications of such ambivalence have consequences for all concerned: for the birth parent(s) who continue(s) to agonise over the decision about agreement/consent and needs to decide whether to instruct a solicitor and apply for legal aid; for the adopters whose anxiety may well be increased by the uncertainty and who may also need to instruct a solicitor if the case is opposed; for the court which needs to know whether or not to appoint a guardian ad litem and may have to set up additional hearings; for the parties' solicitors who, in those cases where agreement/consent is withheld and until told to the contrary, must proceed with the case on the basis that it will be contested through to the final hearing; and for the child whose state of 'limbo' will continue for longer than would have been the case had the birth parent(s) not been indecisive the overall effect of which is to slow down the progress of the case. (We discuss Legal Advice and Practice in Part II, Chapter Four.)

3.2 The Practitioner View

From practitioner's comments concerning the matter of parental agreement/consent it was apparent that problems could arise for:

(i)   the birth parent in deciding whether or not to agree/consent;

(ii)   the prospective adopters and the child where the birth parent(s) is/ are indecisive;

(iii)   solicitors acting in cases which appear to be opposed.

In addition practitioners reported instances where it appeared that both local authorities and solicitors in private practice sometimes exploit delays to gain some kind of tactical advantage in those cases where either one or both of the birth parents is/are withholding their agreement/consent.

Whilst the issue of parental agreement/consent was obviously regarded by practitioners as a problem about which they were concerned, it should be remembered that we are reporting what they see through **their** eyes and not through those of the parents. In that sense the information is second-hand and may be skewed since it is not possible to say how far the practitioners' views are framed within their own professional experience.

3.2.1   Birth Parent(s)

Some birth parent(s) may have a problem in comprehending or accepting the full implications of a successful application. Much can depend on how the social worker involved has discussed the matter with her/them. As one solicitor in the South West put it:

> "Great difficulties have arisen where the mother initially indicates consent then has second thoughts. I have been instructed in more than one case where the social worker involved has not fully emphasised the significance of the original decision (to agree to adoption). In one particular case my client felt the social workers concerned should never have allowed her to indicate her consent to adoption. In the same case by the time the mother had decided to oppose in practice it was too late for her to go back . . ."

This solicitor also suggested that he might have been able to help her more had he been involved at an earlier stage, a point made by several other solicitors.

The parent(s)' doubts may be reinforced or be initiated when she/they is/are visited by the reporting officer. We were told that many find the actual act of signing the agreement or consent form too painful. Even though they might in principle accept that adoption is in the best interests of the child they still see it as "signing away" their child. If they refuse to sign then when the application is granted they can to some extent be consoled in knowing that it was the court which made the decision, not them, a feeling which a solicitor in Birmingham could well understand:

> "In many ways it's probably the best outcome. In later life, the child is not going to get a feeling of rejection because he'll know the parents had their rights taken away and equally the parents will know that the court made the decision and they didn't. It takes away the guilt."

In such instances the practitioners felt that the withholding of agreement/consent may apparently be no more than a token objection in that the birth parent(s) does/do nothing further to oppose the application. However some practitioners said that others can appear to be more actively determined to do so. Then they may instruct a solicitor feeling that by so doing all the relevant facts will be considered and investigated, thus ensuring that the child's best interests will be met. Some solicitors reported instances where the birth parent(s) may appear to oppose the application up to the eleventh hour and then agree/consent or simply not turn up at the court for the hearing. Only a few went on to actively oppose the application in court.

3.2.2   Prospective Adopters and Child

Practitioners thought that the effect on the prospective adopters can be considerable if the birth parent(s) appear(s) to withhold her/their agreement or consent, increasing the uncertainty felt by them. It inevitably delays the date of the final hearing because additional processes will be necessitated, for example the appointment of a guardian ad litem.[1] A social worker in the Midlands described the consequences of a mother's ambivalence in the specific case with which she was involved in the Court Record Survey:

> "We put the (freeing) application in to the domestic court because mother was not contesting the application but at the last minute she changed her mind. A contested case couldn't have two applications in two different courts for the same case. So we withdrew the application to the domestic court and then re-applied to the county court and waited for yet another date. It did delay the case for about three to six months and it did have implications for what was happening to the child and where he would be placed. Mother changed her mind three days before he was due to be placed with the adopters. The introductions were well under way by then. Although we could have placed him they would have run the risk of him being taken away if we lost the application to free. They couldn't bear that. So they didn't have him to live with them but carried on visiting hoping that we would get the court date quite soon. But, because it took so long, four months later they said 'we can't take any more of this—it's causing us too much distress' and they withdrew. They said they would like to be considered if he became free in the near future but wouldn't hold out indefinitely. As it happened by the time the child was freed although they'd been considered for another child they hadn't begun introductions and so therefore they weren't upsetting another child. So they resumed contact with this child and he was placed with them and later adopted. The mother changed her mind about five times before we actually got to the court hearing which was supposedly contested, but she didn't turn up. She did want him adopted but she just didn't want to be seen to be agreeing."

Several solicitors and social workers mentioned the stress caused to the prospective adopters in such circumstances. A number of solicitors said

---

[1]   See Part I, section 8.9 of the Court Record Survey where the length of court proceedings is compared in contested and uncontested cases. Generally speaking we found that for both freeing and adoption, contested cases took longer to complete than uncontested cases.

that they could not say with any certainty to their clients that the adoption order would be granted. As one put it: *"You can be sure to a great extent, but not absolutely certain."*[2]

3.2.3 The Solicitor

Whilst the birth parent(s) continue(s) to withhold her/their agreement or consent the case will have to proceed on the basis that it is actively contested. As a solicitor in the South West said, in such circumstances it

> ". . . makes it into a contested matter and consequently causes court delays unnecessarily. I can't see how you get round it. He or she **can** always turn up on the morning of the hearing and cause confusion, so you must prepare. For example, a mother and father turned up having taken no active part, but acting in person, so we had a barrack room lawyer doing the job. The judge dispensed and the order was made but there were dire problems."

Another solicitor thought it would help if there was an automatic presumption that the birth parent(s) disagree if they have not agreed or consented because the case can then continue on a disagreed basis without further ado.

A case which appears to be opposed involves solicitors in additional work, including preparation of the Statement of Facts. As one explained,

> "Generally speaking it takes about three hours to go through the files, it takes a further two hours to prepare a draft document, and then the various parties will be given the document to test it and approve. It will take a further half an hour to prepare the final document."

Clearly opinions differ as to how much information the Statement of Facts should contain, but its preparation is obviously time consuming:

> "If consent is withheld I have to do a **Statement of Facts** which is, what, one side of A4. And it means reading through documents to summarise and try and reduce it. Certainly Judge C's view (local judge) is that one ought not to try and make the Statement of Facts so heavy that it's a distressing thing for the natural parents. So you are looking to convey enough to enable consent to be dispensed with but not so much that it causes more distress to the natural parent and also it runs the risk of the natural parent being obliged to defend for some reason. So you take a bit of care in trying to balance

---

[2]   However, in Part I, section 2.9, we show that for the majority (89%) of all adoption applications an order was made. With regard to no relation adoptions the proportion of "successful" cases was even higher (96%).

that out when you do the Statement of Facts. But it's only then when you get on and you find there is a realistic opposition that you have to prepare affidavits."

But sometimes it is the social worker who is involved in additional work when a Statement of Facts is required. Several solicitors said they left it to the social worker to prepare:

"I didn't prepare the Statement of Facts. That was prepared by the Social Services Department who of course had their files and all the facts available from that. I approved it and in fact it was done very well. I don't think I needed to suggest any amendments to it at all. There were 50 different incidents noted chronologically in this case. In fact when the adopters first came along they brought their Social Services man with them and he brought along the Statement of Facts which had already been prepared."

Clearly work involved in preparing a case is increased considerably if it appears that the birth parent(s) is/are not agreeing/consenting. This can involve several additional hearings at court. Uncontested final hearings are, generally speaking, very speedy affairs (as we shall explain in Part II, Chapter Six), but obviously a solicitor will need to set aside more time for the final hearing if there is a chance that it will be contested. S/he may well have needed to brief counsel too. The implications in terms of time and money are considerable when we consider the extra input needed by social workers and lawyers and by the court, too, in reserving both court and judge time.

If the birth parent(s) withholds her/their agreement/consent until the last minute but finally agrees, the work which the solicitor, social workers, the court and so on have had to put into the case can suddenly become totally superfluous. But, as a solicitor in Devon put it:

"We all know the reason—the mother can't bring herself to do it so we have to go through all of this procedure where really we know, provided everything's right, it can go through. Justice must be seen to be done—and apparently has to be done in this long-winded way."

3.2.4   Tactical Delays

As we demonstrate throughout this report, the adoption and freeing process is bedevilled by delays. Moreover there is some evidence from our interviews with practitioners to suggest that delaying tactics can sometimes be used by local authorities and solicitors representing the applicants in cases where one or both parents appear to be withholding their consent. The longer the child has been away from its birth parents and in some instances even placed with prospective adopters, the weaker the birth parents' case can become. If such a situation prevails, the granting of the application is often regarded as a fait accompli. This point was made by practitioners in each of the fieldwork areas.

For example, a solicitor in the Midlands who was acting for the prospective adopters in a case where one of the birth parents was opposing the application had had some experience of this. He said:

> "When I first started the case law wasn't settled. Fairly early on, I think it was Lord Justice Ormrod who more or less settled the case law. The essence of it was that if the child to be adopted remained with the adopters for a given length of time then the adoption would follow through virtually automatically. The consequence of that was that people in my position could guarantee to 'win' a case by delaying a case. Obviously I was very uncomfortable with that. I've been at the other end where I have been acting for a natural parent and we haven't been able to succeed because we haven't been able to influence the speed at which a case is going."

Others added that in cases where access was reduced to a minimum or terminated, then the longer the proceedings took the stronger the case became for the applicants because of the length of time when there had been minimal or no contact between the birth parents and child.

In freeing applications, time and delay were perceived by practitioners to favour the local authority and run against the birth parents. In some instances, because of the extensive delays in the freeing process, the child may well have been placed in the adoptive home by the time of the final hearing. In our Court Record Survey (see Part I, section 4.6) we found that in 20% of cases at the time of the freeing application the child had been placed with a view to adoption. Of the remainder, one third were placed in an adoptive home during the course of the proceedings (see section 4.6, Table 4.6(b) in Part 1).

In adoption the placement may have been in progress for a considerable period of time prior to the final hearing. A solicitor in Somerset recognised the advantages of this for the prospective adopters but was concerned that the birth parents had no means of expediting the proceedings in any way to help their cause:

> "Certainly with the adoptions I deal with inevitably there will have been a placement for some period of time before the adoption proceedings are started. The delay is not a terrible problem as far as my clients (adopters) are concerned because it's not as if they are waiting for the child to come to them. Indeed, very often it's a case of saying the longer the child is with you the more helpful it is to the cause . . . But not to the natural parents' cause—that's quite right. I have never acted for the natural parents in adoption. It's the same with all litigation, one side wants to rush things on, the other side is

quite content with delay . . . The natural parents are in difficulties
because almost inevitably in this situation you are going to have
either a care order or a wardship order. In any event they do not
have care and control of the child. They therefore have no control
over when any adoption proceedings are even started so there is
nothing very much they can do about it. They don't have a chance to
have any say until someone decides to start some adoption proceedings. So if it was the view of either the Social Services Department or
the prospective adopters that we'll leave it for a year of so before we
get round to doing it there would be nothing that the natural parents
could effectively do about it other than trying to discharge care
orders or whatever."

A solicitor in the Midlands was one of many who said that what was
required was a time scale built in to the adoption process since the longer
the delay the more the result could be a foregone conclusion. Time scales
would give the birth parents *"more chance of fending off the adoption or pursuing rehabilitation."*

3.3 Comment

Several questions are prompted by what the practitioners had to say about
parental agreement or consent:

(i)   Clearly some parents see giving their agreement to adoption as sym-
        bolically "signing away" their child. Is there some way of
        overcoming this?

(ii)   Is there a way of avoiding the delays, expense and additional work
        solicitors especially face of having to prepare a case as though it will
        be actively contested when the objection is very often no more than
        a "token" one?

(iii)   In cases where parental agreement is withheld or in doubt, is there
        scope for improvement in the way birth mothers and, where appro-
        priate, birth fathers are prepared and consulted?

(iv)   What should be done to reduce the opportunity of exploiting delays
        to gain tactical advantage?

CHAPTER 4 Legal Advice and Practice

4.1   Introduction

4.2   Solicitors' Experience and Expertise in Adoption

4.3   Background Information

4.4   Legal Aid

4.5   Comment

4.1   Introduction

Birth parents and prospective adopters are unlikely to instruct solicitors in an uncontested adoption, as we found when collecting information on cases for our Court Record Survey. Indeed one of the solicitors we saw said he positively dissuaded prospective adopters from instructing him in a 'straightforward' adoption case as he thought it to be unnecessary. There is an increased likelihood that solicitors will be instructed in cases which are likely to be opposed.

Our interviews with practitioners revealed three major problem areas concerning legal advice and practice in adoption. They were:

(i)   Solicitor's level of experience and expertise;
(ii)   Solicitors' anxiety about the paucity of information concerning the case, especially regarding Schedule II reports which they do not have an automatic right to see;
(iii)   Problems involved in proceeding with the case work when parties apply for legal aid.

4.2   Solicitors' Experience and Expertise in Adoption

In an attempt to establish how much of their work concerned adoption, we asked the solicitors we interviewed what proportion of their workload had been involved with adoption in the 12 months preceding the interview. 25% said none of their work had involved adoption. 67% said it was less than a quarter of their workload. Just 4% said it was a quarter to a half. The remaining 4% were unable to say.

We also asked if they could estimate how many actual adoption and freeing cases they had dealt with in the three years prior to the interview. On average they had each dealt with just under nine adoption cases, of which they estimated an average of around two to be step-parent adoptions. Solicitors had far less experience with freeing cases, the average number being less than one (0.4) over the three years.

From these figures it is not unreasonable to conclude that overall the solicitors in our sample dealt with adoption relatively infrequently, a fact about which the solicitors themselves expressed concern.

Some solicitors in private practice as a legal adviser to an adoption agency. In our sample 13% did so; 63% were eligible to do so but did not; 8% had done so previously; 16% were not eligible to do so.

Solicitors were also asked how they normally became involved in adoption work. Just over half (58%) said the instructions usually came from existing clients, for whom they may have acted previously in, say, a conveyancing, or matrimonial matter; 8% came from the CAB; 8% came in 'off the street'; 4% came following advice by the local authority; the rest came by word of mouth, through a voluntary agency or because their name had appeared on a BAAF list.

The apparent lack of experience amongst solicitors who undertake adoption work provoked a number of anxieties amongst the solicitors and social workers alike. Some solicitors said they felt they were handicapped by their inexperience. One in the West Country who was actually on the Child Care Panel explained:

> "I've had very few (adoption) referrals and it is an area of the law which is very important to the client, but if you have little practical experience it's very difficult to exude confidence so that they feel they know what's going on. And certainly, the first couple of step-parenting adoptions that I did we got into one or two tangles and it took longer than it should have done—for instance reasons for pre-ferring adoption as opposed to custodianship. And in one case I know the court had been waiting for me to do something and I was waiting for the court to do something and it was about three months before anything happened. Now I'm not sure if there are any good 'idiots' guides' but it is the sort of thing where that's what one tends to need to make sure you get off on the right track. And I found when talking to Social Services there was often an element of the blind and the blind and the blind . . . dangers of all giving negative feelings to the adopters . . ."

A local authority solicitor in the Midlands who was conscious of the fact that some solicitors dealt with adoption more regularly than others explained that the experience of some could cause problems particularly *"when it comes to understanding the type of evidence that needs to be drawn out and understanding the actual procedure itself."*

Some social workers told us that they had had to *'pick up the pieces'* of what they regarded as ineptitude on the part of some solicitors. For instance a social worker described what happened in a case involving three siblings who were being adopted, two by one family and one by another. She said:

> "One family went to a solicitor near their home. The other family went to a solicitor near to their home but the two sets of solicitors were branches of the same firm. They were to liaise. It became fairly clear that neither of these solicitors had a clue about adoption. One of them left after a few weeks—nobody told me or the the adoptive parents so there was a delay of some weeks. There was then a decision that the solicitor of the other family would act for both fam-ilies and it became even more apparent that he hadn't a clue what he was doing. So we had lots of telephone calls and letters whilst I explained to him what we had to do and how we had to do it."

She went on to explain that once the application had been lodged the solicitor got into a mess *"working out who had to do what when"*, and she ended up compiling the Statement of Facts herself because he *"clearly didn't know what he was doing."* As we explain later this could be because solicitors have no automatic right of access to certain information about adoption and freeing cases.

A social worker in the South West described how, in her area, there was some liaison between local solicitors and herself which she found helpful, even though overall she remained generally sceptical of solicitors' value in adoption cases:

> "Solicitors need the opportunity and time to learn and understand what's involved and to move away from the adversarial stance. I've never felt too much confidence in how they deal with these matters. What is quite useful locally is that the solicitors know me, I know them and they will quite often ring me up and discuss issues. For example in step-parent adoptions they'll ask if they should be encouraging the couple to apply or not. That's been really good. But by and large I often feel they are a waste of time in adoption situations. Very rarely do they say much in court. It seems to me the contribution of the person who writes the Schedule II Report and what the guardian ad litem reports is what matters to the judge, and solicitors are superfluous. They can be helpful at times but unhelpful at others because their experience and knowledge is quite limited."

Inevitably progress in a case can be delayed whilst problems arising from solicitors' inexperience are sorted out. Such delays are no help to the birth parents and prospective adopters can add to the length of time that the child is in a state of limbo, a matter of great concern to many of the practitioners. One local authority solicitor reported what had happened in one of the cases with which she had been involved:

> "We placed the child in 1984; the prospective adopters instructed solicitors in 1984; we were chasing them until 1987, when they told us they hadn't got expertise in dealing with adoption and they were going to recommend the prospective adopters to other solicitors. The adoption order was made in November 1989. There need to be strict time limits for children, no matter what forum the child is coming before."

She felt strongly about solicitors' poor level of expertise in adoption that she contacted her local Law Society to see if they could compile a list of solicitors experienced in adoption work. After they had given the matter some thought, the Law Society responded by saying that they did not anticipate a list being available "in the foreseeable future".

Several practitioners advocated the need for specialist solicitors to undertake adoption work and suggested that panels should be set up similar to those in being for specialists in the field of child care work.

4.3   Background Information

Solicitors were very concerned about the paucity of background information made available to them by the adoption agencies and the courts. This affected their preparation of the case and also, in some instances, their ability to give their client the most appropriate advice.

Many solicitors said they found it a particular handicap not to have sight of the Schedule II report or the guardian ad litem's report. We asked them whether or not they had seen the Schedule II report in the specific case with which they were involved in the Court Record Survey. 43% had done so whilst 46% had not. The remainder could not remember. When we asked if they thought they should have an automatic right to see the Schedule II report, the majority (71%) said they should.

Whilst they have no automatic right of access to the reports, practice was reported to vary from court to court as to whether or not the Schedule II and guardian ad litem report are released to the solicitor. In some cases much can depend on the attitude of the judge. For instance this solicitor in the South West said:

> "I'm not sure that I understand the need for quite the secrecy that surrounds that report [Schedule II Report]. I've had occasion when I've had to call on the social worker to help me with my Statement of Facts. It's the firm view of the local judge that we should not see it. We should also see the guardian ad litem's report. The local judge has been helpful over that of late. At times she has read out chunks that she thought we ought to hear. I've had one or two where she said I could go along to the court and read it but not take it away. So you write down little bits and you might as well have had a copy of it."

Another suggested that whether or not you saw the Schedule II report depended on whether you had *"struck up some sort of rapport with the social worker"* involved in the case.

Solicitors identified some of the disadvantages the present haphazard system concerning access to report creates for them. First, in order to draw up a Statement of Facts in a contested case they need full information otherwise the task can prove impossible to execute. This may well explain why some practitioners told us that the social worker sometimes prepared the Statement of Facts because, as one put it, social workers have *"avenues of information"* that they did not. A solicitor in Birmingham suggested that it would be more appropriate if the local authority prepared Statements of Facts because they always had access to the necessary information.

Secondly, if the solicitor is acting for the adoptive parents he may know little or nothing about the case. A solicitor in the Midlands explained:

"If one is not supplied with a draft copy of the Schedule II report and one just has to go on what the clients know, you are at a total and complete disadvantage. In this case, we were sponsored by the local authority who paid the costs of my clients and who introduced me to my clients which meant that I was in a position to talk to the social worker and we were part of one team. One fundamental problem for a solicitor acting for adoptive parents is that their knowledge of the case is extremely limited."

Thirdly, evidential problems can arise. For instance, we were told of one case where the local authority had to get leave from the wardship judge to release some papers. That had taken some time. The solicitor then received some, but not all, of the papers and not until after the first hearing. He was trying to prove that the birth mother was unreasonably withholding her consent. Crucial to his argument was evidence concerning the mother's mental condition. The Schedule II report sent to him by the local authority had revealed the existence of psychiatric reports. He went on:

"When I wrote and asked the city solicitors for the psychiatric reports, they wrote back and said I shouldn't have had the Schedule II report and you can't have the other reports. I wrote back and said 'why not!' I thought it was some sort of bureaucratic stupidity. They wrote back and said it was the rules! I still don't understand why I was not supposed to have seen it. The persons who had prepared it were witnesses. We were to call these witnesses. We were surely to know what the witnesses were going to say."

In those cases where the solicitor had seen the reports, many were critical of the fact that this had not been until the day of the hearing. One solicitor argued that if he could see them then he saw no reason why they could not have been released earlier.

This would have helped those solicitors who were concerned that if they had known what the reports contained early on in the proceedings, the advice they gave their client might have been different. As one solicitor said:

"In the context generally of representing a party in proceedings involving children, it assists, I think in advising the parents—and preparing the case if it's going to be a fight—if one's got all the information. Sometimes there's a certain amount in the reports which would enable one to suggest to the parent that really it's not the children's interests or their own interests to fight any further."

Many solicitors said that with some knowledge of what the reports contained the view of the client might have been different too. For example, a solicitor in Devon reported that all the way through one case his client had indicated her intention to oppose it. She changed her mind on the day of the hearing "*at the door of the court*". He suspected this was as a result of going through the Schedule II report with her which had only been made available to him on the morning of the hearing.

Another felt similarly about the guardian ad litem's report. He said:

> "I think one thing that does cause a problem is that you cannot always obtain a copy of the guardian ad litem's report unless the court directs . . so for all you know it may say that the adoption shouldn't go ahead . . . And most clients in my experience are happy to accept the advice of an independent, experienced person—as long as they can see that it has in fact been investigated—not just, 'well, I think I'd better agree with him or her'. And it is helpful to know what they say and why they've said it—even if you don't disclose the whole report . . . my client was not aware of the whole report but was aware of the conclusion and aware in general terms of the reason for it and said, 'Now I'm satisfied and I can hold my head up with that child if he or she comes back to me at a later date. I didn't just say I'm not interested any more.'"

Whilst recognising the need for confidentiality in freeing and adoption cases the practice of withholding information from solicitors in the way we have described is at variance with 'normal' litigation practice.

4.4 Legal Aid

Both the social workers and the solicitors mentioned the appalling delays incurred when the parties to a freeing or adoption case apply for legal aid. A major factor here is local authority policy with regard to costs. Some will sponsor the prospective adopters irrespective of need. Others require them to apply for legal aid as a matter of course, but make it known that if the application fails they will meet the costs. But, as some practitioners pointed out, if The Law Society thinks there is a chance that the local authority will foot the bill, it is unlikely to grant the application for legal aid. A 'Catch 22' situation results. One solicitor said that in his experience a case can be delayed for up to 11 weeks whilst *the applicants are forced to go through hoops which are totally futile.*" He felt that a uniform policy was needed. As he put it:

> "Really, it's sheer cussedness in that people from the Lord Chancellor's Department don't seem to be able to sit down with people from local government and decide once and for all how these things are to be funded. So that is a cause of quite unnecessary delay when it crops up."

Waiting for the result of the legal aid application presents the solicitor with something of a dilemma. Some reported 'throwing caution to the wind' and proceeding with the case anyway, sometimes paying the fees themselves as they went along to avoid delay. But others, not unreasonably, felt they could not proceed until the matter of costs had been settled. One solicitor described what happened in the specific case with which he had been involved in the Court Record Survey:

> "The council had resolved that my clients would be supported if legal aid was not granted. In other words, the public purse would support them one way or the other. The difficulty was that we then had to prepare an application for legal aid and we had to wait and wait while that situation sorted itself out before we could get on with the application. We then had to revert to the local authority to ask for their formal confirmation then of their general promise that the costs would be met. The case had to go through the legal aid hoop. As all solicitors, we have to be very cautious about what work we do before we get any guarantee for costs—in all fairness to the clients."

This solicitor was one of several who said that those local authorities who agree to meet the costs still take a considerable time to endorse the payment for costs once The Law Society has refused an application. The appropriate committee has to meet first before a letter of confirmation can be sent to the solicitor.

A practitioner in the South West offered a solution to the dilemma:

> "The easiest way to avoid legal aid problems is for local authorities to take a realistic view and look long-term—for a short-term expenditure of possibly £2,–3,000, they are saving many, many thousands long-term. If they would under-write our costs we could get on directly a client comes in."

Many of the practitioners were particularly worried about the consequences of these delays for the parties and for the child since, as one solicitor said, in such cases you are dealing with *"fundamental emotional matters"*. Some made the point that applicants find the process of applying for legal aid very traumatic and the information they are required to give an invasion of their privacy. This could be particularly galling for those who felt they would probably not be entitled to legal aid, but who were directed to apply for it nonetheless by the local authority.

The effect on the birth parents can be grave and in some instances even affect the eventual outcome of a case as this practitioner explains:

> "They inevitably have problems getting legal aid to defend adoptions. That is not right in any way—it should be an absolute right for any parent to be represented in adoption proceedings regardless of the strength of their case. It's such a fundamental decision that they should be represented. You can get a strange situation where you can have a relatively weak case for adoption but by the time the solicitors for the natural parents have got involved, have applied for legal aid, had it refused, appealed it, got round to a final hearing,

another year has gone by and the adoption has become a dead certainty. So it does cause problems. If a lot more pressure could be put on The Law Society to make sure that parents are properly represented in these cases it would make life considerably easier. It would stop any solicitors from having any excuse for delaying things—legal aid is always a good excuse." (The possible exploitation of delay by practitioners was discussed in Part II, Chapter Three.)

A local authority solicitor who shared this view said that in her experience it was not unknown for a contested freeing application to take a couple of years and by the time the substantive hearing was reached the child had already been placed in an adoptive home (a point discussed in the Freeing Monongraph).[1] She went on to mention a further complication for the birth parents in their conduct of the case:

> "Another problem we've got is that the court here certainly wants to have affidavits filed in a lot of the contested cases. That can create problems because in freeing applications you are often going back over a long history and you are often having to contact people to swear affidavits who are no longer in the area. That in itself causes delay. If the parents want to file affidavits then, because of the problems with legal aid generally, that can cause delay."

4.5 Comment

In considering the issues raised by the practitoners' comments on legal advice and practice we are prompted to ask:

(i)   Should panels of specialist solicitors be established for adoption similar to the Law Society's existing Child Care Panels?

(ii)   Should solicitors have an automatic right to see Schedule II reports and guardian ad litem reports in advance of the hearing to enable them to better prepare their cases and advise their clients?

(iii)   How can the problem of halting work on a case whilst a legal aid application is processed be overcome?

---

[1]   Report of the Research into the Use and Practice of the Freeing for Adoption Provisions (Lowe, 1991).

CHAPTER 5 Courts Administration

5.1   Introduction

5.2   Staffing

5.3   Listing

5.4   Appointment of Reporting Officers and Guardians Ad Litem

5.5   Comment

5.1　Introduction

Once an application for freeing or for adoption has been lodged with the court, the progress of the case will then to some extent rest with the courts administration. We wished to find out, therefore, whether there were any aspects of the process for which the courts are responsible which from their experience practitioners considered might impede the progress of cases. Three major problem areas were identified by them:

(i)　　staffing in court offices

(ii)　　listing cases for hearing

(iii)　　appointment of reporting officers and guardians ad litem

In the Court Record Survey, Part I, section 2.5 we looked at the breakdown of cases in the court proforma sample according to the type of court used. We found that 88% of agency adoption applications and 86% of freeing applications were lodged in the county court. We therefore assume that practitioners' experience of courts administration reported here relates mainly to the county court.

Both the solicitors and the social workers were asked if they had experienced any delays once the application had been lodged with the court in the specific case with which they were involved in our Court Record Survey. Half the solicitors had done so. Although social workers are less likely than solicitors to have direct contact with the court once the prospective adopters have submitted their application to the court, 26% were aware of delays occurring after the application had been lodged; 58% said there were no delays; 16% did not know whether there were any or not.

5.2　Staffing

During the fieldwork phase of the Court Record Survey we were aware that there were staffing problems in some of the court offices. Indeed, concerns about staff shortages were mentioned to us in one Midland area where the problem was particularly acute. The pressure on the existing staff is therefore very great; they are fully stretched and working *"flat out"*. That, coupled with the fact that there is a policy to move staff on from one section of the office to another on a regular basis, results in the kinds of problem reported by solicitors and social workers in each of the areas we visited. Even allowing for possible exaggeration, a solicitor in the Midlands described a very disturbing situation in his local county court, attributing it to a combination of overwork and inefficiency:

> "If you went to X county court now, you'd find 20,000 items of unopened post. It's absolutely horrendous. I've had unanswered post going back eight weeks. I've got bills in for taxation that have been in court for over two years. Everybody has got horror stories.

> They are very understaffed and they've got inexperienced staff. It's a
> gross irritation and a grotesque set-up."

Staff shortages have a knock-on effect, as a solicitor in the West Country
pointed out when he said that in his county this resulted in delays in getting documents issued, waiting for reports and waiting for dates.

The courts administration has to work out some kind of priority for dealing
with the work it undertakes. Staff shortages can only make this more difficult. A local authority solicitor in the West Country was one of several who
were concerned that children's care cases might not be accorded sufficient
priority. He cited an example and went on to explain some of the problems
that he had experienced:

> "We filed the application in April and heard nothing until 5 July
> although they very cleverly stamped the form in May. We didn't
> even get a case number until 5 July . . . We have a difficult relation-
> ship with the court office and often they will fail to serve us (the
> local authority) with the proceedings but will say they've worked
> their fill. That may all be part and parcel of the same disease. They
> always say that we want everything straight away and they say they
> are short of staff. We go up to the court with children's work that
> needs to be dealt with as quickly as possible so obviously we do put
> them under more pressure but I don't think it's unreasonable
> pressure."

Another problem appears to be a lack of administrative staff to back up the
clerk who has responsibility for adoption work. A consequence of this can
be that when the adoption clerk is in court or absent for any reason there is
no-one else available in the office who is sufficiently informed to deal with
any enquiries practitioners might make.

A criticism often made of the staff undertaking adoption work was an
apparent lack of experience, a problem that is exacerbated by what appears
to be the standard practice of relocating court staff on a regular basis. As a
result, by the time a clerk has a modicum of familiarity with adoption work
and is beginning to gain experience s/he will then be moved on as the system dictates. Whatever the justification for such a system, it surely has little
merit in an area of work that in the context of their work as a whole takes
longer to become familiar, since adoption is less likely than other aspects of
their work to feature on a regular day-to-day basis. A solicitor in the West
Country summed up the situation reported in each of the fieldwork areas
when he said:

> "What really seems to be the problem is that as soon as they learn
> their job they get transferred to do something else. I find that it's
> very important for us to have a good relationship with the court
> staff. It's just about the first thing you get taught when you start in

the legal profession—court staff and ushers are the most important people of the lot so that can make life very easy or very difficult for you. Of course the problem is that as soon as you get a good relationship with someone and they know what they are doing you then find that they are transferred to some other department and you have to start all over again . . ."

Because of the length of time it can take for an adoption case to reach a conclusion, practitioners reported that they sometimes deal with as many as three or four different adoption clerks in the course of an application.

Some practitioners said that the resulting lack of familiarity with and understanding of adoption law and practice amongst the court staff could lead to misunderstandings with them about the correct procedures to follow. For instance, a solicitor in the Midlands recalled:

"The county court—even though you sent them a copy of the rules—wouldn't accept that you didn't have to dispense with the consent of a putative father—only if there was a maintenance order or if he were a guardian or whatever. Sometimes it was **very** difficult to persuade them that they were wrong. I used to dread filing there. They used to insist that you had to dispense with consents. I used to say that I accept if he's paying maintenance, then he can be a party to the proceedings but . . we argued about it and kept sending letters to each other. I know in one case the judge dispensed with the "consent" of the natural father although he didn't have to! I remember thinking then "what a waste of time". In the end we'd just carry on . . ."

Another in the West Country said that as a result of what he saw as a reluctance by the court staff in his area to *"follow the Adoption Rules"*, he had to go to the court office to talk to the adoption clerk and agree upon a form that was acceptable to them both. He added that it had taken *"6 to 8 weeks to sort it out"*.

As we reported in Part II, Chapter Four, some of the solicitors who undertake adoptions are themselves unfamiliar with it—all the more reason therefore that adoption clerks should be experience enough to cope with any problems that the solicitors' inexperience can cause. It would also be fair to say that from the court administration's point of view they sometimes need time to unravel and correct errors in procedure made by inexperienced solicitors.

Many practitioners, in recounting their experiences with the courts administration, put in a plea for better prepared and trained staff and for clerks who would become specialists in adoption and who would not be *"moved on"* but *"stick to their job"*.

5.3 Listing

The courts administration is responsible for listing cases for hearing. In considering the work of the courts it was this aspect of it which practitioners in each of the fieldwork areas singled out as of particular concern. Time and time again they expressed their anxiety at what they considered to be the unacceptable length of time they had to wait for a hearing date. In Part I, sections 8.11–8.13 we report an analysis of the length of time that elapsed from the date when an application was lodged in court to the date of the first hearing. Freeing cases generally took longer to reach a first hearing (just over six months) once the application had been made compared with agency adoption cases (just under five months) in cases where the child had not already been freed (Part I, section 8.11 Table 8.11). Overall it was quicker to obtain a hearing date in the magistrates' courts than the higher courts (Part I, section 8.12 Table 8.12). Furthermore contested cases took longer to reach the court for a first hearing than uncontested cases (Part I, section 8.13 Table 8.13).

A local authority solicitor explained how the chronic delays caused by waiting for a hearing date in freeing applications have contributed to her authority deciding to reduce the number of recommendations it makes for freeing. (We shall return to this matter in Part II, Chapter Eight.) She said:

> "If you're talking about freeing applications the problem I see is delay, and that is why the number of freeing applications which we recommend go forward as such in this division has reduced considerably. We find that when we lodge the application—particularly in the county court—that we wait for three months or so for the first directions hearing. We get to the first directions hearing and then it depends whether the judge wants affidavits filed. If he wants affidavits filed by the local authority as applicant, usually there's 28 days to lodge those. Then the respondent has got a further 28 days so that's 56 days on top of the three months and **then** you've got the time delay while you're waiting for the substantive hearing because of the pressures on the court for allotting time. So time I see as the biggest problem in freeing applications."

The researcher went on to ask the solicitor if she saw time as the biggest problem area in adoption too. The solicitor replied:

> ". . . Most certainly, because my understanding of the whole essence of freeing when it was introduced was that it would enable good planning to be undertaken. Because of the time delay—sometimes you're talking about 9–12 months from the time of the lodgement of papers to the hearing—in my view that can't be in the interests of the child. And on the other side there is the trauma to the parents while this is going on! If you're talking about the domestic courts it's **far, far** quicker, but of course you've got the practice direction in

connection with domestic courts where they can't hear matters that are contested. I've got very strong views about it, very strong views."

And a solicitor in private practice described what happened in the freeing case with which he had been involved in our Court Record Survey. In doing so he mentioned, as did many others, the tactical element that the delay in hearing dates can invoke (which we discussed earlier, in Part II, Chapter Four):

"This case which was issued in February of '88 didn't get a hearing until March of '89, by which time the client's bond with his daughter had of course been prejudiced. And that's another problem, because of the length of proceedings it provokes tactics on behalf of the party with statutory care seeking to strengthen its case and quite often they'll reduce access to the bare minimum. In this particular case they actually stopped it altogether. So I think that the contentious element of freeing orders is probably a disadvantage and the present system promotes the contentious aspect rather than trying to see ways to try and minimize that problem in the interests of the child."

As we have explained, most of the comments on courts administration concern the county court. However, when expressing their anxiety about listing and the problems it can cause, several practitioners were keen to include their experiences in the High Court where the problem appears to be even more acute.[1] This local authority solicitor expressed the exasperation felt by many of the practitioners:

"One of the concerns I've got about freeing in particular is where we are dealing with a ward of court. The policy here is that we don't lodge freeing applications in respect of wards of court primarily because we don't want to lodge them in the Principal Registry because, while we complain about the delays up here, the delays in the Principal Registry are in my honest opinion horrendous. I feel so strongly. Where we've got the Official Solicitors involved with a child in wardship, as you know we have to lodge a freeing application in the Principal Registry. I've done that in one case. It was lodged on 4 September 1989. I was particularly cross about this because we were ordered by the Wardship Court to lodge our freeing application within 28 days so you can imagine the trouble that caused. We did it and they've **never** acknowledged it until about two weeks ago (early March 1990) when they wrote and acknowledged it. I'd been writing to them and ringing them and it's driven me mad. That is my one big criticism. The Principal Registry obviously cannot cope. So I really wish that freeing applications where children are warded didn't have to be lodged there. If the Official

---

[1]   See Part I, section 8.12 in the Court Record Survey.

Solicitor is involved, whilst I can understand the logistics of it already being down there and the file referred across to them, there's got to be a better way of doing this. There's got to be. It's just absolutely ridiculous. And because of these experiences we do not free in wardship, unless the Official Solicitor is involved, in which case the adoption application would be lodged in the High Court and we'd face the same problem. We freed in that particular case because we placed the child outside the jurisdiction in Scotland. As it was going to be a contested matter we were advised it would be best to free in this jurisdiction to save all the witnesses having to trek up to Scotland. I knew the delays were terrible, but I didn't realise they were this bad. It's unbelievable. So we will seek leave in wardship to place a child with long term foster parents with a view to adoption—access terminated usually, seek to place and then ask the adopters to lodge an adoption application which, even if it's contested, hopefully access has already been terminated so that decision has been taken, and the evidence will be the stability and security of the placement. This route has proved speedier and successful."

Many practitioners were concerned about the impact on the parents and children of prolonging cases, in this instance because of listing problems. As one solicitor put it:

"It seems that it's not the child's interests and it's not really in the interests of the nautral parents for there to be such a long delay because no one can really get on with their lives. The children are out there with their prospective adopters, but I think it's particularly for the birth parents. They're in limbo, I mean they probably realise in their heart of hearts that there will be an adoption order but they feel they can't consent and they wait for two years, perhaps even after termination of access before finality which is not in their interests."

And a social worker in the West Country describes the effect on one child who, because of the time the case had taken going through the court process, had not only endured a number of changes of foster family, but had not been able to move to a permanent placement. She went on:

I worked with this child on life story work, got him to the stage where he should be ready to move on and I've actually damaged that little boy because the court's not ready to move on. I said I would like to contact the court and tell them what this little boy is suffering because he's a complete mess this child . . . he's confused. Every time I kind of see him he says 'what else is happening? Tell me some more'. We finished off by being on this island where his boat had broken down and I had to bring the mist down and say we can't go anywhere until the mist clears and the mist is still there and this is months and months later. . . I feel it's going to be very, very much harder for me to find adoptive parents for him".

Given their concerns, it is not surprising that a number of practitioners tried to think of ways in which the listing problem might be overcome. For instance, a solicitor in private practice in the Midlands suggested a way in which delays might be reduced in relation to first hearings:

> "We file an application for adoption and then you wait for something like months before you get your first directions hearing. Now why? In most courts, the directions hearing takes place before a judge. **We** believe that first hearing should take place before a registrar, just like it is in wardship cases in the High Court. It ought to go before a registrar—whose very job it is to give directions on cases. That would cut down delays in getting that first appointment."

Social workers, too, suggested ways in which listing might be improved. One suggested that *"getting more judges on the circuit"* would help, whilst another said:

> ". . I've got great hopes that the Children Act will speed things up if the judges and magistrates learn to set timetables and not accept excuses from solicitors."

A local authority solicitor explained how built-in time limits in the procedure might improve matters.

> "There should be strict time limits . . . Clear rules of court for the progress of children's cases. Courts should **not** take matters out of lists, without reference to the parties involved . . . clear guidance needs to be given to the court that when a matter is to be heard again it **is** heard again on the first open date."

5.4   Appointment of Reporting Officers and Guardians Ad Litem

Another criticism voiced by practitioners concerned the time taken by the courts to appoint reporting officers and, where appropriate, guardians ad litem. Of course the reason for any delay in doing so does not necessarily lie with the courts administration. For instance, late submision of Schedule II reports, the ambivalance of birth parents about whether to agree to adoption and so on, can all affect the timing of the appointment. However, the longer that takes, the longer will be the wait for their reports. Again, the time these take to prepare will vary considerably. For instance, much depends on the complexity of the case and the difficulties that may be encountered in locating birth parents, especially the putative father.

Both the social workers and solicitors expressed frustration at the time taken to appoint reporting officers. For instance, a social worker in the Midlands described a case where the papers had been in the court for weeks, but nothing had happened. Eventually the initial hearing date had to be adjourned because the reporting officer had not been appointed owing to *"staffing problems"*. In some areas, a severe shortage of reporting officers/ guardians ad litem was reported.

5.5 Comment

The problems in the courts administration as perceived by the practitioners prompts the following questions:

(i)   Should court offices employ permanent, specialist adoption clerks?

(ii)   How can the perpetual problems of listing be overcome?

(iii)   How can delays associated with the appointment of reporting officers/guardians ad litem be overcome?

(iv)   Should regular time checks be built in to the freeing and adoption processes?

CHAPTER 6   # The Court Hearing

6.1   Introduction

6.2   Practitioners' Views on the Final Hearing

6.3   Are Court Hearings Necessary?

6.4   Some Alternatives to a Court Hearing

6.5   Comment

6.1   Introduction

As we reported in Part II, Chapter Five, some of the obstacles on the path-way to adoption are perceived by practitioners to arise in the court and its administration, resulting in considerable delays and causing stress and anxiety to the parties and children in a process which is often already highly charged. It is also an expensive procedure, involving as it does court administration time, court time, court space, judge time and so on. How-ever, once the final hearing is reached those obstacles are all but overcome, since the overwhelming majority of adoption applications are granted an order at that hearing. (See Part I, section 2.9 of the Court Record Survey in which an analysis is made of the outcomes of our sample of cases). Less than 1% of all applications were refused at the final hearing, these being freeing applications. The large majority (89%) of all applications were suc-cessful, 4% were withdrawn and 5% were pending or adjourned sine die (see Part I, Table 2.9).

It should be remembered that in a high proportion of adoption applications there is only one hearing. In Part I, section 8.4 of the Court Record Survey we showed that three-quarters (76%) of agency adoption applications necessitated only one hearing and this excludes those cases where the child had been previously freed for adoption, all of which required only one hearing to reach an outcome (Part I, Table 8.4).

During our interviews with practitioners we asked a number of questions about the conduct of the hearing. We also asked whether or not they thought a hearing was necessary in all circumstances (see questionnaire in Appendix D and E). From their response, a number of issues arose. They concerned:

(i)   The appropriateness of the venue for the hearing and its conduct (their comments on the adjudication process are given in Part II, Chapter Seven);

(ii)   Whether it was appropriate to have a hearing in all cases;

(iii)   Whether there was any alternative to the court hearing.

Most of their comments relate to the county court since, as we have shown in Part II, Chapter Five, the majority of cases with which the practitioners were involved were heard in that court.

It should be stressed again that the views we report here are those of the practitioners' perceptions of how the parties viewed the hearing. In that sense, they are "second hand". The project on the consumer view of the adoption process, which we shall be undertaking for the ESRC, will pro-vide us with the opportunity to gather the consumers' impressions of the court hearing first hand.

6.2   Practitioners' Views on the Final Hearing

6.2.1   Waiting for the Hearing

Many practitioners voiced concern about the surroundings in which parties
have to wait and the poor facilities they often encounter. They felt that the
atmosphere and surroundings were inappropriate for an adoption hearing,
principally because the courts often deal with criminal matters too.

A solicitor in the South West described the venue in which adoption hearings are heard in his town:

> "One could easily complain about the particular court house where
> the hearings take place. It is disgusting. There are no conference
> rooms . . . Waiting room provision is inadequate. It's thoroughly
> uncomfortable and unpleasant. It's not a suitable place for family
> jurisdiction. We have modern law courts but they have to be
> reserved almost entirely for crime . . ."

In contested cases these inadequate waiting rooms and the consequent lack
of privacy were a particular cause for concern, since they only added to the
discomfiture of all the parties and increased the risk of disclosing the identity of the prospective adopters.

There were frequent reports of a long wait before finally being called into
the hearing. This can often be a problem if children and other family members come along as well. As one social worker said, *"We had to wait in the
court lobby for quite a while with various desperate villains. The wait was not an
easy experience for three lively children."* The parties are often tense before
going into court and this will not be helped by a long wait in uncomfort-
able surroundings.[1]

6.2.2   The Hearing

It would obviously help the parties to some extent if their social workers
and/or solicitors could prepare them for what to expect once they are
called in to the hearing. However this is easier said than done because of
the variation in practice between courts. For instance, the hearing may be
conducted in a court room or in the judges' chambers. The former were
generally reported to be intimidating and daunting for the parties. On the
whole, practitioners and parties alike much preferred the hearing to be
held in chambers. Confusion about who should actually be present at the
hearing was also reported. For example, some courts allow children to be

---

[1]   In earlier research which we undertook on the overlapping family jurisdiction of magistrates' courts and county courts
in domestic proceedings we reported in some detail litigants' views of the courts and their facilities. See the Overlapping Family Jurisdiction of Magistrates' Courts' and County Courts Research Report, Murch, Borkowski, Copner and
Griew (1987), Socio-Legal Centre for Family Studies, University of Bristol.

present whilst others do not. A social worker involved with a couple who were adopting their fifth child asked if the previously adopted children could attend the hearing. The clerk told her that the judge did not like having children there. In another case, it would have helped if the court had made it clear at the outset that the children would not be required. The social worker explained:

> "The children were kept hanging around for a number of hours then told they could go home. The judge hadn't a clue what he was saying because you can't send seven children home and keep their parents in court. That all got very muddly! They did go home and various neighbours were roped in to help and then they all had to come back again the next morning. That was a shame because they'd hyped themselves up for the occasion . . ."

One aspect of the hearing about which the practitioners were able to warn the parties was the possibility that they might well feel a great sense of anti-climax because of the way the hearing was likely to be conducted. Practitioners, particularly the social workers, felt very strongly indeed about this. They attributed it to the speed of the hearing and to the lack of any sense of occasion or ceremony, which they felt was due principally to the way judges conduct the proceedings. As one social worker said, it appears that the courts have not thought through just what an adoption means to the parties concerned. A potentially joyful occasion becomes *"a massive non-event"* for the prospective adopters whilst for the birth parents it will be a sad one. Another said that for many, the final hearing came *"at the end of years and years of a lot of heartsearching, work and effort."* She went on:

> "I think they were prepared for it because I did warn them! Parents can't believe something so serious can be over so quickly. I always say to people 'it will be very, very quick because all the work has been done beforehand.' "

One practitioner told us that in one of the cases with which she was involved, the adoptive father had timed the hearing for his application; it was one minute thirty seconds.[2]

One social worker who had attended several adoption hearings recalled one which was

> ". . . conducted in open court, not in chambers. The mother was called yet again loudly in the corridor so that everyone outside knew the mother's name and knew the reference to the adoption. The child was not spoken to at all. I can honestly say it was one of the—I've been to a lot of adoption hearings that are an anti-climax,

---

2   Due to the inadequacy of documentation in the court files concerning the hearings and the length of time they took, we were unable to make any reliable analysis of this aspect of court procedure in the Court Record Survey.

that's not unusual—but it was cold, it was a huge open court with everyone sitting along one row and was over within three to four seconds. 'I write this order and I hope you have a nice day.' The child was all prepared and ready for it and was quite upset for several days after it. The adopting couple themselves were tremendously upset."

Another practitioner thought that much depended upon whether the judge *"likes children."* If s/he did so, he or she would be kind and encouraging and take time to speak to the family. She continued:

"If you get one who is not particularly interested, they can give a brief grunt and a nod and you can be out before you came in. It makes what is a very serious step for a family something very inconsequential. It's important that they're given credit."

A social worker in the South West said that in his experience, about 50% of the judges conducted adoption hearings *"very well"*, but he was worried about the other 50%, going on to describe one experience:

"We had a case where this was the third adoption (in the family). We waited an hour for the hearing. There were three children aged five, three and one. We walked in, the judge didn't raise his eyes from the paper; he said he'd make the order, and we walked out again. Now that little girl of five, she was very bright, she was very 'in' to all this and it was awful. But it's worse when they are older children and nothing happens."

In the Midlands, a social worker compared his experience of adoption hearings in the magistrates' court with those in the county court. His comments demonstrate the difference some time and care in conducting the proceedings can make:

"One of the complaints people have anyway is that they've been through so much to get to that stage and all of a sudden it's a great anti-climax. Some of the better ones I've been to—in the S. Magistrates Court they made a really big occasion of it—they made it more informal in that they came down from their bench. They got the applicants to take the oath and confirm it was their marriage certificate. They talked to the child. They took half an hour in all and everyone felt something had happened. Judges I'm afraid aren't desperately socially skilled at our level—they are not good at children—at the plebeian masses they belong to—and very often they just come in and ask them an inane question about what their hobbies are. One judge asked somebody if he knew how much a compact disc player cost because his wife wanted one for Christmas. And in another the judge realised the applicant went fishing and asked him if he ever went fishing and he said well done and that was it. That was a real anti-climax . . ."

6.3   Are Court Hearings Necessary?

We asked the social workers: "In uncontested cases is a court hearing necessary?" Nearly three-quarters (73%) thought that it was; 15% that it was not whilst 12% did not know.

The solicitors were asked a slightly different question: "In your opinion are there cases in which a court hearing is unnecessary?" A similar proportion to the social workers (71%) said that a court hearing was necessary; 17% thought there were cases where a hearing was unnecessary; a further 8% thought it was unnecessary as far as they were concerned, but it was necessary from the child and adopters' point of view. Four per cent did not know.

Given practitioners' varied experience of final hearings for adoption applications, the criticisms they made, and an acknowledgement by many that certainly in uncontested cases the application often appeared to go through *"on the nod"*, it was perhaps surprising that the majority thought a court hearing to be necessary.

6.3.1   Why a Court Hearing is Necessary

Many practitioners said that transferring the parental rights from the birth parents to the adoptive parents was one of the *"biggest decisions ever made"*, marking the completion of a lengthy process. They considered it was therefore essential that the application be heard in court. There was support for the view that orders made in respect of children should always be the responsibility of the courts and should not just be *"rubber-stamped in a bureaucratic process"*. A solicitor in Birmingham who thought that a court hearing was necessary for all applications, whether they were agreed or not, said:

> ". . . prime consideration must be that of the child. It could be far worse if there are informal agreements between people for adoption because if something goes wrong—and there will always be one that goes wrong—as soon as that happens everyone is going to come back and start criticising. Then you really will have a court hearing on your hands and a lot of trouble . . ."

Another solicitor who shared the same view also thought that children should be parties to the proceedings.[3] He said,

> ". . . children should be represented on all adoption cases and the advocate for the child should act as **amicus curiae** if you like, just putting the case to the judge to make sure it is in the child's best

---

3   Practitioners' views on whether children should be separately represented in adoption proceedings are reported in Part II, Chapter Ten.

interest even if the parents don't consent. It may not be in this child's best interests to be adopted. It may be best for it to be in long term foster care with a view to adoption. I believe there always ought to be a hearing with evidence given."

A local authority solicitor suggested that the decisions and actions taken in the case could be justified by the court hearing. Some practitioners, whilst acknowledging that many adoptions *"appeared"* to *"go through on the nod"*, nonetheless thought that because of the enormity of the decision a judge was the most appropriate person to make the order. He had authority and *"the weight and majesty of the law behind him"*.

Many practitioners considered that a hearing was seen as essntial by many for the prospective adopters' sake. For one thing it would help impress on the adopters the commitment they were making. For another it was felt that they needed to hear someone say "this is your child", thereby putting a seal on the process. And the point was made again that the sense of occasion and ceremony potentially afforded by a court hearing was helpful and appropriate. As one social worker pointed out, *"the law is quite often used as a ritual and there is something to be said for that."*

It was thought that the hearing was important for the birth family too. One social worker regarded it as a *"funeral"* for the bereaved birth parents. A solicitor in the Midlands who considered the hearing to be of equal importance for birth parents, despite the trauma it involved, went on to describe a hearing he had attended just a few days before our interview with him:

> "... the natural father was there and he hadn't even been granted legal aid but his representative kindly turned up to explain his circumstances and he was invited to the witness box and he was just sobbing uncontrollably in court. He declined to say anything but felt obliged to be there because he didn't want to sign away the child ..."

A court hearing was of some significance, too, for those children who were old enough to have some perception of what adoption means. Some practitioners saw it as a *"legal transaction"* which children were able to understand. Again, it was the sense of ceremony and occasion which were thought to be particularly important. One solicitor described it as a milestone in a child's life, who then had two "birthdays": his actual birthday and his adoption day. A hearing conducted in a way the child could appreciate would be remembered and talked about long after the event. A social worker described one such hearing she had attended:

> "The judge was very good. He had his wig box there and had some Smarties in it. He engaged her (the child who was being adopted) very well and asked her why she had come to see him. Because she was very shy he got her to look at the wig and then find the Smarties inside the box and eventually she said she'd come to be

adopted. He said he thought that was a splendid idea and then talked to her about remembering the day as her second birthday . . ."

6.3.2   Why a court hearing is unnecessary

A solicitor in Devon who had not actually heard of a situation where an adoption application had been refused presumed this was because the doubtful ones were *"weeded out"* before they got to the court stage. In the remainder of the cases all the necessary investigative work was carried out before they got to court, therefore obviating the need for a court hearing *"in any practical sense"*.

Some suggested that providing the birth parents agreed or consented, all those involved were *"100% certain"*, and that there were *"no outstanding issues"*, a court hearing was not just unnecessary, but also an unnecessary expense. One solicitor thought that in cases where agreement or consent had been given or formally dispensed with the hearing was no more than a public relations exercise because any issue the judge might raise should already have been dealt with by the social services.

6.4   Some Alternatives to a Court Hearing

Practitioners suggested several alternatives to the present hearing. One solicitor thought that adoption could be dealt with *"in the same way as divorce, on the paperwork"*. Another suggestion was that the adoption panel be given a "legal mandate" in uncontested cases.

There was some support for the idea that step parent adoptions could be decided *"on an administrative basis"* undertaken by an "independent welfare officer" or guardian ad litem. As a solicitor said, *"the main principle is the child's interests and that should be adequately covered by a guardian ad litem."*

A local authority solicitor suggested that in unopposed cases a registrar could make the order, providing he had checked the agreement to the adoption. He thought that would expedite the procedure considerably. There was some support for this amongst practitioners, one of whom developed the idea further when she suggested that there should be a registrar of births, marriages and adoptions:

> "There has to be something formal and legal to a degree but that could be done in the way that a registrar conducts marriage cere-monies. Where all parties are consenting I think that would be fine. That could even happen in contested cases where the judge has heard all the evidence and is inclined to make the order then he could give leave to go to the registrar to perform the ceremony."

When considering alternatives to the hearing, practitioners also suggested ideas that might help to create a special sense of occasion. A social worker told us that one judge had suggested to her the need for a written script, almost like a marriage ceremony, *"where he was actually saying some things about this family coming together which would have been appropriate and met his needs and the family's needs."*

One social worker who supported the need for a ceremony thought that it should be a two-way process. She was actually in the process of adopting a seven year old girl who saw adoption not just as *"me adopting her but as us adopting each other"*.

Many practitioners thought it would help if the adopters and children were given some kind of certificate:

> "I think what could actually be done is that people could come out with something in their hand. It's a small thing, but people do feel very let down when they just come out—it would be a simple thing to do and helpful to the child too, to come out clutching something. After all you do that when you get married. But with adoption you come out onto the court steps in the rain and wonder whether you should go and have a cup of tea in Lewis's or go back to school . . . it's a damp squib".

A social worker who shared that view thought that the children might appreciate being given some kind of badge too.

Some judges wear their robe and wig whilst others, perhaps in an attempt to make the hearing less formal, wear a suit. Some children express disappointment if the judge is not robed, but one social worker said she knew of one judge who donned his wig and robe specifically for photographs. Having a photograph taken with the judge was also mentioned as something which made more of a sense of occasion, adding a certain flourish to the proceedings.

One social worker compared what she considered a good experience at a court hearing with others which were not so pleasant, summing up many of the points we have already mentioned:

> "I was very impressed. Compared with some it was slightly longer—it took about fifteen minutes instead of seven and a half. Not only was the child addressed, but they took along her brother who was already adopted. Judge C made a point of referring to him—not leaving him out. He was really included in the whole proceedings. It was business-like but informal. Is it all to do with the judge? I mean there was a beautiful bowl of flowers on the table. It was just atmosphere really. But that woman (the judge) has got such personality. I've been to other hearings and it's been awful. You can actually see the children's faces drop. I think there should be instructions given to judges about it because it's a very, very important

thing. There's enormous ceremony attached to weddings and funerals and it's probably the other most major court appearance in a positive way. I went to an awful one in X where he (the judge) sat behind his desk and he came in and he said "Humph—is Mrs. S (social worker) present? Have you got anything to add?" I said "No". And if he'd had a rubber stamp, well that's what it was all about and this little girl's face dropped and that was the end of it. Whereas Judge C had said 'are you too old to have a kiss?' and I thought that was very nice and it really made it."

A social worker mentioned the needs of the birth mothers whom she considered *"get rather a poor deal"* after the hearing. She felt there was much scope for improvement in the way the mother was informed that the adoption order had been granted:

"She just gets the form with most of it crossed off and in the middle it says adoption order granted! I think in a way she needs a more significant thing. Sometimes it's just a half slip torn out of a book—perforated. It's not symbolic. It's not saying this is a very special thing you have done—it's a tear off slip, like a receipt almost."

6.5 Comment

The views the practitioners expressed about the court hearing raise the following questions:

(i)   Is a court hearing necessary in all cases?

(ii)   Could an alternative way be found to grant uncontested adoption applications?

(iii)   Should a short ceremony be created to mark the change in status following the granting of an adoption order?

(iv)   What are the most appropriate fora in which to decide adoption applications?

CHAPTER 7   The Adjudication Process

7.1   Introduction

7.2   Procedural Approach

7.3   The Judicial Role

7.4   The Judicial Manner

7.5   Comment

7.1 Introduction

Despite the fact that the majority of adoption and freeing applications are successful (as we explained in Part II, Chapter Six), difficulties can arise at the hearing stage, sometimes causing confusion and discomfiture which may have an unsettling and damaging effect on the parties to the proceedings, on the child and occasionally on the practitioners. The consequences of these, although unlikely to affect the final outcome, can delay progress of the case. For instance in Part I, section 8.4 of the Court Record Survey we have shown that just over half (54%) of the freeing applications in our court proforma sample required at least two hearings before the decision was made although, as we have said, in 76% of the agency adoption applications (excluding cases where the child had been freed previously) the matter was decided at the first hearing (Part I, section 8.4 Table 8.4). The number of hearings required to reach a final decision appears also to be determined to some extent by whether or not the case is contested (Part I, section 8.5) and the age of the child (Part I, section 8.5).

Prevalent amongst the difficulties the practitioners identified concerning hearings were criticisms of the adjudication process. These related mainly to the county court since, as we have shown in Part I, section 2.5 of the Court Record Survey, 78% of all applications from the mini record sample were made to the county court (Table 2.5b). Three main problems emerged:

(i)   variations in procedural approach;

(ii)   an apparent uncertainty about the judge's role;

(iii)   concern about judge's manner.

Again it should be remembered that we are reporting the practitioners' perceptions of these issues. It was not in our terms of reference to ask members of the judiciary for their views, neither have we yet asked the consumers for theirs.

7.2 Procedural Approach

Those practitioners who had experience of adoption hearings before different judges in various county courts were concerned by the apparent lack of consistency between them regarding several aspects of the adjudication process.

For example some solicitors said that in the county court or High Court, use should be made of the rules enabling affidavits to be filed. However some judges did not see the necessity for affidavit evidence. They considered the Statement of Facts (in contested cases) to be sufficient. The solicitors acting for the birth mother and/or father feel that the lack of affidavit evidence hampers their preparation of the case because the them about it is thus limited. A solicitor who had experience of this dichotomy explained that in his local court:

> ". . . judges tend to go along with affidavits. Because each side knows what the case is about, it enables us to prepare our case and in the long run it shortens proceedings because it cuts down the amount of oral evidence. In other courts, it seems it's a purely oral hearing with very little affidavit evidence filed. That seems totally wrong. The problem is that some judges agree with affidavit evidence, others don't."

A local authority solicitor said that in her experience the requirement to file affidavits appeared to be at judges' discretion. She had mixed feelings about this, recognizing the advantages for the birth parents if they are filed, but worried about the extra time and cost involved:

> "It takes time and adds to the cost because you are then involved in contacting people who no longer work for the local authority. I don't know why the judges have started doing this, but I can certainly see the advantage to the parents in filing affidavits in response to the Statement of Facts because it helps you to identify the actual areas of contest at the end of the day, and you can then decide just how many witnesses you've got to bring in."

Another aspect of the process, about which the practitioners felt the judges were at variance, related to the efforts expected of the social worker in searching for and contacting a putative father. Some judges who consider such efforts to be insufficient tend to adjourn the proceedings so that further investigations can be made. This can be frustrating in those cases where the agency will have gone to what it might regard as considerable and thorough lengths already, which will have been fully described in the appropriate reports. The progress of a case can be held up for several months whilst the additional investigations are carried out and a new hearing date set. One of the social workers who had experienced this described what happened in one of her cases:

> "Some judges feel that the natural father has got to be involved and approached no matter what—it causes delays . . . even where the fellow has been in touch with nobody he still apparently wants efforts made. I think this tends to be particular judges. We had a case the year before last. The father didn't want the mother to place the baby for adoption. He said he wanted it. He was told to see a solicitor straight away. Then he disappeared to Ireland, came back here, went back to Ireland. He did eventually see a solicitor who wrote to us and said he (the solicitor) hadn't heard from him (the father) since, and that was well over 12 months. The guardian ad litem was appointed and the judge was even talking about him going over to Ireland to see this fellow. He was out of the country, we had no jurisdiction over him, so why should he have to do that?

In the end he (judge) decided he'd give us a date and he didn't ever refer to it!"

Another social worker described the frustration engendered by one case in which she had been working with the birth mother. She considered that the judge who presided over the final hearing would have acted differently from the judge who presided over the earlier hearings. In this case the birth parents had been separated for two years, and were in the process of divorcing. The child was conceived between the granting of their decree nisi and decree absolute. She went on:

"... When the applicants went to court for the adoption hearing the judge would not grant the adoption order without the agreement of the ex-husband to the adoption. And the reporting officer went to the ex-husband to get him to sign a paper saying that he agreed to the adoption of the child. When the hearing came the judge would not accept it (the signed paper) and said the ex-husband would have to sign another paper saying the child was not his. So the reporting officer had to go back to the ex-husband and get him to sign another piece of paper which could all have been done at the same time. There was no need for all the delays in that case. I might add the final rider: on the morning of the adoption hearing the judge that had asked for all this information was not available and another judge had to preside who wondered what all the fuss was about and why there had been so many delays!"

Although the social worker considered that the fussiness of the first judge had impeded the progress of the case, the judge may well have been frustrated by what he considered the ineptitude on the part of the social worker and Reporting Officer. In cases where the birth mother is married at the time the child is conceived, whether or not her husband is the father of the child his agreement to the adoption application is required. The judge in this case might have reasonably expected that the adoption agency would have taken the necessary steps concerning this prior to the hearing.

7.3   The Judicial Role

A few practitioners said that from their observations of the varied way in which judges conduct cases they could only conclude that the judges themselves have differing views about their role. For instance, some judges make a point of seeing the children whilst others do not. Judges vary, too, in what they wish to hear about the case and the amount of detail that should be considered. One solicitor summed it up:

"There's an enormous range of approach between those who take the view that it's all been prepared and been thorough and if mother doesn't actually turn up and there is no active opposition, what on earth is the point of rehashing it? It goes through to those judges who feel that they ought to at least have you recite the Statement of Facts, which performs no useful function, because presumably they can read as well as everyone else and it doesn't actually add anything except embarrass the applicants to have read out a catalogue of horrendous activities by the child's parents. And then to those judges who view this as a pretty drastic step and so feel they have to judicially carry it out and so they do. They do it formally in two stages—(i) dispense with consent without the applicants being in the room and hearing some evidence—they usually say to just summarise it and then (ii) the applicants come in and the order is made."

The comment made by this solicitor again prompts the question which we asked in Part II, Chapter Six: how necessary is a court hearing in all cases?

7.4   The Judicial Manner

Practitioners proffered a number of views on the manner in which judges dealt with cases, ranging from good and sensitive to awkward and more akin to criminal proceedings. The effect on practitioners as well as the parties can be considerable.

One social worker described a hearing for a freeing application in the High Court, which the birth mother was opposing. The mother was seventeen and *"heavily pregnant again"* at the time of the hearing. The hearing lasted three days and there were counsel acting for the mother, for the local authority and for the Official Solicitor. The social worker felt that the mother was very isolated with no-one to turn to and was devastated by her experience in court. The social worker, too, found it a difficult experience. She felt that had the judge ensured that the case was conducted with greater sensitivity the mother might have been spared some of her anguish.

A solicitor cited a case in which he had represented the birth father:

"I don't think the judge had read the papers, and I thought he was looking for a quick solution to what looked like a long, drawn-out hearing and really I don't feel that he gave my client the opportunity of stating his case. He interrupted him and criticised him for one or two elements of his lifestyle. The net result was that my client was not only absolutely devastated by the result, which I had tried to get him to anticipate, but because of the judge's comments. My client felt that he'd not really been taken seriously. One of the judge's comments, I think, was 'just like the rest of your life, you've put your own selfish reasons before your child's'—which I felt totally unnecessary and I felt very personally distressed by the way that case was dealt with. I'm not saying the judge was wrong—I'm talking about the way he dealt with it."

Some practitioners felt that judges who were more used to conducting criminal proceedings were unable to adapt their style when dealing with family proceedings. One local authority solicitor explained that practitioners in her area would ask for a case to be adjourned rather than have it heard by one particular judge who was *"not renowned for his sensibilities in children's cases"*. She went on:

> —". . . It does make a considerable difference because it means that when you know you are going before him you are edgy and wondering what's going to happen. He'll pick up on the spelling mistakes or the comments that have been missed out or whisper instructions, so that you are all on edge . . ."

(The judge might have thought that had the reports been carefully checked there should have been no spelling mistakes in the copies sent to the court!)

The solicitor recognised that seeking an adjournment in this way had to be weighed against the possible damage to the child if the case was delayed any further.

Many practitioners spoke of their experience before judges whose manner was kind and sensitive. For instance:

> ". . . I like the judge there. I knew it would be Judge W . . . I think he's very good at this kind of thing—adoption and matrimonial. He's very understanding and patient and appreciates the concerns that to others may seem a bit irrational and foolish."

And a solicitor recalled one adoption where the judge had been *"very good with the child"* as a result of which the child *"remembers it and still talks about the nice judge who said such nice things to him."*

Given their views it is not surprising that several practitioners advocated the need for specialist, trained judges, to deal with adoption. For instance, this social worker said:

> ". . . Judges need to be more aware of the cultural, racial and religious aspect. Judges have a colour blind approach—and this is the issue relating to trans-racial adoption—and need to cater for the holistic needs of a child. Judges need training and awareness courses about racial issues. As you know, judges are usually over 40—well over 50—over 60! To tell you the truth, some of them are out of touch. I'm not trivialising their responsibility."

A solicitor in private practice felt that adoptions would be more appropriately dealt with in a family tribunal by:

> ". . . people who specialise in it all the time, and people who are capable of making reasonable and compassionate decisions and giving a party the fullest opportunity to air their views."

7.5 Comment

The following questions are raised by the practitioners' comments on the adjudication process:

(i)   How can the apparent inconsistencies in judicial practice be reduced?

(ii)   Is the judicial role in adoption proceedings in need of clearer definition?

(iii)   Should adoption applications be heard only by judges experienced in this area of work?

(iv)   Should judges receive some/more training in the conduct of adoption hearings?

CHAPTER 8   # The Legal Process

8.1   Introduction

8.2   Practitioners' Knowledge of the Law

8.3   The Freeing for Adoption Provisions

8.4   Adoption Law

8.5   Whether Adoption Law Meets the Needs of the Parties

8.6   Changes to the Freeing Provisions and Adoption Law

8.7   Comment

8.1   Introduction

In 1989 the Department of Health set up an Inter-Departmental Review of Adoption Law. The present legislation is contained in the Adoption Act 1976 which resulted from the previous review of adoption undertaken by the Houghton Committee. It incorporates many of the recommendations made in that Committee's report, (Report of the Departmental Committee on the Adoption of Children, 1972, Cmnd. 5107, HMSO). The Children Act 1989, which introduces fundamental reforms in child law, incorporates a new range of orders available to the courts in all "family proceedings". Section 8(4)(d) of the Act designates adoption as family proceedings. Once the 1989 Act is implemented it will have the effect of repealing some provisions in the current adoption legislation. These are detailed in the Inter-Departmental Review on Adoption Law, Discussion Paper No 1: The Nature and Effect of Adoption, issued by the Department of Health in September 1990.

With the Departmental Review in mind, we included a series of questions about current adoption legislation in our interviews with practitioners. We also asked what, if any, changes they would like future legislation to incorporate. We report their response here.

8.2   Practitioners' Knowledge of the Law

We began our series of questions by first trying to establish practitioners' level of knowledge of adoption law.

We asked the social workers:

"Do you consider you have an adequate working knowledge of the law relating to adoption?"

62% thought they did; 37% that they did not. Several of those who replied affirmatively qualified their response by saying that if they were unsure they could always look up the law or seek advice from their agency's legal department, their supervisor or colleagues as and when a case demanded. A social worker in Devon put it this way:

> "I feel that in each new case one needs to know the important bits as they appertain to that case. I think it would be very difficult for any one of us who isn't working in adoption regularly to carry all that around. Nor do I see it to be essential. It's essential to know where you can get that knowledge and there is nothing like a case to make you go running looking for it!"

We asked the solicitors:

"Are there areas of adoption law about which you feel you should know more?"

29% said there were. Of those who specified areas about which they should know more, 8% mentioned the freeing provisions and 4% foreign adoptions. 17% thought their knowledge was sufficient for what they were generally asked to do. 8% said there were no areas about which they should know more; a further 30% was made up of some who said that one had to be a 'jack of all trades' in their particular practice, others who said they had only dealt with one or two adoption cases and some who said they needed to know more about all aspects of adoption law; the rest did not know.

A solicitor in the South West who thought his knowledge was adequate explained why:

> ". . . Generally speaking I feel my knowledge, apart from keeping generally up to date, is sufficient for the work I'm normally called on to do. And let's face it, when you come down to it really the vast majority of times if you've got a problem it's to do with dispensing with consent and you are then dealing with fact rather than with law to a large extent. Very often the actual hearing is to do with fact and very often what you are doing is enabling the natural parent to have their say. The outcome is probably a foregone conclusion. We know that and the judge knows and the guardian and litem knows that and you are just giving the natural parent a chance to feel at least they've been given an opportunity to make their point and haven't given up their child voluntarily. But that doesn't require great legal expertise . . . Most of what we are dealing with are human problems and not legal problems but then that applies to all the work I do: human problems and their legal background."

Another solicitor, who had acted in one adoption case in three years, in answering our question said:

> ". . . All of it. I don't get enough to know and I have to mug it up for every case. If I did more I'd have it at my fingertips. It's a dangerous situation because when a new one comes in you are groping until you get the books out and check it all up again, I'm afraid."

8.3 The Freeing for Adoption Provisions

We asked the social workers and solicitors if they could say what they regarded as the most positive and the most negative aspects of the freeing for adoption provisions. Their response is shown in Tables 8.1 and 8.2 below

From these data it can be seen that nearly three-quarters of the social workers (73%) thought there were positive aspects, but 17% related their

Table 8.1
The Social Workers

(a)   Are there positive aspects of the freeing for adoption provisions?

	NO.	(%)
Yes	38	(73)
D/K—not enough knowledge to say	5	(10)
Answer related to process rather than law	9	(17)
ALL	**52**	**(100)**

(b)   Are there negative aspects of the freeing for adoption provisions?

	NO.	(%)
Yes	13	(25)
No	1	(2)
D/K—not enough knowledge to say	5	(9)
Answer related to process rather than law	31	(60)
D/K	2	(4)
ALL	**52**	**(100)**

Table 8.2
The Solicitors

(a)   Can you say what you regard as the most positive aspects of the freeing provisions?

	NO.	(%)
Yes	14	(59)
Not experienced enough to say	6	(25)
Answer related to process rather than law	2	(8)
D/K	2	(8)
ALL	**24**	**(100)**

(b)   Can you say what you regard as the most negative aspects of the freeing provisions?

	NO.	(%)
Yes	11	(46)
No	2	(8)
Not experienced enough to say	6	(25)
Answer related to process rather than law	3	(13)
D/K	2	(8)
ALL	**24**	**(100)**

answer to the freeing process rather than to actual specifics in the legislation; that percentage rose to 60% when they were asked about negative aspects.

As we explained in Part II, Chapter Four, some of the solicitors we interviewed had little or no experience of freeing; that is reflected in the figures above.

8.3.1   The positive aspects

A number of positive aspects were mentioned by the practitioners though many, as we have said, commented on the process or its potential benefits to the parties, rather than on the law itself.

(a)   The Principle of Freeing

Several practitioners voiced their enthusiasm for freeing in principle, seeing it as a *"very good philosophy"*. However all of them without exception added the rider that because of the practical difficulties freeing appeared to involve, principally of delay, it was not being used as much as it might be. A local authority solicitor in the Midlands felt so strongly about this that she was recommending to Social Services less and less that freeing applications should be pursued. A solicitor in private practice in Birmingham who had no doubts that freeing was a *"good procedure"* felt that local authorities did not have the time to deal with it, partly because they did not have enough solicitors in their legal departments. A social worker in a voluntary agency who had previously worked in a local authority where freeing worked well said:

> "Freeing is a good piece of legislation and I'm sad it hasn't been used extensively. The whole aim was to get things done more quickly and to get a clear cut answer to a very important question. If it worked as I think it should do then that would be wonderful. And in some authorities I think it does work. In the local authority in which I used to work it did. That was because freeing applications were made literally the day after the panel had decided. That was because we'd worked with the judges and the courts as soon as freeing came in and so we had that sort of arrangement and the whole department was geared up to it. I know that it can be done. . . ."

(b)   Benefits for the Child

Some practitioners saw freeing in theory as an excellent way to get a clear cut answer to the plan for the child, establishing the principle sooner rather than later, though in practice this was not soon enough in many cases.

It was also thought that it would be a help to the child in the long term because the child would not perceive the subsequent adoption as a battle between its birth parents and adoptive parents, since any "battle" is enjoined between the local authority and the birth parents and settled prior to the adoption proceedings.

There were benefits, too, for so-called 'hard to place' children who had been freed in that as soon as suitable prospective adopters were identified the placement could be arranged without delay.

(c) Benefits for the Birth Parents

Practitioners felt that for the parents of babies freeing was particularly helpful, since it enabled them to complete that part of the process quickly through a relatively simple procedure. Also, as one social worker pointed out, if the freeing process was carried though quickly it was so much more pertinent for the birth parents because the time scale would still be relevant to them. They would not be dealing with something that had happened to them three or four years previously.

(d) Benefits for the prospective adopters

Many of the practitioners thought that the prospective adopters benefited greatly from freeing since it offered some security and reduced their anxiety. A solicitor in the South West explained that the prospective adopters then realise that:

> ". . . subject to the child settling down, there's no bar to adoption. Your lollipop's not going to be removed from your mouth at the last moment. That's very important. It must affect the emotional stability very closely."

The matter of parental consent is therefore dealt with outside adoption and, as a social worker in Birmingham said, it is thus *"an issue between the caring authority and the natural parents rather than the applicants and the natural parents"* and protects them from being embroiled in a court case.

A social worker identified another benefit for those adoptive parents who are not well off. She said she would often suggest freeing in those circumstances because that meant that the department made the application and footed the bill. There could never be any argument about it then. In this way, too, some of the problems encountered when the parties apply for legal aid are avoided (see Part II, Chapter 4).

8.3.2   The negative aspects

The majority of criticism about freeing was levelled not so much at the provisions themselves as at the time it took and the delays involved, thus obviating one of the benefits envisaged when freeing was introduced—that it would expedite the adoption process.

(a)   *The time factor*

Practitioners in each of the fieldwork areas expressed grave concern about the time it took for the freeing process to be completed. In Part I, sections 8.6 and 8.7 of the Court Record Survey we report the length of time taken to complete the freeing applications compared with other types of adoption applications (Table 8.6a and Table 8.7). As we have already said, in some areas a decision had been taken to use freeing less frequently because of the time taken. A social worker in the Midlands explained what had happened in her local authority. Because of the time factor she concluded that there might be advantages in pursuing a contested adoption instead of a freeing application. She said:

> "Two years ago we worked out that freeing took a minimum of seven months[1] which was quite unacceptable and it's led us to make fewer and fewer freeing applications. You have situations where you get a freeing order one week and the family put the adoption application in the next week and it just started to seem something of a nonsense, and where a child was already placed with prospective adopters the prospective adopters were being called to court to give evidence in the freeing application and you start to think well, what have they gained from all this? We might just as well have been doing a contested adoption application. It feels the same, the anxiety is the same, sometimes the involvement is the same and had it been a contested adoption, they would actually come out at the end with an adoption order whereas with the contested freeing, you've then got to start on the adoption application."

(b)   *The disadvantages for children*

Much concern was voiced about children's status between the time they were freed and adopted. They were seen as being in a state of limbo. A solicitor in Devon was worried because freeing broke the tie with the natural family but put nothing in its place. A social worker who agreed was

---

[1]   Table 8.6(b) in Part I, section 8.6 gives an analysis of the mean time taken from date of application to date of order for each type of application by area for all cases sampled in the mini record.

concerned about the implications of having to place the child no later than twelve months after the freeing order has been granted:

> "It creates a legal orphan, doesn't it? The agency become the parent and the agency doesn't make a very good parent. You've only got a year to find a family. If something goes wrong with the placement you have to go through the process all over again—the mother has a right to go back. We don't want to leave children freed in that state of limbo for longer than necessary. I wonder if it's really appropriate if you've got a freeing order to really need to look at it again at all. If it's right that the child should be freed for adoption—it's right! It then seems to be a complication that if they haven't got the right placement in a year the mother then has a chance to revoke."

It was thought by some that the possibility of having to go through further proceedings after a year if no placement had been made could be very hard on children, so-called 'hard to place' children being particularly vulnerable in this respect.

Where a child was a ward of court one solicitor said:

> "If the local authority has decided that it would be appropriate for a ward to be placed with foster parents with a view to adoption, rather than put the onus on the prospective adopters, I feel it would always be preferable for the local authority to free that child for adoption."

(c) *Disadvantages for birth parents*

Some practitioners were worried that the birth parents' distress might be increased because they had no idea where the child was to be permanently placed. One solicitor thought the parents might feel they were being asked to consent or to fight *"in the abstract"*. He went on to say that if parents had some idea of when and with whom their child might be placed they might be more willing to consent, as they would be better able to see that it was in the child's best interests.

A social worker in the South West expressed concern at the way some authorities use freeing and the effect this can have on the chance of any future relationship between the birth parents and the child:

> "It concerns me a little that when other local authorities are looking to place youngsters in adoptive homes in this country that freeing is some-times used as almost part of the normal procedure rather than because it is really necessary. I'm particularly talking about the boroughs that have these fairly aggressive permanence policies where I feel uneasy about how the natural parents of the child are being treated. It seems to me that termin-ation of access followed by freeing is a means of getting them out of the

way. I've sometimes felt that some of the youngsters could retain a relationship with their families of origin, possibly by means of long term foster care or some type of more open adoption rather than the procedure that's taken place. I feel very uneasy about it. . . .."

(d)   *Other concerns*

One solicitor was concerned about the wording of the grounds. In particular, he thought that those which said that the parent(s) had repeatedly failed to discharge their responsibilities to the child to be *"terribly unsympathetic"* and wondered if they could be *"de-legalised"* in some way. He also mentioned what he saw as the rather adversarial approach to the freeing proceedings, a concern echoed by a social worker who said:

> ". . . Not all social workers are comfortable with the adversarial role which freeing brings about. It's not as though the child is with foster parents and the foster parents decide they'd like to adopt. You take the adversarial initiative and that doesn't rest comfortably with some areas of social work. Things are changing, but I think it's part of the social work ethic that we want to take people with us in our plans."

Another solicitor was worried about the declaration procedure.[2] Under S. 18(6) of the Adoption Act 1976 the court must be satisfied that the birth parent(s) have been given an opportunity of making a declaration that s/he prefers not to be involved in future questions concerning the adoption of the child. If s/he signs a declaration they are then denied the possibility of applying for a revocation of the freeing order if the child has not been placed within 12 months of the making of that order. Whilst he saw it as a positive aspect of freeing he was concerned because:

> ". . . I don't think it's discussed enough, particularly by guardians ad litem, with the parents. I've sometimes felt that parents may have considered a declaration further if it had been discussed with them further."

8.4   Adoption Law

We asked the social workers and solicitors if they could tell us what they regarded as the positive and negative aspects of the adoption legislation current at the time of our interviews, a question several practitioners said they found difficult to answer. Well over half (65%) the social workers thought there were positive aspects whilst a half also thought there were negative aspects.

---

2   Data from the Court Record Survey revealed that a declaration had been made in only 17% of the freeing cases in the court proforma sample.

Solicitors felt there was an almost equal balance between the positive and negative aspects of adoption law. The majority felt they had sufficient experience of adoption law to comment, compared with the quarter who had said they were not sufficiently experienced to comment on freeing. (See Part II, Chapter Eight Table 8.2).

Again, the comments the practitioners made relate as much to process as to legislation.

8.4.1   The positive aspects

(a)   *The process and the law*

Several practitioners thought the process was a thorough one, giving adoption proper legal control. One solicitor was attracted by the finality of adoption and the fact that *"you can't muck about with it"*. Several solicitors said that they thought that it was a relatively simple process and that the rules were *"straightforward, easy to follow and reasonably regularly updated."*

(b)   *The benefits to child and adopters*

The security that adoption gave both the child and the adopters was regarded by many as one of the most positive aspects of adoption law. One solicitor said that in addition to the security it gave, it also meant that the child and adopters were *"free from interference from parties who have been involved with the child previously"*. Another who thought that it brought the turmoil to an end went on to say:

> ". . . Whether it's the right decision or not, it says "These kids are no longer embroiled in care, access, revocation, a further revocation, another access application etc." They're out of all that, the uncertainty is over and they're with people with whom hopefully—the figures are pretty high on breakdown these days—they're going to have some permanency at last."

A local authority solicitor thought that it also removed the stigma for those children who were in care.

8.4.2   The negative aspects

(a)   *Process and the law*

In contrast to those practitioners who saw the adoption law and process in positive terms there were many who felt the opposite about it. Some saw it as too elaborate. For instance, a solicitor in the Midlands described it as:

> ". . . Convoluted, complex, lengthy, calculated to upset natural parents. It's calculated to impose an impossible burden on prospective adopters and children. That's pretty bad enough, I should think. But when it's all over, I guess the children are pretty pleased."

He did not like the role he had to play. A solicitor in the South West who also thought it too complex went on to say:

> "People (solicitors) dabble in adoption, which is why I get so many telephone calls, when they should have the courage to say they do not do this. Dabbling is dangerous . . ."

He felt that the law could be simplified, but regretted that he was not clever enough to know how!

(b) Inflexibility

Several practitioners highlighted a number of aspects which they regarded as too inflexible, the most frequently mentioned of these being that the child was cut off from its roots once the order was made. A social worker in Devon spoke for several practitioners when she said:

> "It can be inflexible—we are talking about the birth parents, the natural family. It's a bit cut and dried for everybody. We cut those links, we create those links. It's black and white and the reality is that very often we are not dealing with black and white issues."

Whilst the marital status of prospective adopters relates more to the policy of individual adoption agencies, it was nevertheless regarded as another aspect of the process which suffered from inflexibility. A social worker said that adoption was intended to provide a *"stable unit"* for the child. She felt that nowadays stability could be just as well provided by cohabitees and single applicants as it could by married applicants, and the fact that people were not married should not bar them from applying to adopt. We found from some interviews we conducted with adoption workers when we were setting up our research that attitudes to marital status were now changing and single people and cohabitees are no longer necessarily disbarred. In Part I, section 2.6 of the Court Record Survey we report that only 2% of cases in the court proforma sample involved a single applicant.

Age of potential adopters was a concern—another issue related to agency policy rather than to the legal process. A social worker in Devon summed it up when she said:

> ". . . There's a very unimaginative stance by local authorities over adoption. Very few local authorities will take an application to adopt—unless it's for a special needs child—from a couple after they are thirty five. They are very sceptical of couples who are over thirty. Adoption is quite middle class really. I think adoption agencies are

missing out on a lot of couples who would make good adopters because of the age factor. It's true of the professional middle classes that perhaps they won't start thinking about having a family until they are thirty. By the time they have fertility tests etc., by the time they get to an adoption list they are thirty six/thirty seven. I think that they would bring things to adoption—in the natural world people have children at that age. One of the best adoptions I ever had was with a couple who were thirty two and I just got them in, but there were a lot of eyebrows raised. . . . Local authorities need a kick up the backside about age restrictions. There's nothing about that in the actual law."

In Part I, section 6.9 of the Court Record Survey we discuss data collected on the age of the adoptive mother. An analysis of the court proforma sample (393 agency adoptions) revealed that overall 80% of mothers adopting babies and 68% of those mothers adopting children between the ages of five and ten years were over thirty years of age at the time the adoptee was born. From Table 6.9, Part I, section 6.9 it can be seen that the large majority (82%) of adoptive mothers were aged thirty or over at the time the adoption application was made, with approximately one third aged between thirty one and thirty five, and one third between thirty six and forty. Just under half (44%) of mothers adopting babies were aged between thirty one and thirty five at the time the application was made. Just over one third (34%) were over thirty five. This compares with 57% of those mothers over thirty five adopting children between one and five years of age, and 68% between five and ten years of age. For further analysis of this data (a comparison of the birth and adoptive mother's age), see Part I, section 6.10.

A solicitor in Birmingham was concerned at the lack of flexibility for *"unusual situations"*, the one he cited being if the placement did not work out. A social worker in Birmingham expressed a similar worry:

"Once the adoption process has actually started, it is very difficult to recant and backtrack. I find social workers very reluctant to stop the process and go back to court and say 'look we've made a mistake here'. We need to look at changing circumstances."

(c)   Other concerns

A solicitor in Birmingham was concerned by the absence in the Act of any reference to the child's wishes and feelings, although this was in the Rules. He was also concerned about the grounds for dispensing with parental agreement and thought that the checklist should be extended.

A local authority solicitor in the West Country found *"the actual concept of adoption a difficult one"*, since it deprived birth parents of their parental rights and placed them with someone else.

A solicitor in private practice expressed concern for the plight of the birth mother. He said that because of what might only be a short term predicament she had to make a long term decision and lost her child as a result. A social worker in the South West described a case where the birth mother had made a decision to give up her baby but later changed her mind. She said:

"One of the aspects I found difficult was in a case where a child was placed directly from hospital with prospective adopters and then after about three months the mother changed her mind. That was the first indication she had given that she was wavering. I think probably taking the child back from that couple was the worst thing I've ever had to do. It was a really awful business. I find that no man's land between the application being made to the court and—when the parent is asking for adoption—that's no man's land, but I'm not sure in my own mind how that can be changed because parents should have some time to make up their minds, but on the other hand prospective adopters have a right to be protected. That no man's land, if you play safe it can be detrimental to the child in that they have to wait longer for a placement. It's very difficult and I'm not sure how you get round it."

8.5   Whether Adoption Law meets the Needs of the Parties

As we have already said, many of the practitioners found it difficult to comment on the freeing provisions and on adoption law. However we also asked them whether they thought that adoption law current at the time of the interviews met the needs of children, birth parents and adopters, and this proved to be a question about which many had clear and strong views. Tables 8.3 and 8.4 summarise their response.

From these data it appears that social workers feel that the current legislation best meets the needs of the adoptive parents. Whilst 46% think that it meets the needs of the child, 39% do not. Only 21% think it meets the needs of the birth parents. The majority (60%) think that it does not. Further analysis of this category revealed that 6% of social workers felt that there was a bias towards the birth mother and the birth father therefore fared worse.

The solicitors' view appears to agree with that of the social workers in that the adoption legislation best meets the needs of the adoptive parents, although the same proportion (58%) also think it meets the needs of the child. Again, the needs of the birth parents are considered to be the least well met. 25% thought that it does meet the needs of the birth parents,

Table 8.3
Whether social workers think adoption law meets the needs of the child, the birth parents, the adoptive parents.

	Child		Birth parents		Adoptive parents	
	NO.	(%)	NO.	(%)	NO.	(%)
Yes	24	(46)	11	(21)	36	(69)
No	3	(6)	10	(19)	10	(19)
No—cut off from roots	7	(13)	10	(19)	–	–
No—too slow	4	(8)	–	–	–	–
No—insuffient counselling	–	–	4	(8)	–	–
No—other	6	(11)	7	(14)	–	–
Other	1	(2)	2	(4)	1	(2)
DK	7	(13)	8	(15)	5	(10)
ALL	**52**	**(100)**	**52**	**(100)**	**52**	**(100)**

Table 8.4
Whether solicitors think adoption law meets the needs of the child, the birth parents, the adoptive parents.

	Child		Birth parents		Adoptive parents	
	NO.	(%)	NO.	(%)	NO.	(%)
Yes	14	(58)	6	(25)	14	(58)
No	2	(8)	3	(13)	3	(13)
No—cut off from roots	–	–	3	(13)	–	–
No—other	3	(13)	2	(8)	–	–
Other	1	(4)	3	(12)	–	–
DK	4	(17)	7	(29)	7	(29)
ALL	**24**	**(100)**	**24**	**(100)**	**24**	**(100)**

compared with 34% who did not. Just over a quarter of the solicitors did not know whether the legislation meets the needs of the birth and adoptive parents.

8.5.1   The needs of the child

Many of those practitioners who felt that the legislation current at the time of the Practitioner Study did meet the needs of the child said that the child's interests were put first. However, a social worker in Birmingham who shared that view added that she felt that whether the child's needs were met depended much more on how Social Services Departments were organized, staffed and worked in relation to their adoption work than on the law.

Several said that the legislation had inbuilt safeguards and provided reasonable checks and balances which, as one social worker put it, helped *"guard against overzealous authorities,"* thus protecting the child.

A social worker in a voluntary agency said that the legislation allowed for the possibility of open adoption and the provision of post-adoption support to which her agency was committed. As a result families were *"not left high and dry"*. But another was concerned that even though there was mention in the legislation of the provision of post-adoption support, local authority adoption agencies were less likely than the voluntary agencies to provide it.

A solicitor in Devon who thought that the legislation met the needs of babies and *"undamaged children"* had grave doubts as to whether the law met the needs of children in complicated cases, and was concerned that in those cases the procedure did not provide the right degree of protection for the child. Two solicitors did not think that adoption law was child focused.

Several practitioners expressed concern for older and 'hard to place' children. A major reason why their needs were perceived as not being met was because there are no time limits built into the legislation and it *"just goes on and on"*. As a social worker in the Midlands explained:

> "I believe it still lingers on in the belief that the adoptive child is a six week old baby in a cot and it doesn't matter how long you take to do an adoption, it doesn't affect them anyway. I don't think it has adjusted to take on board the needs of the eight, nine, ten year old children that are being placed for adoption now to whom we simply don't operate within the child's sense of time spans. We accept as adults that twelve months is not an unacceptable delay . . . It is a very drawn out process."

A solicitor in the Midlands also thought there was a danger that the views of older children *"are not being sufficiently taken into account"*.

Other practitioners said that for older children particularly, the legislation did not meet their needs because adoption in so many instances meant that they were cut off from their birth parents and extended family. More careful account should be taken of the child's history and whether some kind of "open" adoption would be appropriate.

8.5.2   The needs of the birth parents

A solicitor in Birmingham felt that the needs of the birth parents are met because they are entitled to legal aid and to being represented. He thought they had the opportunity to show that they were not unnecessarily withholding their consent. Another added that it enabled a child to be placed for adoption *"without fault being placed on the birth parents"*.

On the other hand several practitioners thought that no consideration whatsoever was given to the birth parents—they were just not taken into account. A solicitor in Devon who shared this view said:

> "They're just there; they almost don't count. You go through the fiasco of saying are you prepared to consent? How many parents who object, how many succeed in stopping it? Nobody cares at all about birth parents. They wouldn't because all the statute law says the children are of paramount importance and therefore it's almost interpreted as saying therefore the birth parents are of no importance at all—their feelings or welfare."

Another in the Midlands felt it was *"horrendous"* for the birth parents when they were asked to *"sign away their children"*. A social worker in Birmingham with sixteen years' experience of adoption work said:

> "In all the adoptions I've dealt with over the years I have never seen a mother part from her child without heartbreak. It takes a noble person to give her child to someone else."

Another social worker recognised that difficulties could arise because what was in the interests of the child might conflict with what was in the interests of the birth parents.

One social worker who thought that the law was *"written for babies with the implied consent of mothers"*, felt that this was an irrelevance for the majority of adoption agencies. She also expressed concern for the lot of the putative father, a view shared by another who said:

> "As far as fathers go, if it's adoption at the parents' request we listen to the mother, we counsel the mother. We don't always press the issue of what the father might want. Social workers tend to say that putative fathers haven't got any rights. Well, they have, and adoption deprives them of them and quite often adoption happens without them knowing about it and that's wrong. Many putative fathers disappear over the hills and far away, but not all and the fact that some run away is no excuse for not knocking on doors and saying what's your view about it. They have the right to say they'll look after the child themselves."

(This view possibly conflicts with those expressed by some other practitioners who wre critical of judges whom they considered to be somewhat overzealous in their concern to seek out putative fathers. (See Part II, Chapter Seven.))

Other practioners doubted whether adoption could ever meet the needs of birth parents. Many were concerned at the apparent differences in interpretation of the legislation. For instance a social worker in Somerset cited the test of reasonableness as an example of what he meant:

"You read court appeals, judgements, that have found family A unreasonable in withholding their consent, and you'll read another case where the appeal has been upheld. It's down to interpretation. . . ."

A social worker in the Midlands regarded the process as "*respectful to birth parents*". However, there appeared to be a sting in the tail for she went on to say:

". . . In reality the dice are loaded against the parents. Quite often, we're acting a part in a play. You know the ending but parents in contested adoptions really believe their wishes and feelings are going to be taken into consideration. It's set up to treat people properly—it depends on the personalities involved as to how well the parents come out of it."

Several practitioners said they thought the odds were stacked against parents who were opposing.[3] A local authority solicitor in the Midlands thought it was very difficult for birth parents to challenge a freeing application because long term decisions had already been made. She said:

". . . I've no experience of representing parents, but it may all seem like a fait accompli. The applications are lodged and they are obviously faced with a Statement of Facts that goes back often over a large number of years, a barrage of this stuff, and they've suddenly got to oppose that. But quite how we change that when we've got the child at the forefront of our mind, when we've all got views as to what is best for that child, is very difficult."

Of major concern was the fact that so often birth parents were completely cut off from their child once the adoption order had been made. A solicitor who said he often thought about birth parents, was concerned by the "*finality*" of adoption for them; the adopted child at least had the opportunity on reaching eighteen years of age to find out "*who their birth parents were*". Some felt that matters would be improved if the birth parents had a built-in right to some kind of on-going information. As a social worker in Somerset said:

"I think it asks a lot of birth parents and older children to actually give up contact and offers them very little, nothing at all, in return. Even if there's no contact there might be some means of providing them with some information—if not regular information—at some stage in the child's life to give them reassurance. I'm sure a lot of natural parents would say that. If that choice were open to them they could of course choose themselves whether they wanted to take it up or not."

---

3   See Part I, section 2.15 of the Court Record Survey where analysis of data on contested cases in the court proforma sample suggested that contesting an application appears to have little effect on the outcome of the case, the vast majority of applications resulting in an order being made.

Another, in Birmingham, suggested that a *"central information exchange"* should be set up to which adoptive parents could be asked to send reports about the progress of the child. Then, if the birth parents wanted to know how their child was getting on that information could be made available to them. This would have been a great help to a birth mother in Devon who was having doubts about giving up her child for adoption. Her social worker went on:

> ". . . she (birth mother) said, when she was having doubts, she said I actually would be happy with giving up my baby but I would like to know perhaps once a year the baby is alright and growing well. It seemed such a simple request and both the other social worker and myself thought let's go ahead with that. When we actually came down to practical details, it was impossible for whatever reason, for administrative reasons, to actually accede to that and it seemed very unreasonable."

Again many felt that the provision of post adoption support was of pre-eminent importance. A social worker in Devon who was concerned about this thought that in general birth parents were *"damaged by giving up their child for adoption"*. Post adoption support was therefore vital for them. Perhaps this on-going need is well illustrated by the social worker who told us:

> ". . . In one case where a baby was adopted the child must now be about five years old. The mother still gets in touch with me. For example she came to see me after she had dreamt that the child had been drowned and she needed to put her mind at rest. I was able to assure her that the child was fine."

8.5.3   The needs of the adoptive parents

As we showed in Tables 8.3 and 8.4 above, the legislation was thought to best meet the needs of the adoptive parents and the practitioners' comments reflect this view. However, some reservations were expressed, the main one being the provision of post adoption support for them. Some practitioners thought that this should be available on a long term basis. It could be particularly valuable if the adoptee decided at eighteen plus to search for his/her birth parents. As a social worker in Devon put it:

> "We demand a lot from adopters—particularly childless adoptive parents where the motive to adopt is very much wrapped up with infertility—we trade on their possessiveness. We want them to offer this total commitment to a child and at the same time we say that they've got to very carefully sit down and explain to the child that he's not really theirs at all, and I'm not sure we help them enough with that. It's difficult because a lot of them get the adoption order and don't want a social worker to continue being around after that.

But I don't think we've got to grips with post-adoption support yet and offering it in a way that is meaningful beyond saying at the door of the court "if you ever need help . . ."."

Some other points were raised by solicitors. Adoptive parents: (i) should have sufficient access to information *"to enable them to bring up the child properly"*; (ii) should be *"looked at more closely in court"* to help determine their ability to care for the child; (iii) are not allowed to play an active part in contested cases, particularly in serial number cases, and should be enabled to do so.

8.6   Changes to the Freeing Provisions and Adoption Law

We asked practitioners if they would like to see changes made to the freeing for adoption provisions and adoption law. Many felt they did not have enough experience to say; others again related their answer to the process rather than to the law.

8.6.1   Freeing for Adoption Provisions

We summarise the points raised by practitioners.

(i)   Time limits should be built in to the legislation to enable the proceedings to be expedited. Practitioners felt it likely that the provisions would be used more often if delays inherent in the present proceedings could be drastically reduced.

(ii)   The Schedule II report may not be the most appropriate document for use as a "basis" for freeing? The Statement of Fact might be better.

(ii)   The Schedule II report may not be the most appropriate document for use as a "basis" for freeing. The Statement of Fact might be better.

(iv)   The termination of access issue should be dealt with by the same court and should be a part of the freeing proceedings which would help save time.

(v)   Freeing orders should allow for the provision of access to continue between the child and its birth family where appropriate.

(vi)   The rights of the child should have more weight than the test of reasonableness.

(vii)   The present test of the unreasonable parent is confusing and needs to be clarified.

(viii)   If not placed one year after the order is made, the child who had been the subject of a care order at the time the application was made should automatically become the subject of a care order again.

(ix)   The twelve month period to place the child after the order is made should be extended to eighteen months because it is not necessarily long enough for "hard-to-place" children. A report should be made to the birth parents after twelve months.

(x)   The procedure to revoke needs to be tightened up. As one local authority solicitor said, the present procedure is *"very airy fairy"*. The procedure to be followed is not clearly stipulated in the current legislation.

(xi)   Freeing applications for wards of court should be lodged in the county court, not the High Court.

8.6.2   Adoption law

One solicitor made it quite clear that he would not welcome any changes when he said:

> "For God's sake don't change any more law. We've got to know it—keep the set of laws. I am fed up with the law being changed day after day so that none of us can keep up with it . . . Six months with no legislation whatsoever. Give us all time."

However, his view contrasts with those of many other practitioners who did make suggestions for change. These are summarised below.

(i)   There is a need for time scales to be built in to proceedings. A solicitor in the South West voiced the thoughts of many practitioners when he said:

> "I don't see any reason why we shouldn't be completing an adoption application within the same sort of time structure as you complete a care case. I don't see any reason why, if the Social Services have got the information—which they should have if it's gone through the agency—you shouldn't be able to complete an adoption application in three months subject, of course, to the natural parents. In a case that's "properly" contested then that would extend it. But one where you've just got nominal non-consent I don't see any reason why you couldn't do it in three months.
>
> As I said earlier, there should be automatic reviews at certain intervals during the process. They are tending to do that in wardship now. The court locally will not adjourn proceedings generally but will always adjourn it for another directions

hearing in say, two months' time. So it's always coming up for review. It shouldn't be too difficult to set up a system."

(ii) Solicitors should have an automatic right of access to all reports such as Schedule II reports and guardian ad litem reports.

(iii) The Schedule II report should be made available to adoptive parents. parents.

(iv) The legislation needs to be more flexible; it should discriminate between the different types of adoption such as step parent adoptions, baby adoptions, older children adoptions, etc. As a social worker in Somerset said:

> ". . . they are all very different but all subject to the same rather inflexible procedure and some outcomes and consequences. So I think more flexibility really. It makes me feel like a kind of bureaucrat really—going through a process which very often I find is quite irrelevant to the actual situation I'm dealing with."

This flexibility should extend to same race placements. A Devon social worker explained:

> "Also I think we have to be realistic about trans-racial and international adoption. I would hate to see a child be deprived of the benefit of a family life just because we can't get one of the same racial group. Race is like other things— you aim for the rooftops. You are not going to get perfect adopters. By aiming for the very very best you can miss out on something that is quite good enough."

(v) The law should stipulate that only experienced social workers (equivalent to approved social workers in mental health cases) should undertake adoption work.

(vi) The procedure should be more child-focused. A solicitor in Birmingham explained:

> ". . . I think a child's wishes and feelings and a child's cultural and ethnic background, that should be in the Act. Not in any kind of rules, or in any kind of case or social work policy document—it should be in the Act."

(vii) The checklist on the grounds for dispensing with parental agreement akin to those under Section 1(3) in the Children Act 1989 should include for example:

(1) Wishes and feelings of children
(2) Physical, emotional and educational needs
(3) Age, sex, background, any characteristics

(4)   Cultural and ethnic background

(5)   Capability of parents

(6)   Any harm which the child has suffered and so on

(viii)   Adoption proceedings should not be separate from other proceedings. For example one solicitor said:

> "If you have a wardship judge hearing a whole case he ought to be able to make a freeing order."

(ix)   It should be possible to issue High Court proceedings locally in district registries. One solicitor added that he would be inclined *"to get rid of the Official Solicitor completely"*.

(x)   Children's attendance at the hearing should be dispensed with unless they wish to be there.

8.7   Comment

Arising from the views the social workers expressed about the legal process concerning freeing to adopt and adoption, we ask:

8.7.1   Freeing

(i)   Is freeing used in the way in which it was intended?

(ii)   Should any changes be made to the freeing provisions/process?

(iii) Should the freeing provisions be maintained?

8.7.2   Adoption

(i)   Is adoption law/process too inflexible, for example regarding ongoing access, marital status of prospective adopters, age of prospective adopters?

(ii)   Does adoption law meet the needs of the child, the birth parents, the adoptive parents?

(iii) Should any changes be made to the adoption law/process?

CHAPTER 9   # Open Adoption

9.1   Introduction

9.2   The Practitioners' Views About Open Adoption

9.3   Practitioners' Experience of Openness in Practice

9.4   Implications for Practice and Legislation

9.5   Comment

9.1   Introduction

Under the Adoption Act 1976, it is possible to attach conditions to an adoption order (S. 12/6), formally setting out access arrangements or some kind of on-going contact between the adopted child and members of its birth family. The Children Act 1989, s. 8, makes provision for a contact order to be added to an adoption order and also to a freeing order. Contact could mean anything from the exchange of letters or cards on special occasions such as birthdays and Christmas, to enabling the child to have staying access.

Orders made with conditions attached are something of a rarity, a fact confirmed by the data collected in the Court Record Survey. An examination of applications for adoption (excluding freeing) in the mini record sample revealed that where an order was made the vast majority (89%) had no condition attached to the order. In very few cases (1%) was an adoption order granted with conditions attached. (See Table 2.9 in Part I of this report). These findings tend to reinforce a "traditional" approach to adoption in that, once the order has been made, the child severs connections with members of its birth family.

Despite the lack of formal arrangements, there is some evidence to suggest that informal arrangements are made, as Thoburn and Rowe reported in 1988.[1] The on-going contact they encountered was not necessarily in the form of visits between the child and its birth family members, but perhaps in exchanging letters and cards from time to time. Such arrangements were made in only a very small proportion of the cases they studied. Data from the Court Record Survey lends some support to their findings. Fratter (1989)[2] also reported on cases where openness had been involved.

Information from the court proforma sample showed that at the time the application was made, 1% of children in adoption cases had contact with their birth mother, compared with 28% of children being freed. In the adoption cases the contact was most likely to occur with older children, (10–18 years old). In the freeing cases 12% of babies had contact with their mother compared with 37% of children aged between one and five and 50% between 5 and 10 years of age. 1% of children involved in adoption had contact with their father whilst 16% had contact in the freeing cases, (although it should be remembered that whether or not the child is legitimate may have some bearing on contact).

There was some contact with maternal grandparents (3%) in adoption cases, less with paternal grandparents (1%). In the freeing cases about 2% had contact with their maternal or paternal grandparents. As for contact

1   Thoburn J and Rowe J (1988), *"A Snapshot of Permanent Family Placements"*, Adoption and Fostering, 12.3.

2   Fratter, J (1989) *"Family Placement and Access: Achieving Permanency for Children in Contact with Birth Parents."* Barnardos

with siblings, in adoption cases 9% had contact, and the older the child the more likely it was that contact occurred. Nineteen per cent had contact with siblings in the freeing group; again the older the child the more likely it was that contact occurred. It should be noted that a proportion of those siblings would be living in the same households as part of a sibling group placement.

Once the order had been granted the contact decreased. Contact with the birth mother continued in 1% of adoption cases and 3% of freeing cases. However in 30% of the freeing cases it was not clear from the information available whether or not contact continued. The contact with fathers was less than 1% in adoption cases and 2% in freeing. There was no contact with paternal grandparents, whilst in 2% of the adoption cases some contact with maternal grandparents was maintained. Sibling contact was more frequent, with 7% of children in adoption cases having contact, (this does not include 8% of children who lived in the same household with their siblings) and 4% in freeing, although again in 25% of the freeing cases no definite information about sibling contact was available.

A more open approach to adoption has evolved in other parts of the world, most notably in New Zealand where "some form of on-going contact between the birth family and the adoptive family is the norm[3]". The on-going contact can range from the exchange of photographs through to visits between the child and members of its birth family. Corcoran[4], in discussing research into the development of openness in adoption there which was undertaken by Clare Dominik, notes

> "Our experience, now supported by research, is that information carefully given is never harmful, and that meetings between birth parents and adoptive parents, carefully prepared for, are positively beneficial to both parties."

In Australia the possibility of open adoptions is recognised in the State of Victoria, where the Department of Community Services has provided information for the period 1988–89 showing that 42% of healthy baby adoptions involved access, 27% information exchange only and 31% neither access nor information exchange. For children with special needs the figures were 80%, 7% and 13% respectively and for children in permanent care 61%, 3% and 35% respectively.[5]

The issue of openness in adoption in this country has taken on a greater significance in recent years given the way adoption has changed. For example, an increasing number of older children, many of whom will have been in care, are now being adopted. Many of these are likely to have an

3   France, Ellen *Inter-Departmental Review of Adoption Law*, Background Paper No. 1, *International Perspectives*, Department of Health, September 1990.

4   Corcoran A, "*Open Adoption*" 1988, *Adoption and Fostering* No. 3.

5   France, Ellen, op. cit.

established and significant relationship with their birth family members, for instance with birth parents, siblings and grandparents. There has also been an increase in the number of children with special needs who are being adopted. This change, together with growing trends abroad towards a more open approach, has led those involved in adoption in this country to question the part openness could play in the future. It is an issue, too, which the Inter-Departmental Review on Adoption Law is currently considering.

For these reasons we took the opportunity to explore with social workers and solicitors their views on openness in adoption. From their comments the following points emerged:

(i)   practitioners are ambivalent about open adoption;

(ii)   open adoption may be more suitable for older adopted children than for babies who are adopted;

(iii)   the provision of pre-adoption and post-adoption support would be vital to the success of openness, possibly necessitating some legislative changes too.

9.2   The Practitioners' Views about Open Adoption

Social workers were asked what they thought about the principle of open adoption which had been recommended in some recent cases. A third (33%) reacted positively, 11% negatively. Just over half (54%) responded positively and negatively. The remainder (2%) had no view.

We did not ask the same question of the solicitors. However, when we asked them whether or not they had any experience of cases where access had continued after an order had been made, some expressed a "general" view about open adoption.

It was clear from the practitioners' response that open adoption was a subject of great concern to them but one with which they found it difficult to grapple. Some had very clear views for or against but most expressed a great deal of ambivalence.

9.2.1   The principle of open adoption

There was much support for the view that the principle of open adoption was *"worth pursuing"*, though it was acknowledged that it represented a *"tremendous challenge"* to the existing system. A social worker in a voluntary agency in the Midlands said:

> "I think we are all in favour of the children and the families having contact with the past. I think that most specialist adoption workers would be of similar mind, that contact with birth families, previous carers, siblings, grandparents, whatever, should be taken on board certainly at the time when the children and new families are introduced and shortly thereafter . . ."

But it was stressed by others that a flexible approach was necessary because each case was different and needed to be assessed individually:

> "You don't have a blueprint on this because every human situation is different and each situation has got to be tailored to suit the situation. . . . I suppose what I'm looking for is flexibility and sensitivity about the needs of all the parties concerned. . . ."

An individual approach was important since in some instances no more than some kind of regular *"information exchange between families—perhaps photographs, and cards on special occasions"* would be appropriate, whereas for others some kind of visiting or even staying access would be appropriate.

The "traditional" assumption that access should nearly always be terminated on adoption was seen by many as a *"hangover from the past"*, when the majority of those adopted were babies. One social worker went on to explain:

> "But I think now that we are beginning to look at adoption for a far wider age range of children we have to take on board the fact that these children have got a considerable life experience prior to coming into care and prior to being adopted—not all of which is bad and they should be protected from."

But others expressed some anxiety at what they saw as a growing trend towards open adoption which they feared might be no more than *"the flavour of the month"*. Several solicitors voiced their concern. For instance:

> I can't in my heart quite accept the theory of actual access of staying and seeing because it goes against the whole principle of adoption which is to take over the parental rights of that child. I find it difficult to accept although I know there are moves towards it."

Some regarded adoption with access as equivalent to long term fostering, the only difference being that the *"adopters have the legal papers"*. One solicitor was perturbed by the prospect and asked, *"If you're willing to have open adoption, why have adoption at all?"*

Many practitioners, whilst accepting the concept to some degree, were adamant that it would be totally inappropriate in vigorously opposed cases and positively dangerous in others:

> "If you had a very nasty contested case with distressed natural parents who don't want to lose their children it would be difficult to

envisage how that might work constructively in the future although, having said that, one of the reasons why they might be so distressed is because they know they are not going to see their child."

9.2.2   Implications for the child

There was little support for on-going contact in baby adoptions, especially where access had been virtually non-existent from the time of birth. The practitioners felt that the child could be very confused, as one put it, *"by having loyalty to two parts of the triangle."*

As a social worker in the South West said:

> "If you want to look at the philosophy of open adoption for babies I think you need to start now and perhaps in four or five years time be considering it seriously. To be considering it now without the appropriate preparation, thought and philosophy behind one—I think you're into very crystal ball stuff, too much risk. . . ."

However, there was far stronger support amongst practitioners for an open approach being considered for the older child, who may well have established a bond with members of the birth family prior to the adoption. As one said:

> "I'm all in favour personally. I think especially for older children it's very hard to cut off somebody from their family where bonds have been made and where really significant relationships have been established and then expect a child to bond with another family as though nothing had gone before and then expect them to feel that's right. If we are looking for what is in the child's best interests, is it right to cut them off . . .?"

Another spoke for the abused older child:

> "I used to think it was crass stupidity even to consider it but the more I work with damaged children the more I think it is worthy of consideration and more research."

A social worker in Birmingham who viewed the principle as *"very sound"* also raised the point that keeping in touch with a birth parent in some way could help to prevent the child from developing *"fantasies about what a birth parent is like"*.

This social worker went on to stress the importance of maintaining contact with siblings whenever appropriate. She thought that would be *"workable in most cases"*, a view shared by many practitioners. A social worker in Somerset advocated sibling contact even in those instances where the sibling relationship did not appear to be particularly good or meaningful, since she felt it was difficult to measure such relationships, many of which can, on the face of it, appear quite hostile.

Another was anxious to ensure that wherever possible in cases where two or more siblings were to be placed for adoption, ideally they should be placed together. She pointed out that if a child is separated from its siblings at placement then its adult relationships are diminished.

Some practitioners foresaw problems with openness once the adopted child reached adolescence. A social worker who felt that adopted children would be confused by on-going contact with the birth family said:

> "I think apart from confusing them, it could also add problems in adolescence when all children go through the problems of hating their parents and wanting to go somewhere else and if there's another family waiting in the wings, what better? So it could actually disrupt the adoptive placement at that stage. . . ."

This could be likened to the children of divorced parents some of whom may move between their two families during adolescence particularly.

Many of those who took a positive view were influenced by the counselling work they had undertaken with adoptees who, on reaching the age of eighteen, were anxious to trace their birth family. A social worker in a voluntary agency said:

> "Why go to the trouble of terminating access, weaning the child away from its (natural) family and then at fourteen/fifteen/sixteen years of age you've got to build it all up again. It's an awful process weaning that child to accept separation and get used to a new family. . . ."

She felt that children would be better able to cope if they had some kind of contact with their birth family. Another social worker had seen the effects on adoptees who had been totally cut off from their birth families and she thought there was probably more to be gained than to be lost if some contact, such as exchange of information, was maintained since this would help to ease the process of making actual contact at eighteen plus, if the adoptee so desired.

On the other hand, some felt that eighteen plus was quite soon enough for adoptees to start finding out more about their birth family. One social worker who was herself adopted, said she would have been very confused by any contact with her birth family prior to the age of eighteen, up to which time the life-story book had been adequate to answer her questions about her family.

9.2.3   Implications for the birth parents

Some practitioners thought it would be a great help to the birth mothers in particular if some kind of contact was maintained. In the first instance, knowing something about where the child was placed and perhaps meeting the adopters could be very healing for them and help them to cope with their bereavement.

Subsequently, providing the birth mother with some information about the child's progress and possibly giving her a photograph from time to time could be enormously helpful and comforting to her. Several social workers said that they were occasionally contacted by anxious birth mothers. One mentioned a mother who dreamt that her adopted child had been drowned. She went to the social worker for re-assurance that all was well. Another had been visited by a mother when her adopted child's birthday was approaching. She talked about her feelings and anxieties at some length and said she would feel better able to come to terms with the situation if she could be informed about the child's well-being from time to time.

9.2.4   Implications for the adopters

Those who recognised the advantages in some kind of continuing contact in appropriate cases felt that even so it was asking a lot of the adopters. For many this would be a threat to their security, causing them stress and anxiety. A solicitor could not envisage many prospective adopters wanting to take on a child *"with strings attached"*. Another who had thought long and hard about the issue of open adoption, had never come across adoptive parents who were prepared to say they would *"welcome the birth parent visiting"*. Indeed, practitioners felt that adopters saw the birth parents as the greatest threat amongst the birth family members although they might more readily agree to consider on-going contact with siblings and grandparents. Foster parents who went on to adopt their foster child were considered most likely to be able to cope with openness, since some would simply be continuing or adjusting the arrangements that had existed during the period of fostering.

One social worker, whilst acknowledging that contact with the birth parents could be threatening to the adopters, felt that there could be advantages for them too:

> "That's a very threatening thing for the adopters—thinking they (birth parents) might come round, knock on the door, drive up and down the street. But I'm sure it would make adopters feel more comfortable if they didn't feel that there was someone looking over their shoulder but could be reconciled to it and could also pass that image on to the child later on. . . ."

Another social worker who was an advocate of open adoption spoke with first hand knowledge of the anxieties continuing contact with the birth family can cause adoptive parents. She was herself in the throes of adopting her foster child and worked with and kept contact with the child's family:

"I think for the child it's very, very good indeed. She knows where she is, who her family are. She's got a very clear idea of herself in terms of who she is and where she comes from. But as far as I'm concerned, even with the skills and knowledge and the fact that I've known the birth family for years, there are times when you approach a visit to grandparents or a visit to brother or sister with a sinking heart and all of your professional training—what you do every day of the week— doesn't impinge on that at all. You still feel it. And I wonder what sort of adopters we are going to get and what sort of massive amount of training—there has to be an acknowledgement of that. For me that should be a comfortable situation, but I have to acknowledge as an adopter it isn't, which makes me aware of where our families are going to be in this. There needs to be an acknowledgement that however much training you put in you are not going to take that sinking feeling away."

9.3 Practitioners' Experience of Openness in Practice

Several practitioners had experience of cases where contact of some kind had been maintained on an informal basis. The examples which follow reflect the views expressed above.

9.3.1   In the first example, a social worker describes a case in which the local authority accepted the need for the child to have continuing contact with her brother, but in so doing ruled out adoption as an option for that child.

"I know of a case that has just been turned down because the child wanted to be adopted by her foster parents. She'd been sexually abused by her father but her brother was still living with his parents. Social Services wanted access to continue with the brother and the girl. It was decided that adoption wasn't in her best interests because of the residual link with her brother. It's changed into long-term fostering which I think is an awful shame."

9.3.2   Next a practitioner describes a case in which the adopters had said that they would be willing to meet the birth mother, but the child's social worker felt that this might result in a disruption of the placement, a conclusion which the interviewee regretted and felt to be a possible reflection of the social worker's resistance to the idea of open adoption:

"I had a case that went to court last week after a wait of 15 months. The child's mother—who'd got a long history of violence—prison sentence—has actually asked to see the adopters. The adopters would be more than happy to meet her but the child's social worker has vetoed it because she said the birth mother might go and disrupt the placement at the moment. It's sad really. Very sad."

Another social worker reported a case in which four adopted siblings maintained access with their paternal grandparents. The family moved away from the parent authority and the adopters, who were enthusiastic about the access, went to considerable trouble and expense to ensure that it continued despite the distance between them created by the move. The social worker said he had a lot of trouble getting the parent authority to agree to the access.

9.3.3   In another case the birth mother of the child had died quite suddenly four weeks after his birth. The maternal grandparents did not feel able to care for the child themselves, but did not wish to lose contact with him either. The social worker described what happened:

> "The grandparents didn't feel able to take on the child. They thought for a long time—they were both in their fifties—and very very reluctantly decided they couldn't take on this child but it grieved them a lot to know that they would never know about him again, so we talked to the adoptive couple and since then every birthday, every Christmas, they send photographs and write to the grandparents who in turn send gifts to the child. So we've kept that up for eight years. The adopters are living abroad but are coming back to live in England permanently and have offered to take the child to see his grandparents. But the grandparents are taking a long time to make up their minds; they can't decide whether they can do it or not. It's been wonderful. The adoptive mother writes the most wonderful letters describing what the child has been doing."

9.3.4   A social worker described a case concerning a baby with Downs Syndrome. She felt that had the birth parents been assured from the outset that open adoption was a realistic possibility, a lot of trouble could have been spared. She felt it had been an ideal case for an open adoption:

> "It involved a little boy with Downs syndrome. His parents felt totally unable to cope with what they saw as a multi-handicapped child. It wasn't really going to be that but they just rejected him on that basis. He was placed with short-term foster parents whilst the parents decided whether or not they felt able to care for him. They didn't want to give him up completely for adoption and they didn't want to lose him and they didn't feel able to care for him themselves which ultimately led us to possibly having to go for a freeing order. We didn't because in the end they reluctantly agreed to adoption. They actually met the adoptive parents and asked if they would keep them informed at Christmas and birthdays of how the little baby was progressing. But I think all difficulties in that case would have all been resolved if the natural parents had known that they could once a year or whenever have seen their child and maintained much more contact with him."

9.3.5   Another case concerned an older child who was in care. The social worker who told us about it stressed the importance of not dismissing the child's life before he was taken into care as a totally bad experience: some aspects of his life had been good and this was reflected by the fact that access between the child and his mother appeared to work well. The social worker explained:

> "We are talking about an excellent foster home. The child needs the security of adoption—he wants to be absorbed into this family—but he is also aware that he has a mum who lives ten miles away whom he has been seeing every two weeks. Access seems to work for both of them, but both he and his mum have accepted that she cannot change sufficiently within his time spans to allow her to resume full-time care. That child is a ward of court, and I went to [. . .] High Court in May and put forward the concept of an open adoption, to which the judge is being quite receptive at the moment. He has given the freeing order; he has also recorded in his judgement that he thinks that the child's needs would be for an open but defined access order to be made with the adoption."

9.3.6   A social worker in a voluntary agency described the case of a child whose mother had died, and the efforts the agency had made to maintain contact between the child and her six half brothers and sisters:

> "She was one of seven children and they'd gone separate ways. The children had different fathers. She was a mixed parentage child and some of the others were white, others were a different mix. We set up six monthly meetings of all the children and again I think that is valuable. We do that at Thomas Coram in London. Some of the others have been adopted, some are in children's homes. The two oldest are in foster care. They're about 16 and 14. All the adopters and the children meet up. From my adopters' point of view, it's more beneficial for the other children who were very much left to look after the younger ones when their mum was ill. There is quite a bond between the older ones and the one we placed. They've suggested the older ones come and stay at weekends occasionally."

9.3.7   Finally a social worker described how continuing contact between an adoptee and her father had helped her when she was older:

> "Very many years ago, I placed a girl who was five. Her mum was dead. She's nineteen now. Her father maintained contact amd eventually broke it, when she was about twelve. She recently got in touch with me because she wanted to talk about dad—and mum. It was much easier for her because he had kept in touch. The adopters felt it was no threat."

9.4 Implications for Practice and Legislation

Several practitioners said that a developing trend towards open adoption would have implications for practice and legislation.

Many felt that as a start individual practitioners needed to move away from the "traditional" concept of adoption by allowing their attitude to develop and grow with the changing needs. A solicitor in the West Country put it this way:

> "In my personal view the child's natural parents are one of its most important resources in its life. . . . We've got this notion of adoption that it's a final curtain and it's in the interests of the child to have its links with the past severed otherwise it won't develop properly. I'm not sure that I agree with that myself. . . . I think that overall we ought to question the way in which we bring up children . . . and see there's nothing wrong with having an adoptive father and a natural father and an adoptive mother and a natural mother etc. and wider relatives of both adoptive and natural . . . because quite often you find a case where you might have natural grandparents who just never get to see their child . . ."

In developing a more positive approach to the possibility of open adoption themselves, practitioners would be better able to help the parties involved to do likewise. A social worker in the Midlands explained:

> "A big issue in open adoption is that we are so brought up with the idea that adopters don't have to deal with continued access that we don't sell it to them very positively at the moment when we are training them. So what we are getting a lot of is 'I can cope with this child being in touch with siblings who might have been adopted by other people and I can just about cope with the idea that when Johnny is 18 he might want to seek out his natural family', but what nobody at the moment will jump at is having anything to do with the natural parents. It's all part of us not selling it very competently. We have to pass on confidence whereas at the moment we are allowing them to shut off."

It was recognised that in cases where open adoption was being considered it was crucial that from the outset prospective adopters were made aware of this. Careful preparation and the right degree of support and reassurance could do much to ease the anxieties that on-going contact can produce. One social worker described a case in which she felt that better preparation work with the adopters at the outset would have enabled them to cope with the subsequent developments. She said:

> "I've got a little girl with a family at the moment. We've had a lot of ups and downs with her. At a recent session with a psychologist and social worker we got out a picture of her birth mother and she was

absolutely delighted and the adopters are finding it quite hard. You know—the bad people who didn't look after her and we've done our best—and now she's absolutely thrilled. She's seven and she's been with the adopters for nearly two years. It's very important to her but hard for the adopters."

Several practitioners said that for open adoption to work the birth parents, too, would need to be prepared and counselled before the order was made. Post adoption counselling for birth parents, adoptive parents and the child would play a vital part in its continuing success. Later on, if the child or the birth parents felt they wished to withdraw from any arrangements that had been made, then support offered by post adoption counsellors would help them to do so.

A social worker with a lot of experience of cases involving on-going contact, whilst recognising pre and post adoption support to be essential, said that in her experience maintaining successful contact depended to a large extent on the goodwill of those concerned.

"I think open adoption has always happened and certainly I've been instrumental in many cases where adopters have had on-going contact with birth parents for years—on an informal basis—by choice, goodwill. I think we've learned enough through the divorce courts to know that contact can only work successfully with the goodwill of the parties involved and there is no way that agencies can dictate goodwill. It's about preparing the families but it is also about not burdening those families too much. I'm very well aware the sorts of children we are placing who have been grossly abused—they are never going to be normal families. . . . I can see that the new Children's Bill is addressing that issue to some degree. But it doesn't matter what law exists. If the practice isn't good enough, it isn't good enough."

Some social workers felt that, whilst the legislation made provision for the possibility of open adoption, it was important that it also included some kind of provision enabling the parties to return to court if any problems arose. A social worker in the Midlands said:

"We don't want the pendulum to swing too much the other way either and risk undermining the adoption placement. Adoption has built-in instabilities anyway. Bringing up children is a huge task even if you set out with all the advantages. Adoption is an extra task over and above that. It requires a lot of commitment and thought and care to steer through some of the issues that are going to arise throughout a child's upbringing. So there are more tasks involved over and above those of bringing up natural children. An adoptive child goes through self-questioning and the sensation of having a bit of jigsaw missing and wanting to either find it, or understand it and grasp it. Now if you can do that most effectively by having contact or access then maybe that would actually lead to better adoptions. But it's a delicate thing and you could be screwing it up completely if mismanaged. That's why the legislation has got to get it right and safeguards have to be built in and the means to go back to a higher authority, to the courts."

9.5 Comment

Having considered the practitioners' comments on open adoption we ask:

(i)   Should some kind of on-going contact be more routinely considered for older children who already have an established bond with their birth parents and/or other family members?

(ii)   Should ways and means to be found to provide birth mothers in particular with periodic progress reports about their child after adoption?

(iii)   If provision is made for open adoption, what kind of supportive arrangements would be needed for children, birth parents and adopters?

CHAPTER 10   Remaining Issues

10.1   Introduction

10.2   Separate Representation for Children

10.3   Guardians ad Litem in Uncontested Cases

10.4   Legal Representation for Guardians ad Litem

10.5   Distinctive Roles of Reporting Officer and Guardian ad Litem

10.6   Ascertaining the Child's Wishes and Feelings

10.7   Comment

10.1 Introduction

In the preceding chapters of Part II of this Report, we have presented an account of those issues and obstacles concerning the freeing and adoption process which were most frequently mentioned by the practitioners and which appeared to be of particular concern to them. However, there were some other issues that arose during the interviews which we think it would be helpful to report here even though the practitioners did not have quite so much to say about them. They concern:

(i)   whether children should be separately represented in freeing/adoption;

(ii)   whether a guardian ad litem should be appointed in uncontested cases;

(iii)   whether guardians ad litem should be legally represented;

(iv)   whether it is necessary to have the distinctive roles of reporting officer and guardian ad litem;

(v)   whether the wishes and feelings of the child are ascertained.

10.2 Separate Representation for children

We asked both the social workers and the solicitors: *"Should children be separately represented by a lawyer in freeing and adoption proceedings?"* We give their response in Table 10.1 below:

Table 10.1
Whether children should be separately represented in:

(a)   Freeing

	Social Workers			Solicitors		
	No.	**(%)**		**No.**	**(%)**	
Yes	23	(44)}		8	(33)}	
Yes—if contested	13	(25)}	69%	–	–}	50%
Yes—older children	–	–}		4	(17)}	
No	6	(11)}		8	(33)}	
No—if GAL appointed	–	–}	11%	1	(4)}	37%
Other	5	(10)		3	(13)	
Don't Know	5	(10)		–	–	
ALL	**52**	**(100)**		**24**	**(100)**	

(b)   *Adoption*

	Social Workers			Solicitors		
	No.	(%)		No.	(%)	
Yes	19	(37)}		4	(17)}	
Yes—if contested	16	(31)}	68%	–	–}	34%
Yes—older children	–	–}		4	(17)}	
No	9	(17)}	17%	10	(42)}	46%
No—if GAL appointed	–	–}		1	(4)}	
Other	5	(10)		3	(12)	
Don't Know	3	(5)		2	(8)	
ALL	**52**	**(100)**		**24**	**(100)**	

One of the local authority solicitors said separate representation was necessary in both freeing and adoption cases; three said it was unnecessary in both types of case and one did not know.

The figures suggest that solicitors felt that it was more important that children should be separately represented in freeing cases than in adoption cases. A greater proportion of social workers than solicitors considered separate representation to be more necessary in both freeing and adoption cases.

Amongst those practitioners who thought that separate representation was necessary, several mentioned the importance of keeping, and the need to keep, separate the child's interests from those of the birth parents. As one put it, under the present system *"the child inevitably gets logged with the (birth) parents"*. A social worker who was on a panel of guardians ad litem also said that from the guardian ad litem's point of view separate representation would be useful

> ". . . because if you do go against the local authority it's just you, your feelings. You're not backed up by any lawyer, solicitor, whatsoever."

Others were concerned that *"nobody listens to the children"*. One solicitor said that he always made a point of interviewing children who were old enough to have some understanding of what was happening. Others who felt the same stressed that a lawyer *"should always argue the case on behalf of the child"* because in that way the best interests of the child were safeguarded.

Those practitioners who considered separate representation to be unnecessary felt that it might only complicate things and make the process more adversarial. One solicitor said *"there are enough parties looking at the case without having another lawyer shoved in"*.

10.3   Guardians ad litem in Uncontested Cases

We asked the social workers: *"Should there be a guardian ad litem in uncontested cases?"* and the solicitors: *"Should there be a guardian ad litem in cases where parental agreement has been given?"* Table 10.2 below shows their response.

Table 10.2

Whether there should be a guardian ad litem in uncontested cases or cases where parental agreement has been given

	Social Workers			Solicitors		
	No.	(%)		No.	(%)	
Yes	5	(10)}	20%	4	(17)}	46%
Yes—ensures checks/ safeguard	5	(10)}		7	(29)}	
No	14	(27)}		6	(25)}	
No—RO fulfils task	10	(19)}	65%	1	(4)}	29%
No—built in safeguards in process	10	} (19)}		–	} –}	
Yes and No	–	–		4	(17)	
Other	3	(5)		–	–	
Don't Know	5	(10)		2	(8)	
ALL	**52**	**(100)**		**24**	**(100)**	

Three of the local authority solicitors thought a guardian ad litem should be appointed. Two took the opposite view.

These figures suggest that the solicitors (46%) felt much more strongly than the social workers (20%) that a guardian ad litem should be appointed in uncontested cases. Nearly half the social workers (46%) thought it unnecessary compared with just over a quarter of the solicitors (29%).

The reasons given in support of the need for a guardian ad litem in uncontested cases were: the interests of the children, birth parents and adopters would be served by having an independent view; guardians ad litem could bring a certain objectivity to the case, something that social workers embroiled in it might find a little difficult; guardians ad litem would provide a necessary check to the high standard of work essential to adoption.

The reasons against the appointment of a guardian ad litem were: the reporting officer adequately fulfilled the task of conveying the implications of adoption to the birth parents; the appointment of yet another person could add to the birth parents' distress by making it even more difficult for them to cope with the system.

It might be helpful to note here that a guardian ad litem was appointed in ten of the specific cases about which we interviewed social workers. In only one of these did the recommendation of the guardian ad litem differ from that of the social worker.

10.4   Legal Representation for Guardians ad Litem

The solicitors were asked whether they thought guardians ad litem should be legally represented in all courts. A third of those in private practice said they should be whilst almost two-thirds (63%) said they should not. The remainder did not know. One local authority thought they should be, one did not. Another said it should be a matter of choice for the guardians ad litem. The response of the other two local authority solicitors was not recorded.

Most solicitors took the view that guardians ad litem were more than capable of "standing up for themselves", some adding that the guardian ad litem's experience of adoption was likely to be greater than that of some solicitors.

10.5   Distinctive Roles of Reporting Officer and Guardian ad Litem

Solicitors in private practice were asked whether they thought it was necessary to have the distinctive roles of reporting officer and guardian ad litem. The majority (63%) did not think it was necessary, but 12% thought it was. A further 12% said they were unable to answer the question because they were not clear about the distinction between these roles. The rest did not know. Three of the five local authorities could not see the necessity for distinctive roles. The others took the contrary view.

Some solicitors saw value in keeping the roles distinct whilst others felt that if the parents changed their minds about agreeing to the application, it made sense for the original reporting officer to take on the role of the guardian ad litem. This would have the probable advantage of averting the delay that might ensue whilst a different person was found and appointed to act as guardian ad litem.

10.6   Ascertaining the Child's Wishes and Feelings

Given that the interests of the child are of paramount importance in freeing and adoption proceedings, we wanted to know whether practitioners saw it as part of their role to ascertain the child's wishes and feelings and, if not, whether anyone else did so. We therefore asked both the social workers and the solicitors a series of questions concerning these matters related to the specific case with which they had been involved in the Court Record Survey.

10.6.1   Practitioners' Role Regarding Child's Wishes And Feelings

Firstly, we asked the practitioners whether they regarded it as a part of their role to ascertain what the child's wishes and feelings were about his/her situation. Over two-thirds of the social workers (70%) explained that in the specific case the child was too young to do so. Of the remainder, 19% said they did see it as part of their role, 4% that it was not. The rest were unsure. Nearly half the solicitors (46%) said the child in the specific case was too young. Of the remainder, 14% saw it as part of their role, but 29% did not. The rest were unsure.

These figures suggest that if the child is old enough, social workers are more likely than solicitors to regard it as a part of their role to ascertain the child's wishes and feelings.

Many solicitors pointed out that if they were, say, acting for the applicants, they were therefore representing them; that did not include the child. They saw ascertaining the child's wishes and feelings more as a role for the guardian ad litem. One made the point that different skills were required to interview children and he did not think it was appropriate for him to "*play the role of social worker*". He fel that ultimately it was the duty of the judge to take into account the child's wishes depending, of course, upon the child's age. Another solicitor said that if he had any doubts about the case concerning the child he would bring in an independent social worker.

10.6.2   Whether The Child's Views Differed From Those of The Practitioners

In the few cases where the social worker and, to a lesser extent, the solicitor, had endeavoured to ascertain the child's wishes and feelings, we asked if the child's view had differed from their own. One of the social workers and one of the solicitors reported a difference of view. In each of these instances the child was old enough to have formed an attachment to his birth family. One of the social workers said:

> "They're people. Most children have a tremendous loyalty to the parent who has cared for them from birth. Whereas as an adult I'd be very paternal and say that in the child's long term interest it wouldn't be appropriate for the child to stay with the natural parent,

that child vehemently wants to stay, even though it gets beaten or sexually abused or whatever."

And another said however much the professional input in a case, you could not *"take away the child's right to care for its parent"*.

Others spoke in general about the difficulties they encountered. For instance, one social worker was in the process of finding a home for a "difficult child" with behavioural problems. The child had declared *"I'd like a family just like the one I've got!"* Another spoke of the conflict between the need for the social worker to act in what s/he considers to be the best interests of the child and what the child him/herself considers to be in their best interests. She went on:

> "An example of this—a black child says to me as a black social worker, "I want to be with a white family". I understand what the child is saying, but their reason for saying it I would not see as in the child's best interest. There are children who have been in the care system who see a white family as better than a black family and who see white as being good. I've been dealing with children who've hated me for being black. They're black children of course but they've said "I don't like him because he's black". They would want to be with a white family. This is a real situation. So it's all about self image, identity, self esteem, feeling O.K. about themselves and so on."

10.6.3   Who Explained Adoption To The Child

We asked the social workers whether they or anyone else had explained the meaning of adoption to the child in the specific case. In nearly three-quarters of the cases (74%) the child was too young, but in the remainder it was either the social worker we interviewed, the child's social worker, the foster parent, or a combination of these. A few solicitors "assumed" that the guardian ad litem had explained the meaning of adoption to the child.

The social workers felt that a few of the children to whom adoption had been explained understood the meaning of it, but felt it was difficult to know whether the rest had done so. One said:

> "I don't think so. She was more interested in the ice-cream van. She was very interested in her black shoes. I mean, classic. But she did understand the concept of a new mum and dad. "I'm going to belong to somebody." She had a favourite bear. I said, "just like you like that bear, they're going to like you." How do you work with little children? I can only hope she understood."

10.7   Comment

On the basis of the practitioners' response there would appear to be some justification for re-considering whether children's interests would be better served if they were parties to the proceedings and could be separately represented in freeing and adoption. This is only possible in the High Court at present.

For the same reason we also wonder whether consideration should be given to appointing guardians ad litem in all cases, whether contested or not. This might be important, given that some practitioners see it as a part of a guardian ad litem's role to provide an independent check for the child and also, where the child is old enough, to ascertain his/her wishes and feelings about their situation.

An argument could be made for the need for some kind of passage agent for the child, someone who would act as 'children's friend' throughout the whole process. This might also benefit the child in that s/he would only deal with one person throughout the proceedings rather than with a number of different ones as the case progresses.

PART III

Conclusions

Conclusions

Reflections, Speculations and Proposals

1 Introduction

2 Reflections

3 Speculations

4 Proposals for Reform

1   Introduction

Policy-related research of the kind which we have undertaken often serves more to illuminate the context of a subject than to provide specific solutions to particular policy issues. Even so it has been suggested that we should round off this report with some general comments about the system of adoption and the pathways through it so as to highlight the broad thrust of the findings as we see them, before suggesting some possible reforms.

2.   Reflections

Acknowledging the various limitations of the study mentioned in the Preface, in particular the absence of a consumer perspective to represent the views of birth and adoptive parents and older adopted children, we take as our starting point the following basic observations:—

(i)   *Avoidable Delay*

First, as our court based data shows, the procedures and processes of adoption can take a remarkably long time—sometimes a matter of years rather than weeks or months. There is of course an important distinction to be made between the length of proceedings and the concept of avoidable delay. Obviously every care must be taken in selecting, investigating and confirming a child's new adoptive home. Also the vital interests of the child's birth family must be considered. These considerations should not be rushed. Nevertheless, evidence from our practitioner interviews suggests that there is sometimes a substantial element of avoidable delay. As we have seen, social workers preparing Schedule II reports often attributed it to the fact that adoption had to take a lower priority than urgent work such as child abuse. In the hurly-burly of a busy Social Services Department there is a tendency for adoption to be pushed to one side.

We were not able to ascertain whether, and if so how far, poor court administration contributes to delays. The evidence of solicitors suggests that this is an important factor in some areas. Yet there are indications that court officials themselves blame the local authorities. Had we been able to interview guardians ad litem we would have been able to take account of their views about the respective contributions of the adoption agencies and the courts to the delay problem. All we can say is that, whatever the causes, there are grounds for serious concern, given the principle under Section 1[2] of the Children Act 1989 that **"delay in determining a question which relates to the upbringing of a child is likely to prejudice his welfare."** (Discussed further below). At all events we would be appalled if there were any truth in suggestions made to us that some solicitors and local authorities take tactical advantage to exploit delay against the interest of birth parents who oppose the adoption of their children.

(ii)   *Practically all applications result in orders*

As we have seen from the Court Record Survey, it is remarkable that virtually all adoption applications, whether opposed or not, eventually result in the order being granted. With respect to contested cases, this raises a nagging question whether the system is too heavily biased in favour of the authorities, or is it merely that the preliminary machinery is so thorough that the chances of a birth parent successfully contesting an application have been virtually eliminated? Another possibility is that agencies only take 'good risk' cases to court; in which case 'poor risk' cases presumably continue in long-stay care.

(iii)   *The changing pattern of adoption*

The pattern of adoptions in 1990 is very different from that in 1970. The overall number of orders has fallen from 22,000 per year to under 8,000, with a dramatic decrease in the number of 'baby adoptions' (OPCS (1972, 1990)). Children adopted from care now make up almost half the total, while a further third involve step parent and other relation adoptions. Each of these categories of adoption reflect different kinds of family history. In general, it seems to us that the most contentious cases arise where local authorities use adoption as part of their policy of placing older children in permanent homes, having previously removed them from their birth families as a result of care or wardship proceedings.

(iv)   *Fragmentation and elaboration*

Given the hard information from our Court Record Survey and the more qualitative information from the Practitioner Study, it is difficult to avoid the conclusion that modern adoption is both too elaborate a process and too fragmented in execution.

Overall, the number of cases dealt with is now relatively modest compared, for example, to the total numbers of children 'at risk' coming to the notice of local authorities, or to the number of children involved in divorce proceedings (about 150,000 per annum). Fewer numbers suggest advantage in concentration of effort by fewer practitioners, especially if experience is to be built up rapidly and retained. Should therefore the process be reorganised on a more specialist basis or would this risk reinforcing what some regard as the mystique of professional adoption services? If so, the result could be yet another category of 'experts' who surround themselves with unnecessary bureaucracy and rules to heighten their sense of professional importance and to draw power unto themselves. At present the reality seems to be that we get the worst of all worlds—a service which practitioners believe requires expertise which is sometimes provided by specialists (some of whom rightly or wrongly see themselves as 'experts'), and sometimes by generalists who can feel inhibited by the existence of specialists and who often do not have access to or the time to absorb such specialist knowledge as exists.

A related question is whether adoption policy and practice should be differentiated from other kinds of child-care provision. Are the fundamental differences between long-term fostering and adoption, including the crucial one concerning adoption's permanent change of legal parenthood, such as to merit a separately organised system? Certainly the prospect of a possible increase in the use of 'open' adoption would tend to qualify the traditional view that adoption represents a complete and final break with a child's birth family. Such developments reinforce the view that traditional adoption and 'open' adoption be seen as just part of a range of child-related court orders available to courts within a procedural framework aimed at closer integration of child care and adoption work—a 'seamless robe' of child care provision integrating the provisions of the Children Act 1989 with a reformed adoption legislation—all of course subject to due process of law with proper recognition and protection of the rights of the adults and children involved.

The welfare reporting aspects of adoption are much criticised for unnecessary duplication and elaboration. At the present time each major step in the process requires a separate welfare report, often prepared by different people. The Adoption Panel draws on the BAAF Forms E and F. Once the application is made to court a Schedule II report is required, in addition to which if the case is contested there has to be a separate accompanying Statement of Facts. These are then followed by reports from either a reporting officer or guardian ad litem, sometimes both. Most of the basic information in all these reports is the same. In practice the later reports tend to elaborate and amplify the information in the preceding ones. We of course recognise that it may be necessary to have a second opinion, particularly in cases which are disputed or following a change of circumstances. But to require all these reports in *every* case seems on the face of it extraordinarily cumbersome and professionally muscle-bound. It must often appear quite baffling to the parties, and even a cause of additional anxiety, to say nothing of the cost. Our research shows clearly that social workers dislike having to do Schedule II reports in their present form, a number being bothered by the level of detail which is nearly but not quite the same as required in other reports. Consequently many are unclear as to their real value and purpose. Accordingly, we consider the rationale for each type of report now needs to be clarified and their retention only justified by their practical utility in the decision-making process.

A further problem is that the current inflexible uniform procedural process seems to us to take insufficient account of the very different kinds of adoption which now occur. For example, Thoburn and others have drawn attention to the differences between consensual baby adoptions and disputed cases of older children with long and turbulent care histories (Thorburn (1990)). The context and history of the case will inevitably define the way adoption is seen and understood. Should procedures be adapted to take account of such considerations? Could some way be found to sift out the straightforward cases and streamline and simplify their route through the system in order to avoid indiscriminate use of the whole system? We wonder whether some kind of diversionary procedure could be devised to prevent such cases getting entangled in the administrative barbed wire that currently bedevils the civil courts and which has been the subject of so much criticism, not least from the Civil Court Review, and by the Home Office's scrutiny of the magistrates' courts chaired by Mr. Le Vey. As our other researches have shown, there are at present many administrative problems endemic in the family justice system. These include poor case-scheduling practices, rapid turn around of court staff, and a lack of coherent management information systems which prevent court staff from knowing enough about their case loads, the case flow and case-related unit costs. (Murch, Borkowski, Copner and Griew [1987], Hooper and Murch [1989] and [1990]). The Children Act 1989, when implemented later in the year, together with its various related administrative measures, will address a number of these issues in the wider context of the administration of family justice. Accordingly, we belive that every effort should be made to adapt adoption law and practice so that it complements the new law. Proposals that we make later for better scheduling and timetabling of cases follow from this principle.

3.   Speculations

The research team, with support from the ESRC, will soon begin a further two year "consumer" study of the adoption process, based on the views of a sample of birth and adoptive parents and some older children. Until that study is complete we are hesitant to argue too strongly for definitive changes. Nevertheless, we believe that the Pathways Study has already identified a number of obstacles which call for a new approach. The length of the process, the elaboration and fragmentation of procedures, and the diversity of practice, to say nothing of inconsistencies and gaps in the substantive law, all suggest that a major rethink is required.

First, we question whether local authorities should continue in their present form to have primary responsibility for adoption agency practice. We are seriously worried by the evidence, particularly from local authority social work practitioners, which pinpoints problems about prioritising adoption work; by its reported allocation to inexperienced staff who may themselves be supervised by colleagues with little or no adoption experience; by the widely held view that adoption needs a more knowledgeable approach than can be provided; by the evident policy variations between authorities concerning such matters as provision of adoption allowances and post adoption support; and last but not least by the reports of inadequate clerical back-up and support.

Notwithstanding the dangers of creating a professional mystique, we suggest that, taken at face value, all these factors point to a need for a better managed and properly resourced network of adoption agencies. They possibly indicate the need to remove adoption work from individual local authorities altogether—an option which should at least be considered. Whether improved management could best be achieved by a consortium of local authorities say on a regional basis, or by voluntary agencies acting on behalf of the local authorities, or even entirely separate from them, is not for us to say. We also realize that such suggestions would reverse the trends of recent years, and may accordingly be difficult to engineer.

Nevertheless, given the increasing use of adoption for children with complex care histories, rearrangement on the lines suggested above might well have the additional merit of separating the earlier proceedings and the local authorities' involvement in them, from the new adoption proceedings. We suspect that for many children and their parents, this would help to mark off symbolically the often bitter wrangles associated with earlier care and access termination proceedings since the new agency should be seen as less biased. Moreover the introduction of a new forward looking agency concentrating solely on the future of the child might well help to convert what would otherwise be regarded as the "last battle" into a new positive beginning for the child. What is required is a crucial change of emphasis and focus. We envisage that once the Adoption Panel had recommended to free or place the child for adoption, the subsequent handling of the application including the finding of a long term placement or adoptive home would be taken over by the specialist agency. We believe such an approach, coupled with the security of an adoption order and provision for 'open' adoption whenever there are important family links needing to be preserved, would reduce the number of contested cases and much of the accompanying sourness. In floating such an idea we recognise that more detailed consideration would clearly need to be given to such questions as what would happen if the agency did not succeed in placing and how the arrangement would work for straightforward 'baby' placements.

Another related idea which we are currently debating is the notion of providing the child placed for adoption with the continuing support of a "passage-agent" throughout the whole process, and if necessary for a period afterwards while the adoption is consolidating. In our view such a provision would counteract the tendency to have a number of professional social work faces each looking at and dealing with a particular fragment of the social care task—Schedule II report writer, reporting officer, guardian ad litem, etc. It goes without saying that such an approach should go hand in glove with efforts to cut out duplication of report writing.

When it comes to the court machinery, as we have already suggested, there is a strong case for reviewing its purpose and function and in particular for examining whether non-contentious cases could be more expeditiously dealt with. One approach might be to divert them from the court system altogether by using an alternative mechanism such as the Registrar of Births, Deaths and Marriages, thus reserving the court for specifically justiciable issues. This could be in line with the view of the Lord Chancellor, given in the recent parliamentary debate on the Law Commission report on Divorce, that courts should concentrate on what they are good at:

> "namely, the resolution of disputes where an authoritative judicial decision has something positive to contribute to a family's well-being."

(Lord MacKay of Clashfern, *Hansard*, HC, Vol. 525, No. 36. 31.1.91. Col. 799).

Against this it has been suggested to us that because it can be argued that there is always a potential conflict of interest between the parties to adoption proceedings, and because in non-freeing cases birth mothers have the right to withdraw their agreement right up to the making of the order, judicial scrutiny will always be necessary. We are not sure we accept that view. We do not see why time limits should not be set after which, subject to appropriate safeguards, it would not be possible to challenge a hitherto consensual application.

Perhaps a suitable compromise between these two approaches would be achieved if uncontested cases were dealt with by District Judges while Circuit Judges working in the new Care Centres were reserved for the contested issues. We elaborate these ideas below.

Whatever approach is adopted the need for ceremony should be considered. Here we are inclined to accept the views of those social workers who thought it important to retain and even develop some ceremony to mark the child's change of status and confirmation as a full member of a new family. Even so, we question whether this has to be performed by an over-worked judiciary, not all of whom relish and are skilled at family work.

We fully accept that because we have not had first-hand opportunity to study the way courts conduct hearings of adoption cases, our evidence in this regard is mostly second-hand and on that account should be treated with caution. For this reason, while we are clear that the role of the court needs to be reconsidered, especially in uncontested cases, and possibly looked at in the context of a broader review of the conduct of court hearings in family matters, we refrain from making firm recommendations as to alternatives.

4.　Proposals for Reform

We turn now to some of the more obvious pointers to the reform of the adoption law.

(i)　*Imposing Timetables*

It seems to us that a priority need is to find some way to speed up the adoption (and especially the freeing) process. Indeed, since s. 1[2] of the Children Act 1989 (which clearly applies to adoption and freeing proceedings), directs the courts to have regard to the general principle that delay is likely to prejudice the child's welfare, the process will have to be speeded up. We note, however, that unless a s. 8 order is specifically applied for, the duty to prescribe timetables for the progress of a case, under s. 11[1] of the 1989 Act does not seem to apply to adoption or freeing proceedings.[1] We think that timetabling provisions in adoption and freeing proceedings are needed. Such a procedure would clearly satisfy the need to avoid unnecessary delay and would call practitioners to account if they failed without good reason to keep to the time limits. Furthermore, the new procedure would inevitably mean that there would have to be a directions hearing in every adoption or freeing application. This in itself would help to speed up the process by enabling the issues to be clarified at an early stage. The application of the timetabling powers under s. 11[1] to adoption and freeing proceedings would not require legislation and could be done via a Practice Direction. We think this should be done ahead of the final report of the Adoption Law Review and preferably upon implementation of the Child Act 1989.

(ii)　*Allocation and Transfer of Proceedings*

It might also help to speed up the process to limit the number of courts able to deal with adoption and freeing applications. If this were done, the designated courts would become more familiar with the procedure and therefore able to process applications more quickly.

Moreover, such courts would become more expert in recognising and dealing with difficult cases—the need for increasing judicial expertise, particularly in relation to freeing cases, was a point repeatedly made to us during the research. In this respect we note the creation of the Family Hearing Centres at the county court level to which adoption and freeing cases will be allocated. As already mentioned in respect of contested cases we would suggest that consideration be given to limiting jurisdiction to the new Care Centres. Indeed, if the decision is that uncontested cases should not be diverted to non-judicial machinery then, following our logic through

---

[1]　Though it may be argued that the s. 11 timetabling powers apply to *any* "family proceedings", on the basis that the court can of its own motion make a s. 8 order; see Chapter 5 of the *Report of the Research into the Use and Practice of the Freeing for Adoption Provisions* (Lowe, 1991).

and given the relatively small number of applications, a plausible case could be made for providing that all adoption and freeing cases, at any rate those brought by adoption agencies or involving agency placed children (see further below), have to be made in a designated Care Centre. As mentioned above this would be coupled with the provision that the District Judge be empowered to allocate uncontested cases to himself, contested cases to the designated or nominated judge of the Care Centre, or to transfer cases (for example, those involving an international element, illegal payments or placements in need of important points of law) to the High Court.

The suggestion that the District Judge hear the uncontested application himself is offered here as an alternative and less radical suggestion to that made earlier (*ante* p. 245), that non-contentious cases be dealt with by the Registrar of Births, Deaths and Marriages. The advantage of vesting such power in the District Judge is that it would provide for a more efficient use of court time and judge power, whilst at the same time allowing for the transfer of proceedings to a designated or nominated judge should, for example, parental agreement be unexpectedly withdrawn.

Of course, if all adoption and freeing applications were allocated or transferred as suggested above, magistrates would lose their adoption jurisdiction. A less radical suggestion, and one which would reflect the current use of the courts (see Part I, section 2.5 above), would be just to restrict adoption agency applications and those involving agency-placed children. In other words, adoption applications for step parents and relatives would be left unrestricted.

(iii)   *Other Procedural Reforms*

Both the timetabling and allocation issues are prompted by the Children Act and there are other points that arise out of the need to harmonise adoption proceedings with the 1989 Act. For example, it is unclear whether the courts have a duty in adoption and freeing proceedings to consider making alternative orders under s. 8 (viz in particular residence orders).[2] Although we found little or no evidence of custodianship orders being made instead of adoption (see Part I, section 2.10 *ante*), this was no doubt due in part to the tortuous provision of s. 37 of the Children Act 1975 which made the alternative difficult and unattractive.[3] The section 8 alternative seems much more straightforward and we see no reason why the courts should not clearly be placed under a duty to consider it.

---

[2]   See the discussions in White, Carr and Lowe: "*A Guide to the Children Act 1989*", para 11–20. Where a child is previously the subject of a care order, it could be argued that since an adoption order would discharge the care order, a duty to consider s. 8 alternatives does arise because such proceedings fall under s. 1[4](b) in which the statutory checklist under s. 1[3] (and in particular under s. 1[3](g) where the court has to consider its . . . of powers before deciding what, if any, order to make), have to be considered.

[3]   See the discussion in Bromley and Lowe's "*Family Law*" pp. 372–3.

It would also be within the general spirit of the Children Act to make adoption procedure more open. Accordingly we endorse the view put to us by practitioners that we interviewed, that solicitors should have an automatic right of access to all reports such as the Schedule II Report and that of the guardian ad litem. Indeed, there seems a strong case for the advance disclosure of the reports (subject to the need for confidentiality), to all the parties.

Other useful reforms, in our view, would be to allow the child to be a party in all proceedings regardless of court level.[4] On the other hand, there could be more flexibility in the powers to dispense with the need for the child to attend the court hearing in person. Alternatively, or if the guardian ad litem and child disagree, provision should be made giving the guardian ad litem the right to be legally represented.

(iv)   *Increasing Practitioners' Expertise*

Apart from improving the process we think that there is a clear need for increasing the expertise of all those involved in adoption work. We have already mentioned the need for more specialisation to be achieved through reorganisation of agency practice. In addition our foregoing suggestion about limiting the number of courts able to hear adoptions would help to develop judicial expertise. With regard to solicitors we wonder whether a system akin to the Law Society's child care panel should be applied to adoption. We also endorse the suggestion made to us by one practitioner that only experienced social workers (equivalent to approved social workers in mental health cases) should undertake adoption work.

(v)   *Substantive Reforms*

(a)   **Step-parent Adoptions**

Mention was made earlier in this chapter that the uniform procedural process takes insufficient account of the different kinds of adoption. A case in point is step-parent adoptions which require a full Schedule II Report, which necessarily involves a local authority. Although adoption is unique in irrevocably transferring legal parentage, and although our research evidence from practitioners is not strong on the point because none of the cases about which they were interviewed involved step-parent adoption, one can question the need for local authority scrutiny and involvement at least in consensual step-parent applications, particularly in the light of the 1989 Act's emphasis on private ordering between individuals. The basic issue is whether step-parent adoptions should be regarded as falling within the domain of either private or public law. There is an argument that of all

---

4   Under the current law a child can only be made a party in the High Court: Adoption Rules 1984 rr 4[2](g) and 15[2](k).

kinds of adoption they are most akin to other proceedings concerning the private ordering of family relationships, such as the appointment of guardians, where there is no mandatory welfare check. On the other hand under the 1989 Act the child's wishes and feelings have to be taken into account. Without an independent welfare check the risk is that a step-parent adoption is used to sever a child's legitimate links with the non custodial parent's family. Yet it should not be forgotten that, unlike agency adoptions, in step-parent applications there is no proper provision for any welfare check. Thus if step-parent adoptions are to be regarded as essentially a form of private ordering, the continuance of Schedule II reports is commonly regarded by social workers as a burdensome task and is particularly onerous in step-parent cases which otherwise have not involved local authorities. We have already suggested that the number of separate welfare reports at various stages in the process needs to be reviewed. Accordingly we recommend that particular attention is paid to the current reporting requirements in step-parent adoptions.

The foregoing suggestion pre-supposes the continuation of step-parent adoption, but the question may be asked whether they should continue and, if so, in the same form. Our research has little to offer on this subject although it may be significant that the Court Record Survey shows that the number of applicants withdrawn (10%) is much higher than in any of the other categories of adoption (see Table 2.9 *ante*). Nevertheless we venture the following suggestions for possible reform. First,[5] consideration might be given to providing for some kind of tripartite "parental responsibility agreements" along the lines provided for, as between unmarried parents, under s. 4 of the 1989 Act. Secondly, if step-parent adoptions are to be continued, consideration might be given to ending the need for the parent to adopt their own child (a concept which anecdotally we have heard puts some parents off the procedure). In other words, the order should only relate to the step-parent.

(b)   Freeing the Child for Adoption

As we discuss in detail in our Monograph on Freeing,[6] the provisions to free children for adoption have not lived up to expectations. While the provisions were initially envisaged as contributing towards the speedy resolution of straightforward adoption cases, our research has shown that it is a lengthy process riddled with delay, the common use of which is with respect to contested or otherwise difficult cases. Again, while freeing was envisaged as being a process to be used before the child's eventual placement, our research has shown that in a significant proportion of cases (20% in our sample, with a further 9% being placed during the course of the freeing applications), the child had already been placed in the adoptive home before the freeing application was made (see Part I, section 4.6).

---

5   For the arguments that step-parents should automatically be vested with some responsibility, see e.g. Masson in "*The State, the Law and the Family*" (ed M D A Freeman) 1984, ch. 14: "Old families into new: a status for step-parents", pp. 237 et seq.

6   Report of the Research into the Use and Practice of the Freeing for Adoption Provisions (Lowe, 1991).

It is tempting to say that the freeing provisions have failed. Nonetheless, as we report in our Freeing Monograph, the practitioners that we spoke to, though disappointed with their operation, did not themselves advocate the abolition of the process. It seems to us that, while there is a desperate need to improve the process, not least by speeding it up, the case for its abolition, <u>at any rate within the current overall scheme of things</u>, has not been made out. The process currently has an important role with respect to contested cases. Indeed, agency workers that we spoke to were adamant that it was a benefit both to the potential adopters and to the child that the "final battle" with the parents should be fought by the agency. In addition, freeing might also be seen to have a useful role in enabling "hard to place" children to be placed more easily, and to enable those parents who so wish to divest themselves of parental responsibility more quickly.

The question remains, however, whether the current system could be changed so that the perceived advantages of freeing could be accommodated in some other way. One possible change is to allow the agency to be a party to the full adoption application—indeed to be able to make the adoption application on behalf of the would-be adopters. Were this to be done, the need to free the child already placed for adoption would surely be eliminated, and furthermore might provide the preferable forum for fighting contested cases. Whether this change alone would remove the need for freeing altogether can be debated. In our view, however, there may still be cases where it is worthwhile having two stages—the one dealing with the parents' position, the other dealing with the child. Such a two stage process would be made more attractive, however, if the initial stage was speedy and the second stage a more ceremonial hearing, (unless problematic in some way), before either the Registrar of Births, Deaths and Marriages or the District Judge as previously recommended.

If freeing is to be maintained then, as we discuss in our Freeing Monograph, it is important to clear up the status of a freed child, clarifying such points as whether a freed child is in agency care, what rights of succession there are, and to make clear that following a freeing order the birth parents cease to be "parents" for the purposes of the Children Act 1989 so that they do not have a right to apply for section 8 orders.[7] Consideration also needs to be given either to some form of automatic revocation if the child has not been placed for some time, and/or to permit the adoption agency itself to apply to revoke the order.

(c)   Conditions and Orders

The change in procedure for ending contact with children in care under s. 34 of the Children Act 1989, coupled with ability to consolidate proceedings under Schedule 11, should end the current complications caused, for example, by termination of access proceedings and freeing proceedings

---

7   As Hershman and McFarlane argue in [1990] *Family Law* 322–3 and discussed in Chapter 5 of the Report of the Research into the Use and Practice of the Freeing for Adoption Provisions (Lowe, 1991).

often being dealt with in different courts.[8] This should bring back much needed rationalisation and simplification. However, the 1989 Act will not resolve the extent of the court's powers under s. 12[6] of the Adoption Act 1976 to add conditions to adoption orders (but not freeing orders), about which there is confusion.[9] Indeed, the 1989 Act will add the complication that s. 8 orders may also be made.[10] The extent of s. 12[6] of the 1976 Act and its inter-relationship with the s. 8 orders under the Children Act 1989 needs to be clarified.

(d)   Miscellaneous Points

Among other suggestions for reform made by practitioners to us are:

(1)   the present test of the "unreasonable parent" is confusing and needs to be clarified. This of course raises the whole question of what the dispensing grounds should be, but our research has little to add to this debate;

(2)   that there should be a checklist of factors, akin to those under s. 1[3] of the Children Act 1989, applicable to dispensing with parental agreement;

(3)   that the weighting of the child's welfare needs re-examining. Again, our research has little to offer regarding this latter point, though we would venture the view that once parental agreement has been given or dispensed with, there seems no reason in principle why the child's welfare should not become the court's paramount consideration.

Finally, we should like to add one point of our own. Under s. 105 of the Children Act 1975, the Secretary of State is directed to keep under periodic review the operation, inter alia, of the adoption provisions. Although s. 58A of the Adoption Act 1976 and s. 83 of the Children Act 1989 empower the Secretary of State respectively to publish information provided by every local authority and approval adoption society, and to commission and assist research into the adoption process, there is no duty to keep the operation of adoption law under periodic review. We think that there should be such a duty.

---

8   Though the new regime under s. 34 should make it more difficult for local authorities to end parental contact, which in turn could lead to more actively contested freeing and adoption applications.

9   See, for example, *Re D (A Minor)* (1991) Times 23 January, overruling *Re F (A Minor) (Adoption Order: Injunction)* [1990] 3 WLR 505.

10   See the discussion in White, Carr and Lowe: "A Guide to the Children Act 1989", para 11–22.

Bibliography

Bromley P M and Lowe N V (1987) *Bromley's Family Law (7th edition)* Butterworths.

Corcoran A (1988) Open Adoption: the child's right *Adoption and Fostering* 12.3.

Davidoff L (1984) *Statistics of Domestic Proceedings in 1983* in Research and Planning Unit Paper No. 28, Home Office.

France E (1990) Inter-Departmental Review of Adoption Law, Background Paper No. 1 *International Perspectives* Department of Health.

Fratter J (1989) *Family Placement and Access: Achieving Permanency for Children in Contact with Birth Parents* Barnardos.

Freeman M D A (1984) (ed) *The State, the Law, and the Family: critical perspectives* London: Tavistock Publications.

Hershman D and McFarlane A (1990) The Children Act 1989: Access or Contact with a Child Freed for Adoption *Family Law 20* (September 1990).

Hooper D and Murch M (1989) *Developing Support Services for the Family Jurisdictions* Socio-Legal Centre for Family Studies, University of Bristol.

Hooper D and Murch M (1990) *The Family Justice System and its Support Services* Socio-Legal Centre for Family Studies, University of Bristol.

Lowe N V with Borkowski, M, Copner R and Murch M (1991) *Report of the Research into the Use and Practice of the Freeing for Adoption Provisions* Socio-Legal Centre for Family Studies, University of Bristol.

Murch M, Borkowski M, Copner R and Griew K (1987) *The Overlapping Family Jurisdiction of Magistrates' Courts and County Courts* Socio-legal Centre for Family Studies, University of Bristol.

Murch M and Griew K with Borkowski M, Copner R and Lowe N (to be published) *Monograph on Charting the Pathways to Adoption* Socio-Legal Centre for Family Studies, University of Bristol.

Office of Population Censuses and Surveys (1972) *The Registrar General's Statistical Review of England and Wales 1970* Part II London: HMSO.

Office of Population Censuses and Surveys (1989) *Population Trends 58* Winter 1989 London: HMSO.

Office of Population Censuses and Surveys (1990) *Marriage and Divorce Statistics 1988* FM2 No 15 London: HMSO

Report of the Departmental Committee on the Adoption of Children (1972) (Chair: Sir William Houghton until his death and subsequently chaired by His Honour Judge F A Stockdale) Cmnd 5107 London: HMSO

Thoburn J (1990) *Review of research which has a bearing on Adoption or Alternatives to Adoption* Government Review of Adoption Law, Department of Health Report.

Thoburn J and Rowe J (1988) A Snapshot of permanent family placements *Adoption and Fostering* 12.3.

White R, Carr P and Lowe N V (1990) *A Guide to the Children Act 1989* Butterworths.

APPENDIX A

List of Courts Covered in the Fieldwork Areas in the Mini Record Sample

DEVON

County Courts

Barnstaple
Exeter
Newton Abbot
Plymouth
Torquay

Magistrates' Courts

Axminster
Barnstaple
Bideford & Gt Torrington
Cullompton
Exeter
Exmouth
Honiton
Kingsbridge
Okehampton
Plymouth
Plympton
South Molton
Tavistock
Teignbridge
Tiverton
Torbay
Totnes
Wonford

SOMERSET

County Courts

Bridgwater
Taunton
Yeovil

Magistrates' Courts

Frome
Ilminster
Sedgemoor
Shepton Mallet
Somerton
Taunton Deane
Wells
West Somerset
Wincanton
Yeovil

BIRMINGHAM

County Courts

Birmingham

Magistrates' Courts

Birmingham
Sutton Coldfield

WALSALL

County Courts

Walsall

Magistrates' Courts

Aldridge & Brownhills
Walsall

LONDON

County Courts

Bow
Bloomsbury
Clerkenwell
Lambeth
Wandsworth
Woolwich

Magistrates' Courts

Camberwell Green
Highbury Corner
Thames
Greenwich
South Western

APPENDIX B

PATHWAYS TO ADOPTION—MINI-RECORD   Court Case No. ☐☐☐☐

1. Research Number ☐☐☐☐   1

2. Court Type ☐   5

3. Location ☐☐   6

4. Date of Application ☐☐☐☐☐☐   8

5. Type of Application ☐   14

6. Child's date of birth ☐☐☐☐☐☐   15

7. Sex of child ☐   21

8. Legitimacy of child at birth ☐   22

9. a) Is application made with agreement of natural mother? ☐   23

9. b) If legitimate
   Is the application made with agreement of natural father? ☐   24

9. c) if illegitimate
   i) Has the putative father been awarded a custody or guardianship order over this child or is he a testamentary guardian? ☐   25

   ii) If YES, which type of order? ☐   26

   iii) Has the putative father been given notice of this application? ☐   27

   iv) Has the putative father been asked for his agreement? ☐   28

   v) If so, has the putative father given his agreement? ☐   29

10. Outcome of application. ☐   30

11. If order made:
    a) Type of order ☐   31

    b) Date of order ☐☐☐☐☐☐   32 ... 38

    c) Number of hearings ☐   40

    d) i) Was final hearing contested? ☐   41

       ii) If so, by whom? ☐   42

12. Type of adoption agency ☐   43

13. In Adoption Proceedings only
    a) Relationship of applicant to child

    b) Has the child been freed for adoption prior to adoption application? ☐   44

    c) If so, date of order ☐☐☐☐☐☐   45 ... 51

14. Is the child of different racial origin to that of the proposed adoptive parents? ☐   52

15. Has the child been brought to this country from abroad in order that it might be adopted? ☐   53

16. i) What is the child's status immediately prior to this application? ☐   54

    ii) Has the child been involved in other child-related proceedings prior to this application? ☐   55

    iii) If so, how many proceedings? ☐☐   57

    iv) List chronologically those proceedings according to date and final order (from left)

17. i) Are there other siblings who have been or are involved in child related proceedings? ☐   73

    ii) If so, how many? ☐☐   74

18. Is the child a ward of court at time of application? ☐   76

19. i) Has access to the child been terminated prior to this application? ☐   77

    ii) If so, to whom? ☐   78

    iii) Date terminated to mother ☐☐☐☐☐☐   79
        Date terminated to father ☐☐☐☐☐☐   85

20. a) i) Has the child lived with its birth parent only at any time? ☐   91

       ii) If so, with whom? ☐   92

20. b) i) Has the child lived with its birth parents together at any time? ☐   93

       ii) If so, for how long? ☐   94

20. c) i) Has the child lived with other parties only at any time? ☐   95

       ii) If so, with whom? ☐   96

20. d) i) Has the child lived with its birth parent and other partners at any time? ☐   97

       ii) If so, how many partners?

APPENDIX C

PATHWAYS TO ADOPTION

COURT PROFORMA

Draft 5

2
Research Number:

Research Number

Court Type

Location

Court Case Number

Serial Number (if applicable) . . . .

A.   THE CHILD

A.1   To which racial group does the child belong?
(NB Must be actually stated).

If other, specify: . . . .

A.2   To which religion does the child belong?

If other, specify: . . . .

A.3   Is the child known to have one or more of the following disabilities?

   (i)   Longterm physical illness or disability

   (ii)   Mental handicap

   (iii) Emotional or behavioural difficulties
          requiring specialist services

   (iv)   Learning difficulties requiring
          specialist school

A.4   Brothers and sisters
      (Write NONE if no brothers/sisters)

Date of birth	Sex	Relationship to child	Subject to parallel appln.

3

Research Number:

A.5 Access to child
Did the child have access to any member of its natural family?

a) At the time of the application:

Member of family	Access to child	If yes, type of access
Natural mother		
Natural father		
Maternal grandparents		
Paternal grandparents		
Siblings		
Other relations		
Other		

b) At the time of outcome of application:

Member of family	Access to child	If yes, type of access	If yes, was the intention to continue?
Natural mother			
Natural father			
Maternal grandparents			
Paternal grandparents			
Sibling(s)			
Other relations			
Other			

4

Research Number:

B. THE BIRTH PARENTS

	Mother	Father
B.1 Date of Birth		
B.2 To which racial group do they belong?		
If other, specify		
B.3 To which religion do they belong?		
If other, specify		
B.4 Occupation at time of child's birth (post code)		
B.5 (i) Marital status of parents at time of application		
(ii) If married, date of marriage		
(iii) If divorced, date of divorce		

5
Research Number: ⸤⎵⎵⎵⎵⸥

C.   THE PROSPECTIVE ADOPTIVE PARENTS
(omit this section if child has not been placed for adoption)

C.1 (i)   Type of application

C.1 (ii) If single application or child
           living with single person, what
           is that person's situation?

C.1 (iii) If joint application or child
           living with married couple, what
           is the date of marriage?

                    Mother   Father

C.2 Date of Birth

C.3 Racial Group

     If other, specify . . . . . .

C.4 Religion

     If other, specify . . . . . .

C.5 Occupation at time of application
     (post code)
     . . . . . .

C.6 Relationship to child

6
Research Number: ⸤⎵⎵⎵⎵⸥

C.7 Profile of other children in family
     (at time of application)

     (If none, write NONE across question)

     Date of birth   Sex   Status

C.8 Name of Local Authority of residence
     . . . .

C.9 Is an adoption allowance to be paid?

7

Research Number: [   ]

D. CARE HISTORY OF THE CHILD

D.1 (i) Is the child in care at the time of this application?

   (ii) If so, how did it come into care this time?

   (iii) How many times has it been in care previously?

D.2 Details of previous court orders relating to this child.

Type order	Date of order	Interim/full	Court type

D.3 (i) Is the child the subject of a parental rights resolution?

   (ii) If so, date resolution made

D.4 Date of decision by Adoption Panel to make this application

8

Research Number: [   ]

E. DETAILS OF PLACEMENTS

E.1 Current placement (at time of application)

   (i) Date current placement began

   (ii) What was the original purpose of this placement?

   (iii) If answer to (ii) above is 3, did the placement become long-term prior to the decision to adopt?

   (iv) Date of decision to make this a placement for adoption if different from (i) above

E.2 (i) Is there any change in child's situation during the course of these proceedings?

   (ii) If so, what change?

   (iii) If placed for adoption during course of proceedings, date placed for adoption

9

Research Number:

E.3 Previous placements
(i) Number of previous placements involving this child

(ii) Details of previous placements:

Type of placement | Date placed | Date removed

E.4 (i) Has any attempt been made at rehabilitation?

(ii) If yes, number of attempts

10

Research Number:

F. COURT MOVEMENT (this Application)

F.1 Application

(i) Is an application made to dispense with parental agreement?

(ii) If so, on which grounds?

If other, specify

Mother   Father

F.2 Date Schedule II Report lodged with the Court

F.3 Reporting Officer/Guardian ad Litem

(i) Was a reporting officer and/or Guardian ad Litem appointed?

Reporting Officer   Guardian ad Litem

(ii) If so, date appointed

(iii) Number of reports filed

(iv) Dates reports lodged with court (in date order)

11
Research Number: |_|_|_|_|

F.4 Respondents

Who were made respondents in these proceedings?
(from left)

|_|_|_|_|_|_|_|_|

F.5 Legal Aid

Was Legal Aid granted to:

	Yes/No/Not known	If so, date granted
(i) Natural mother	|_|	|_|_|_|_|_|_|
(ii) Natural father	|_|	|_|_|_|_|_|_|
(iii) Prospective adopters	|_|	|_|_|_|_|_|_|
(iv) Other relations	|_|	|_|_|_|_|_|_|
(v) Other (specify)	|_|	|_|_|_|_|_|_|

F.6 Other comments on court movements

12
Research Number: |_|_|_|_|

G. COURT HEARINGS

(Each hearing should have a separate sheet)

(If no hearings, then code hearing number as 00)

Hearing Number (in date order) |_|_|

G.1 Date of hearing	Type of hearing	Outcome of hearing
|_|_|_|_|_|_|	|_|	|_|

If other, specify ....

G.2 Adjournments

If the hearing was adjourned to a later date, what was the reason? |_|

G.3 Length of hearing

Is there any record of length of time hearing took? |_|

If so, record length (i.e. court sitting time) to nearest 15 minutes. |_|_|_|_| (minutes)

G.4 Name of Judge/Bench

....

(to be postcoded)

G.5 Other comments on hearing

13
Research Number:

H.   FREEING FOR ADOPTION APPLICATIONS

H.1 Declaration

(i)   Has the parent/guardian of the
      child made a declaration under S14(7)
      of the 1975 Act or under S18(6)
      of the 1976 Act that (s)he prefers
      not to be involved in future questions
      concerning the adoption of the child?

(ii) If so, declaration made by whom?

H.2 Revocation

(i)   Is there evidence that the former
      parent applied for a revocation of the order
      freeing the child for adoption?

(ii) If so, application made by whom?

(iii) If an application has been made,
      was a revocation order made?

Appendix D

PATHWAYS TO ADOPTION RESEARCH
SOCIAL WORK QUESTIONNAIRE

1.   Interviewee's reference number:

2.   Interviewee's sex

3.   Specific case—research case number:

4.   Reference number of other social worker(s) who also prepared the
     Schedule II report:

5.   Type of specific case:

6.   GAL appointed/No GAL appointed in specific case.

7.   In **adoption** cases: adoption application preceded by freeing order

8.   Type of agency involved:

9.   Name of agency/ies involved:

10. Hearing held in:

1.   PROFESSIONAL QUALIFICATIONS, TRAINING AND
     EXPERIENCE

1.1 How many years have you worked as a social worker?

1.2 How long have you been working in the child care field?

1.3 What proportion of your workload in the last 12 months was
     involved with adoption?

1.4 Please describe the range of work you have undertaken in the last 12
     months in relation to adoption.

1.5 How many Schedule II Reports have you prepared in the last 12
     months?

1.6 (i)   Is your adoption work supervised?
     (ii) If yes, by whom?
     (iii) Does this person have specialized knowledge on adoption?

1.7 (i)   Is there someone whom you can consult if you need advice and
           support in your adoption work?
     (ii) If yes, who?
     (iii) Does this person have specialist knowledge on adoption?

1.8 To whom do you turn for help if you need advice about legal aspects
     of your work?

1.9 (i) Do you have any social work or other qualifications relevant to child care work?

(ii) If yes, list qualifications and year obtained.

1.10 (i) Since becoming a social worker, have you attended any training courses specifically related to adoption and the preparation of Schedule II Reports which you have found particularly helpful?

(ii) If yes, list course; whether in-house, or organized by outside agency.

1.11 How do you keep abreast of changes in the law?

1.12 What is your date of birth?

2.   ORGANISATION OF ADOPTION WORK IN THE AGENCY

2.1 (i) How do you feel about the way your authority/agency organizes adoption work?

(ii) Are there any particular problems?

2.2 Can you give me the name and designation of the person who has key management responsibility for adoption work in your agency as a whole?

2.3 (i) Do you have any difficulty in obtaining adequate administrative/secretarial assistance for your adoption work:

(ii) If YES, what effect does this have on the work?

3.   SCHEDULE II REPORTS—General

3.1 What do you see as the main purpose of Schedule II reports/

3.2 (i) When preparing a Schedule II report, do you usually find the information contained in the case files sufficient?

(ii) Do you usually have to seek some of the information you require from sources other than the case file?

(iii) If yes, from which sources?

3.3 What is your view about the amount of information required in Schedule II reports?

3.4 (i) In adoption cases do you think sufficient time is allowed for preparation of the report?

(ii) If no, can you explain why not?

3.5 (i) Are there other general problems that arise concerning the preparation of the Schedule II reports?

(ii) If yes, what are they?

4.   THE SPECIFIC CASE

Research Case Number:

4.1   May we now turn to the specific case we mentioned for which you prepared the Schedule II report? Could you answer the next questions in relation to that please?

4.2   How did you come to be responsible for the preparation of the Schedule II Report in this case?

4.3   (i)   Did any problems arise when preparing the Schedule II report in this case?
        (ii) How were they resolved?

4.4   In particular did any problems arise in obtaining information about:

        (i)   The birth mother?
        (ii)   The birth father?
        (iii) The child?

4.5   (i)   Did any problems arise because the task of writing the Schedule II Report was shared with 1/2 other(s)?
        (ii)   If yes, what kind of problems?
        (iii) Could they have been avoided?

4.6   Do you know why freeing was considered inappropriate in this case?

4.7   What did you expect freeing/adoption as opposed to any other option to achieve in this case?

4.8   (i)   Did you regard it as part of your role to ascertain what the child's wishes and feelings were about his/her situation?
        (ii)   If yes how did you find out what these were?

4.9   (i)   Did the child's wishes and feelings differ from your own view of what was best?
        (ii)   If yes, how was this resolved?

4.10   Did someone explain the meaning of adoption to the child?

4.11   Did you feel the child understood the meaning of adoption?

4.12   Did you explain your role to the child?

4.13   (i)   Was access terminated in this case?
        (ii)   If YES, to whom/
        (iii) when was it terminated?
        (iv)   By whom was it decided to terminate access?
        (v)   Why was it terminated?
        (vi)   If NO does the child see any members of his/her birth family?
        (vii) If yes, with whom
        (viii) Does this work well?

4.14 Did you attend the adoption panel meeting at which it was decided:
    (i)   that freeing/adoption would best meet the needs of the child?
    (ii) to match the adopters with this child?

4.15 Are there any comments you wish to make about the role of the adoption panel in this case?

4.16 (i)   Were costs a consideration in deciding the child's long term future?
    (ii) If yes, how?

4.17 (i)   Did you have any contact with a RO in the case?
    (ii) How did you view the RO's role?

4.18 (i)   Did you have any contact with a GAL in the case?
    (ii) How did you view the GAL's role?

4.19 (i)   Was the GAL's recommendation the same as yours in the Schedule II report?
    (ii) If no, which recommendation was followed by the court?

4.20 Do you know why this application was made to the: Magistrates' Court/County Court/High Court

4.21 (i)   Did you have any direct contact with the court's administration?
    (ii) If yes, did any problems arise?

4.22 (i)   Did any delays occur once the application had been submitted to court?
    (ii) If yes, what was the cause of the delay?

4.23 (i)   Did you attend the court hearing?
    (ii) If no, were you informed of the outcome of the case?

4.24 Have you any comments on the way the case was conducted in court?

4.25 (i)   Did you have to give evidence in court?
    (ii) Did you feel that this was worthwhile?

4.26 (i)   Did any other problems arise in relation to this case which you have not already mentioned?
    (ii) If yes, what problems?

4.27 What was the effect of these proceedings on your relationship with:
    (i)   The birth parents?
    (ii) The adopters?
    (iii) The child?

5.   THIS SECTION TO BE ANSWERED BY SOCIAL WORKERS WHO
      REFUSED TO ANSWER QUESTIONS CONCERNING THE
      SPECIFIC CASES

5.1   Do you explain your role to a child in a freeing/adoption case?

5.2   (i)   Do you regard it as part of your role to ascertain the child's
            wishes and feelings about his/her situation?
      (ii) If yes, how do you find out what they are?

5.3   Would someone explain the meaning of adoption to the child?

5.4   Are there any comments you wish to make about the role of adop-
      tion panels?

5.5   (i)   Are costs a consideration in deciding a child's long term future?
      (ii) If yes, how?

5.6   How do you view the role of the RO in freeing/adoption?

5.7   How do you view the role of the GAL in freeing/adoption?

5.8   (i)   Have you had any direct contact with the courts' administration
            in adoption cases?
      (ii) If yes, in which courts?
      (iii) Have any problems arisen with the courts' administration?
      (iv) How could they be resolved?

5.9   Have you any comments on the conduct of adoption cases in court?

5.10 (i)   Do any problems arise when more than one person is involved
            in the preparation of the Schedule II Report?
      (ii) If yes, what kind of problems?

6.   OPEN ADOPTION

6.1   You probably know that there have been some recent cases where
      the principle of open adoption has been recommended. What do you
      think about this principle?

6.2   Do you know of any instances where adoption with access has:
      (a) worked well?
      (b) caused a problem?

6.3   Do you know of any instances where the issue of access has delayed
      the adoption process?

7.   ADOPTION PROCEDURE

7.1   (i)   Have you experienced any delays in freeing and adoption
            cases?
      (ii) If yes, what causes the delays?
      (iii) How could these delays be avoided?

7.2   (i)   Would it improve the process if applications to adopt had to be submitted to the court accompanied by the Schedule II report?

     (ii) Why/Why not?

7.3   (i)   In *un*contentested cases, is a court hearing necessary?

     (ii) Why/Why not?

     (iii) If no, by what alternative means could the application be decided?

7.4   (i)   Should there be a GAL in *un*contested cases?

     (ii) Why/Why not?

7.5   (i)   Should children be separately represented by a lawyer in adoption/freeing?

     (ii) Why/Why not?

7.6   (i)   Do you consider adoption to be an over-elaborate process?

     (ii) If yes, how could it be simplified?

8.   ADOPTION LAW

8.1   (i)   Do you consider you have an adequate working knowledge of the law relating to adoption?

     (ii) If no, in what areas do you feel it is inadequate?

8.2   Could you say what you regard as:

     (i)   the most positive aspects of the freeing provisions?

     (ii) the most negative aspects of the freeing provisions?

8.3   Could you say what you regard as:

     (i)   the most positive aspects of adoption law as it is now?

     (ii) the most negative aspects of adoption law as it is now?

8.4   Do you think adoption law as it is at present meets the needs of:

     (i)   the child?

     (ii) the birth parents?

     (iii) the adoptive parents?

8.5   Would you like to see changes made to the freeing for adoption provisions?

8.6   Would you like to see changes made in adoption law?

8.7   (i)   Do problems arise if any of the parties involved apply for legal aid?

     (ii) If yes, what kind of problems?

8.8   Could the legal framework be made more user-friendly?

9.   OTHER OBSTACLES

9.1   (i)   Finally are there any other matters you would like to raise in
               relation to the adoption process which you think are in need of
               change or improvement?

        (ii)   If yes, what?

10.   INTERVIEWS WITH BIRTH PARENTS/ADOPTERS/CHILDREN

10.1   Do you think it would have been possible in the specific case we
        have talked about to have interviewed:

        (a)   the birth parents?
        (b)   the adopters?
        (c)   the child?

10.2   Generally speaking do you think it would be possible for us to seek
        interviews with:

        (a)   the birth parents?
        (b)   the adopters?
        (c)   the child?

10.3   If we were to ask your help in a few months time, would you be
        willing to inform us then of any new adoption cases with which you
        had become involved?

APPENDIX E

PATHWAYS TO ADOPTION RESEARCH
PRIVATE SOLICITORS QUESTIONNAIRE

1.   Interviewee's reference number:

2.   Interviewee's sex

3.   Specific case—research case number:

4.   Type of specific case:

5.   GAL appointed/No GAL appointed in specific case.

6.   In **adoption** cases: adoption application preceded by freeing order

7.   Type of agency involved: Local Authority

8.   Name of agency/ies involved:

9.   Hearing held in:

1.   PROFESSIONAL QUALIFICATIONS, TRAINING AND
        EXPERIENCE

1.1   (i)   When were you admitted?
        (ii) How old are you?
        (iii) Have you been in continuous practice since then?
        (vi) If NO, how long was the break between practices?

1.2   What is your status in this firm?

1.3   How long have you been with this firm?

1.4   How long have you personally been dealing with legal problems
        relating to children?

1.5   Are you a member of the child care panel?

1.6   Are you an adviser to an adoption agency?

1.7   How many adoption cases do you estimate that you have dealt with
        in the last:
        (a)   12 months?
              Of these how many were step-parent adoptions?
        (b)   3 years?
              Of these how many were step-parent adoptions?

1.8   In how many of your cases in the last 12 months
        (a)   was parental agreement formally given before the hearing?
        (b)   was parental agreement still withheld at date of hearing but the
              case was not actively opposed?

(c) was parental agreement formally dispensed with by the court?

(d) Was parental agreement withheld and not dispensed with?

1.9   What proportion of your workload in the last 12 months was involved with adoption?

2.   Could you tell me very briefly what you see as the main problem areas of adoption?

3.   HOW ADOPTION WORK IS ACQUIRED

3.1   How do you normally become involved in adoption cases:
(a) following approaches of private clients?
(b) following instructions by local authority?
(c) following instructions by voluntary adoption agency?
(d) following instructions from the GAL
(e) other—specify

4.   THE SPECIFIC CASE

Research Case Number:

4.1   May we now turn to the specific case we mentioned when we contacted you? Could you answer the next questions in relation to that please?

4.2   How did you come to be involved in this case?

4.3   At what stage did you become involved in this case?

4.4   How urgent was the case?

4.5   How long was it between the lodging of the papers and the hearing?

4.6   (i)   Did you decide which level of court to apply to?
(ii)   If YES, give reason for choice
(iii) If NO, who decided?

4.7   Did any legal problems arise when preparing this case?

4.8   Did any evidential problems arise when preparing this case? In particular were there any problems in obtaining the information you needed; for example, in your preparation of the Statement of Facts.

4.9   How long did it take you to prepare the Statement of Facts?

4.10   Did you see the Schedule II report?

If no, do you think you should have an automatic right to see the Schedule II report?

4.11   (i)   Was your client legally aided?
(ii)   If YES, were there any problems obtaining it?
(iii) If NO, did LA pay their legal costs?

(iv) If YES, did that cause any problems?

(v) Were there any other problems re costs?

4.12 (i) Did you regard it as part of your role to ascertain what the child's wishes and feelings were about his/her situation?

(ii) If yes how did you find out what these were?

4.13 (i) Did the child's wishes and feelings differ from:
 (a) those of the Schedule II reporter?
 (b) Your own view of what was best?

(ii) If yes, how was this resolved?

4.14 Did you feel the child understood the meaning of adoption?

4.15 Did you explain your role to the child?

4.16 How often did you see your client in your office?

4.17 (i) Did you see the client at their home?

(ii) If YES, what was the purpose?

(iii) If NO, why not?

4.18 (i) Was there a GAL in this case?

(ii) Did you have any contact with him/her?

(iii) Did you see the GAL's report?

(iv) How did you view the role of the GAL in this case?

4.19 Were there any problems associated with filing the application?

4.20 How long was it between you first seeing your client and filing the application in court?

4.21 (i) Did any delays occur once the application had been submitted to court?

(ii) If yes, what was the cause of the delay?

4.22 Have you any comments on the way the case was conducted in court?

4.23 (i) Did any other problems arise in relation to this case which you have not already mentioned?

(ii) If yes, what problems?

5.   THIS SECTION TO BE ANSWERED BY SOLICITOR WHO REFUSED TO ANSWER QUESTIONS CONCERNING THE SPECIFIC CASES

5.1   At what stage do you generally become involved in agency adoption cases?

5.2   To which level of court do you generally apply in adoption cases?

5.3   In a typical case how often would you see your client in your office?

5.4   (i)   Would you see your client in their home?
        (ii)   If YES, what was the purpose
        (iii) If NO, why not?

5.5   Can you recall particular legal problems arising when preparing a case?

5.6   Can you recall particular problems arising in obtaining the evidential information you needed? In particular were there any problems in obtaining the information you needed; for example, in your preparation of the Statement of Facts?

5.7   (i)   Are your clients normally legal aided?
        (ii)   If YES, are there normally any problems obtaining it?
        (iii) If NO, do the LA's normally pay their legal costs?
        (iv)   If YES, does that cause any problems?
        (v)   Are there any other problems re costs?

5.8   Do you normally see the Schedule II report?

5.9   (i)   Do you regard it as part of your role to ascertain the child's wishes and feelings about his/her situation?
        (ii)   If yes, how do you find out what they are?

5.10   How do you view the role of the GAL in freeing/adoption?

5.11   (i)   Have you experienced any problems associated with the filing of an application?
        (ii)   How could they be resolved?

5.12   (i)   Have you experienced any delays once the application has been submitted to court?
        (ii)   If yes, what was the cause of the delay?

5.13   Have you any comments on the conduct of adoption cases in court?

6.   ADOPTION PROCEDURE

6.1   (i)   Have you experienced any delays in:
               (a) freeing
               (b) adoption cases?
        (ii)   If yes, what causes the delays?
        (iii) How could these delays be avoided?

6.2   (i)   Would it improve the process if applications to adopt had to be submitted to the court accompanied by the Schedule II report?
        (ii)   Why/Why not?

6.3   (i)   In your opinion are there cases in which a court hearing is unnecessary?
        (ii)   If yes, by what alternative means could the application be decided?

6.4   In your opinion is it necessary to have the distinctive roles of Reporting officer and Guardian ad Litem?

6.5   Should there be a GAL in cases where parental agreement has been given?

6.6   (i)   Have you experienced cases where parental agreement has not been given at the date of the hearing but where the parent is nevertheless not actively contesting the case?
       (ii) If YES, does this cause particular problems?

6.7   (i)   Should children be separately represented by a lawyer in all adoption/freeing proceedings?
       (ii) Why/Why not?

6.8   Should GAL's be legally represented in all courts?

6.9   (i)   Do you consider adoption to be an over-elaborate process?
       (ii) If yes, how could it be simplified?

7.   ADOPTION LAW

7.1   Could you say what you regard as:
       (i)   the most positive aspects of the freeing provisions?
       (ii) the most negative aspects of the freeing provision?

7.2   Could you say what you regard as:
       (i)   the most positive aspects of adoption law as it is now?
       (ii) the most negative aspects of adoption law as it is now?

7.3   Do you think adoption law as it is at present meets the needs of:
       (i)   the child?
       (ii) the birth parents?
       (iii) the adoptive parents?

7.4   Do you know of cases where access has continued after an adoption order has been granted:
       (a)   as a result of the court order about access?
       (b)   informally?

7.5   If yes, do you know of any instances where adoption with access has:
       (a)   worked well?
       (b)   caused a problem?

7.6   Do you know of any instances where the issue of access has delayed the adoption process?

7.7   Would you like to see changes made to the freeing for adoption provisions?

7.8   Would you like to see changes made in adoption law?

7.9   Could the legal framework be made more user-friendly?

8.   OTHER OBSTACLES

8.1   Have other people's lack of competence/experience caused any
        problems?

8.2   How do you keep abreast of changes in the law?

8.3   Are there areas of adoption law about which you feel you should
        know more?

8.4   (i)   Finally are there any other matters you would like to raise in
              relation to the adoption process which you think are in need of
              change or improvement?
        (ii) If yes, what?

9.   INTERVIEWS WITH BIRTH PARENTS/ADOPTERS/CHILDREN

9.1   Do you think it would have been possible in the specific case we
        have talked about to have interviewed:
        (a)   the birth parents?
        (b)   the adopters?
        (c)   the child?

9.2   Generally speaking do you think it would be possible for us to seek
        interviews with:
        (a)   the birth parents?
        (b)   the adopters?
        (c)   the child?

9.3   If we were to ask your help in a few months time, would you be
        willing to inform us then of any new adoption cases with which you
        had become involved?

Printed in the United Kingdom for HMSO
Dd296374 6/93 C20 G531 10170